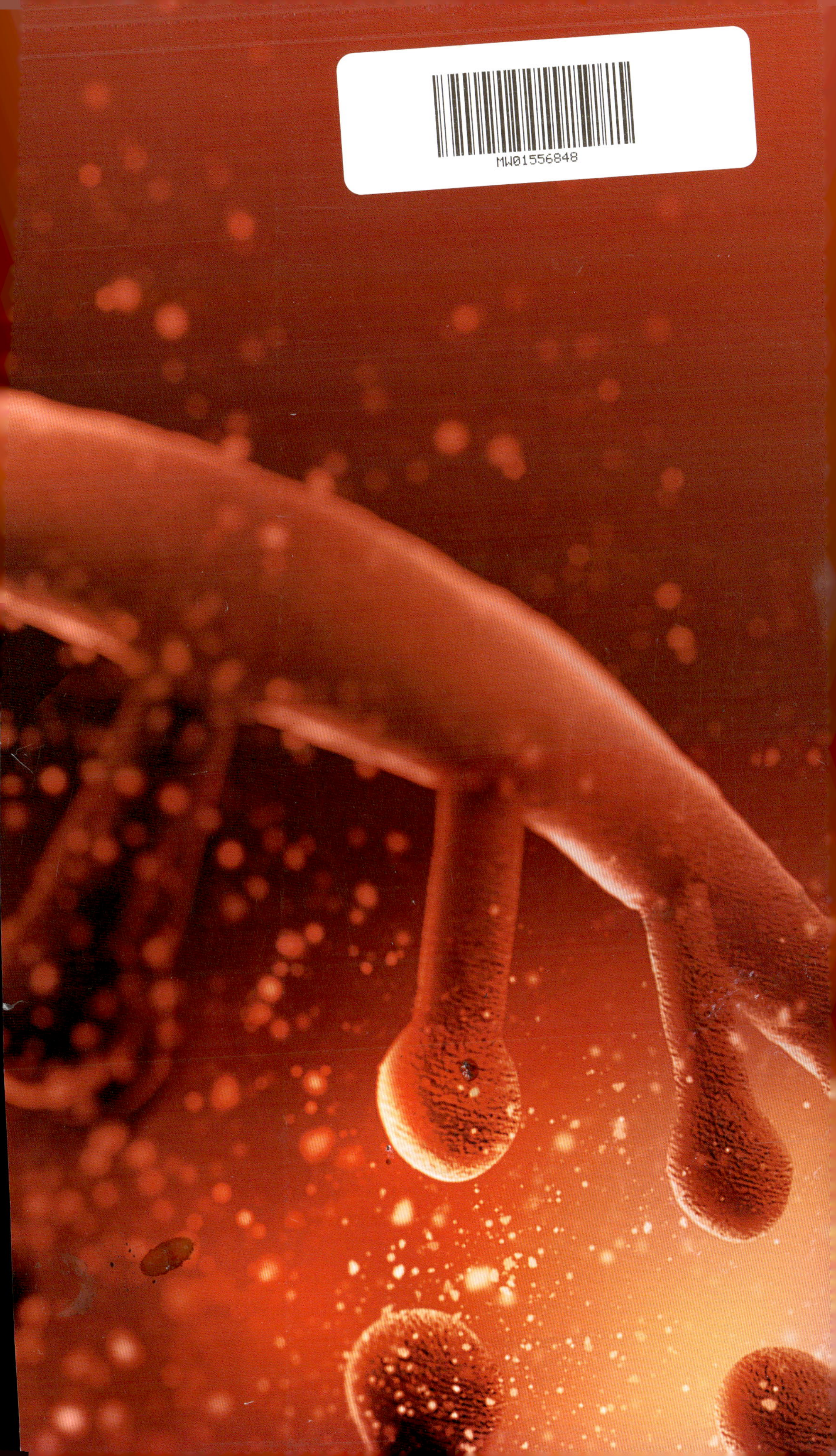

Crick & Watson

Writer	:	Lewis Helfand
Illustrator	:	Naresh Kumar
Colorists	:	Pradeep Sherawat and Ashwani Kashyap
Editors	:	Sourav Dutta and Shabari Choudhury
Letterer	:	Bhavnath Chaudhary
Designer	:	Mukesh Rawat
Cover Artists	:	Naresh Kumar, Vijay Sharma and Pradeep Sherawat

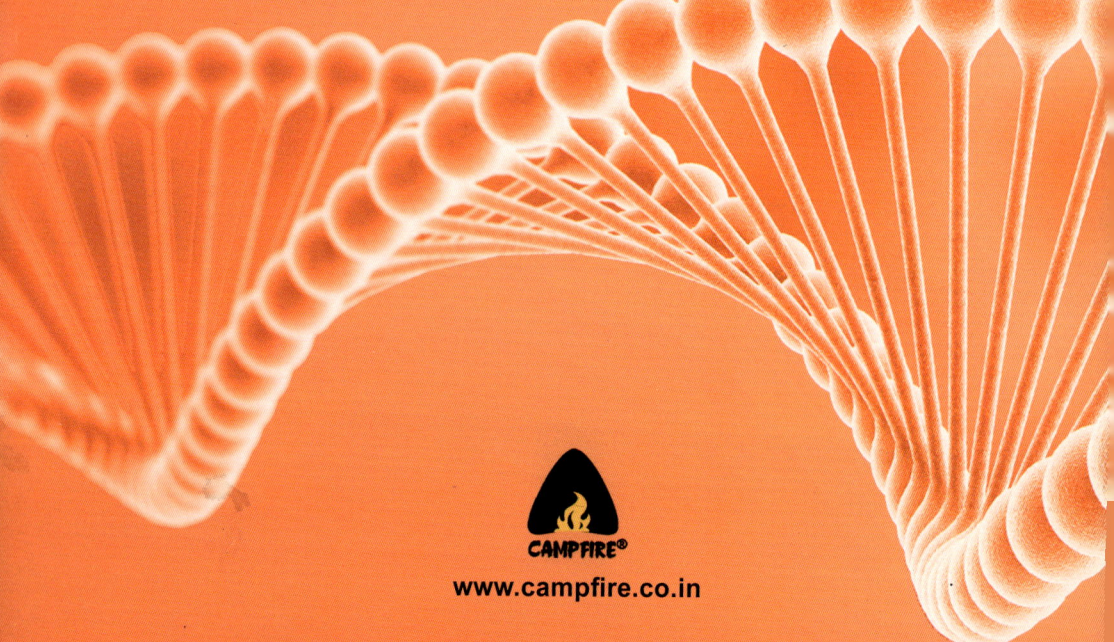

CAMPFIRE®
www.campfire.co.in

Mission Statement

To entertain and educate young minds by creating unique illustrated books that recount stories of human values, arouse curiosity in the world around us, and inspire with tales of great deeds of unforgettable people.

Published by Kalyani Navyug Media Pvt Ltd
101 C, Shiv House, Hari Nagar Ashram,
New Delhi 110014, India

ISBN: 978-93-81182-21-5

Copyright © 2016 Kalyani Navyug Media Pvt Ltd

All rights reserved. Published by Campfire, an imprint of Kalyani Navyug Media Pvt Ltd.

No part of this publication may be reproduced, stored in a retrieval system, or transmitted in any form or by any means, electronic, mechanical, photocopying, recording, or otherwise, without written permission from the publisher.

Printed in India

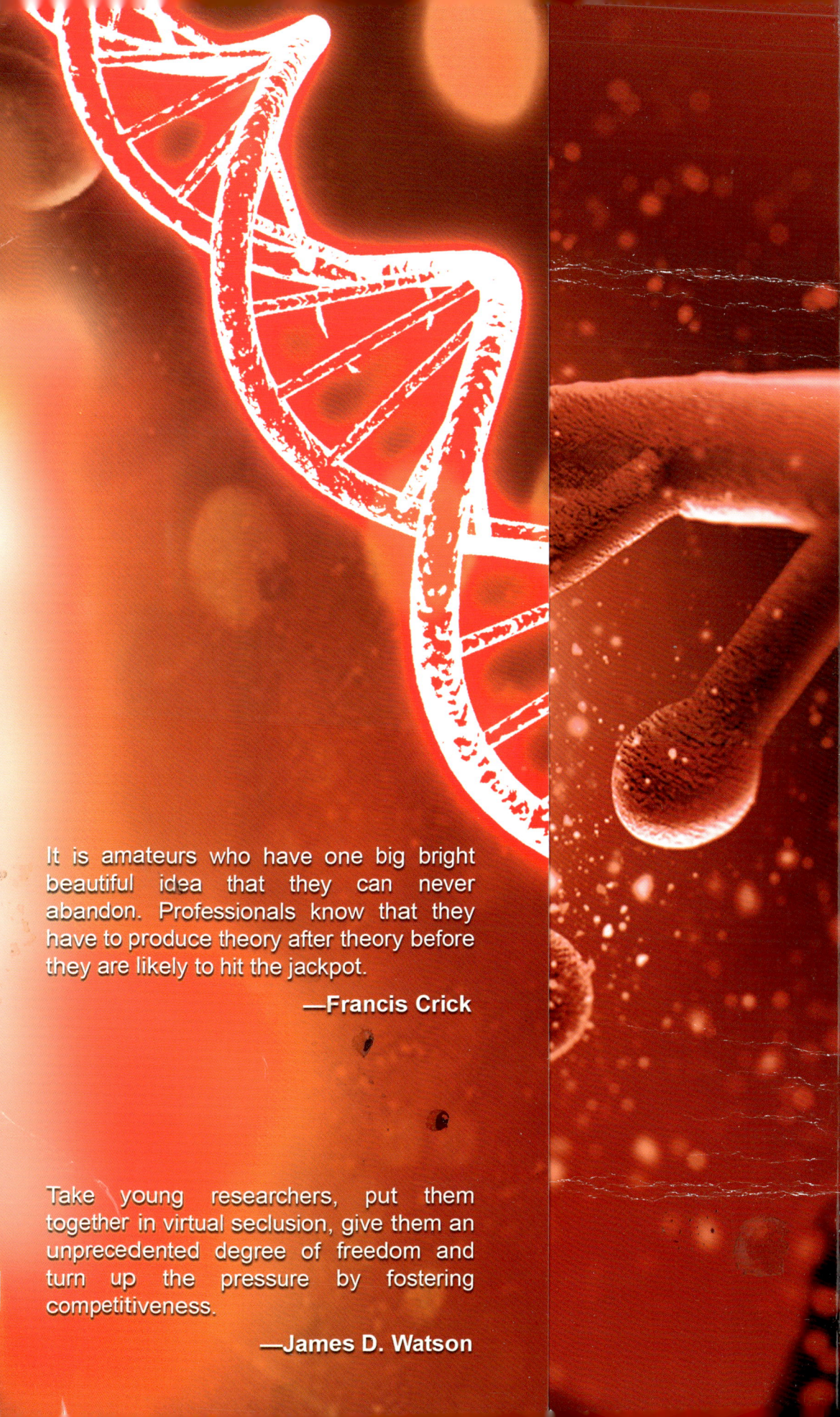

> It is amateurs who have one big bright beautiful idea that they can never abandon. Professionals know that they have to produce theory after theory before they are likely to hit the jackpot.
>
> —Francis Crick

> Take young researchers, put them together in virtual seclusion, give them an unprecedented degree of freedom and turn up the pressure by fostering competitiveness.
>
> —James D. Watson

CAMPFIRE®
Heroes

THEY CHANGED THE WORLD

Crick & Watson

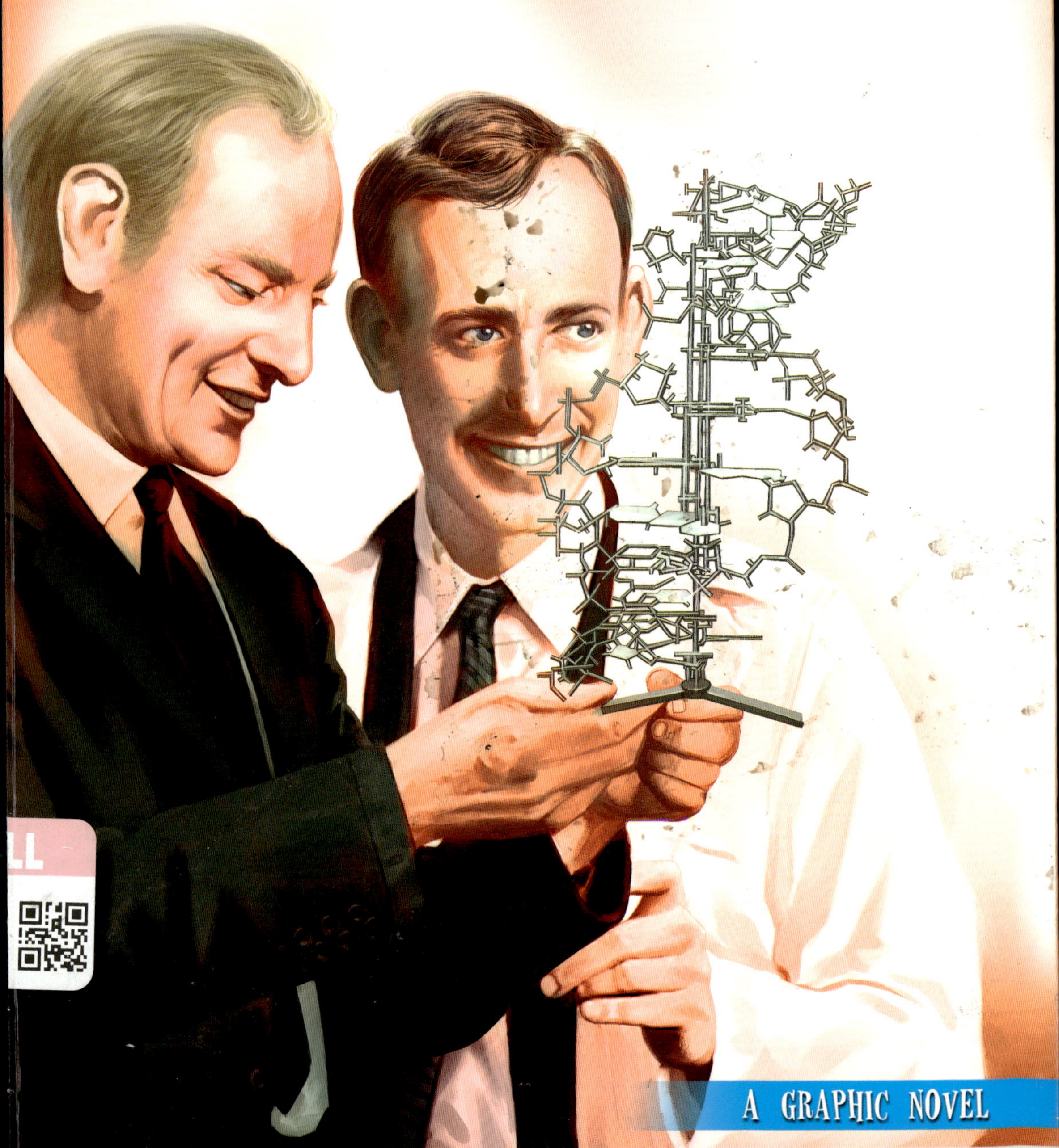

A GRAPHIC NOVEL

WRITTEN BY LEWIS HELFAND

ILLUSTRATED BY NARESH KUMAR

THEY CHANGED THE WORLD

Crick & Watson

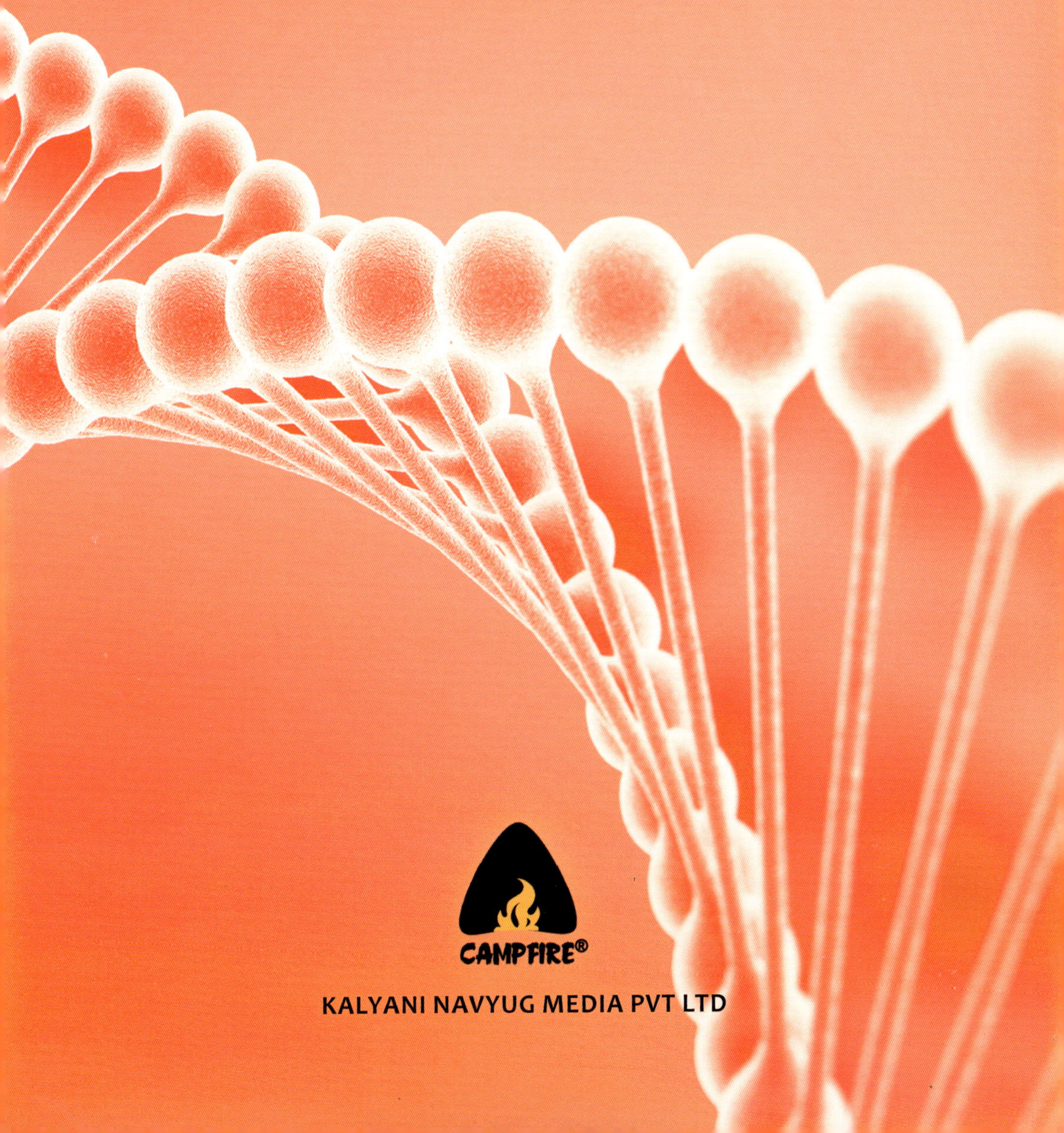

CAMPFIRE®

KALYANI NAVYUG MEDIA PVT LTD

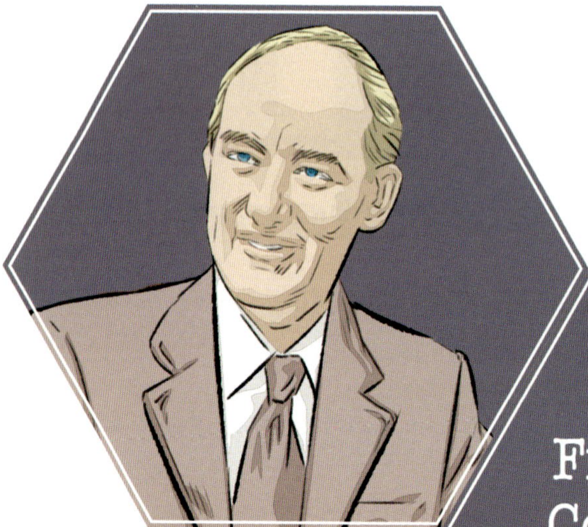

Francis Harry Compton Crick (1916-2004)

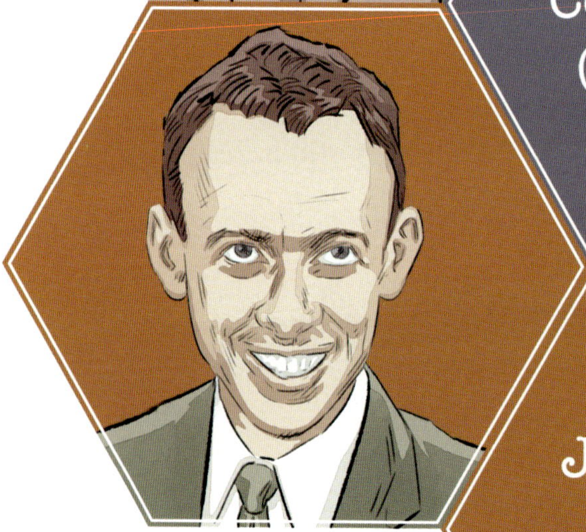

James Dewey Watson (1928-)

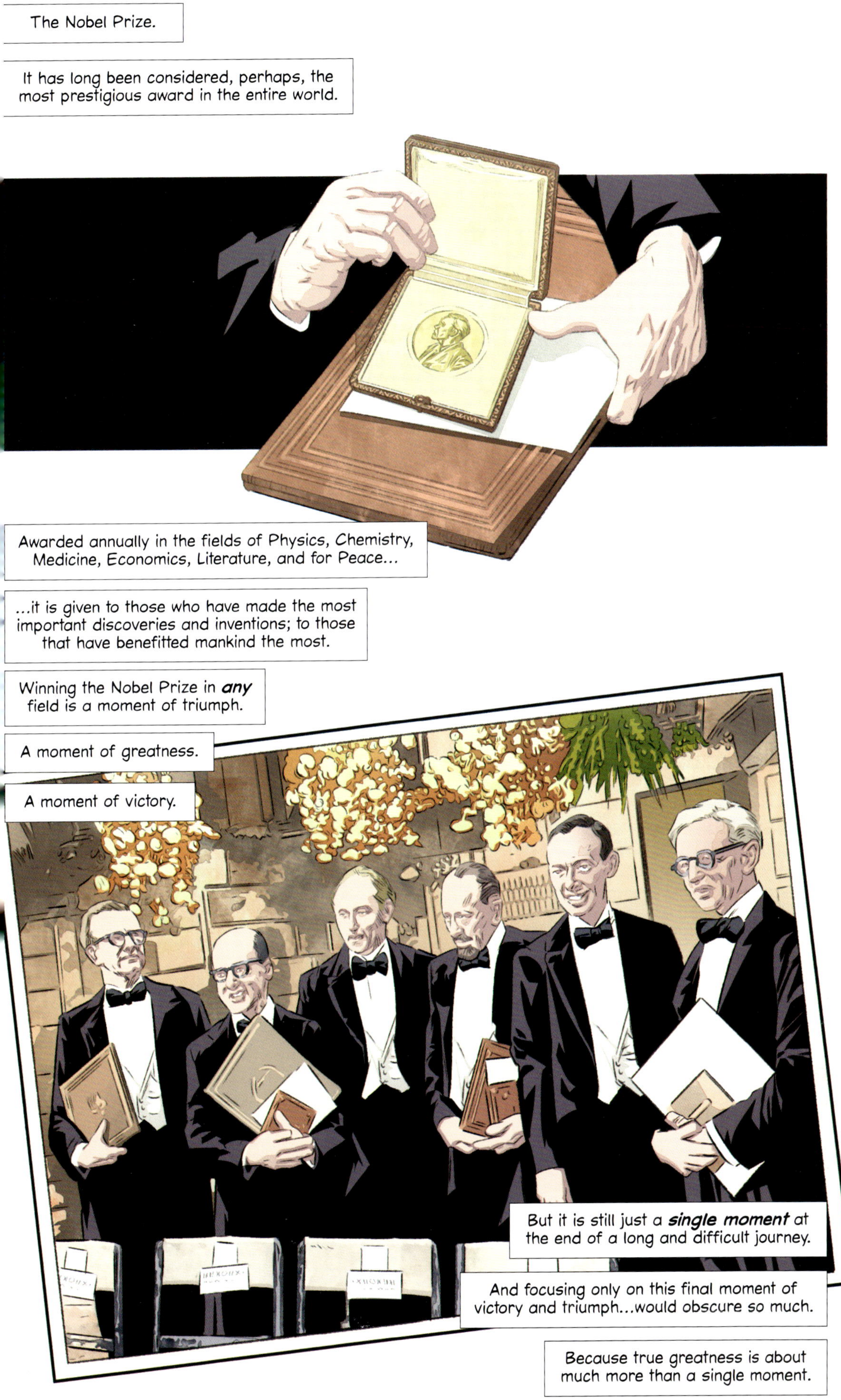
The Nobel Prize.
It has long been considered, perhaps, the most prestigious award in the entire world.
Awarded annually in the fields of Physics, Chemistry, Medicine, Economics, Literature, and for Peace...
...it is given to those who have made the most important discoveries and inventions; to those that have benefitted mankind the most.
Winning the Nobel Prize in ***any*** field is a moment of triumph.
A moment of greatness.
A moment of victory.
But it is still just a ***single moment*** at the end of a long and difficult journey.
And focusing only on this final moment of victory and triumph...would obscure so much.
Because true greatness is about much more than a single moment.

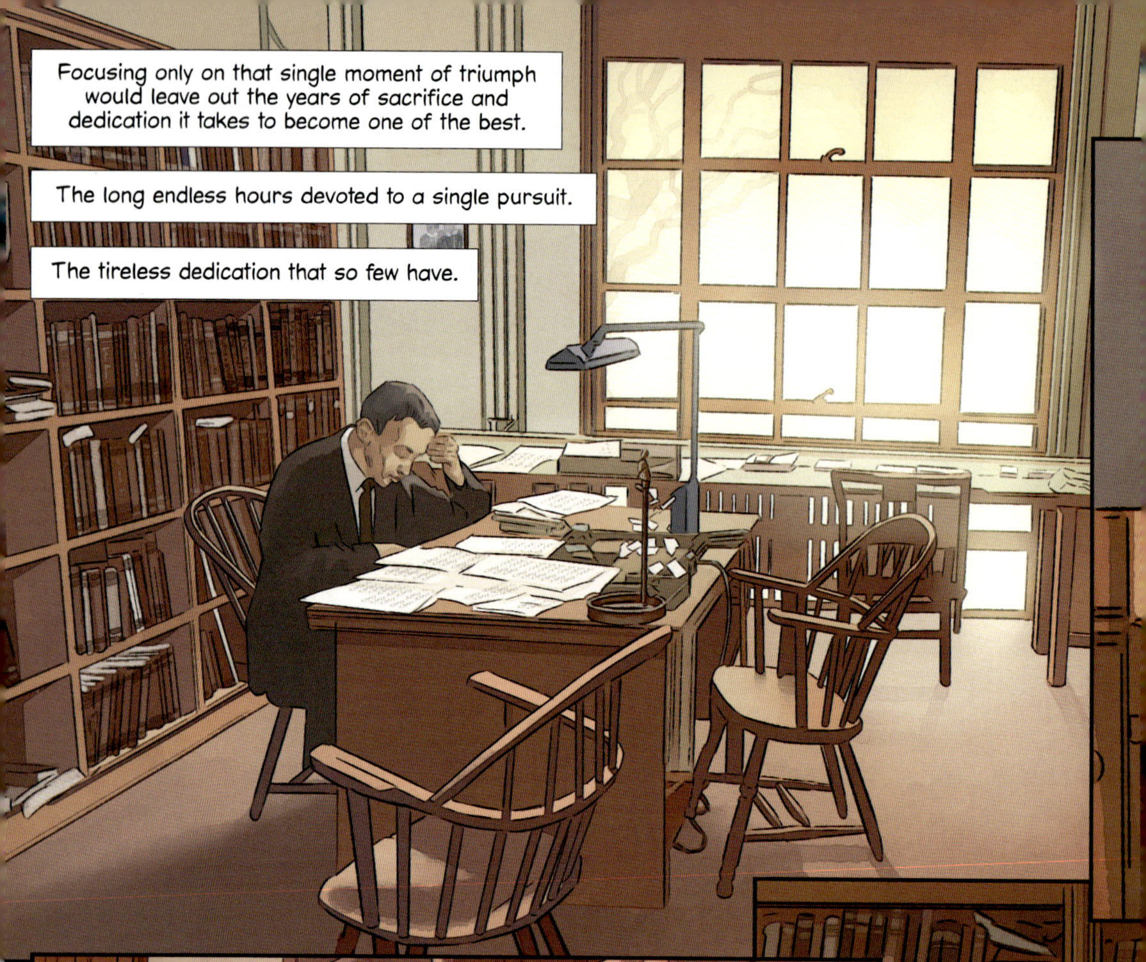
Focusing only on that single moment of triumph would leave out the years of sacrifice and dedication it takes to become one of the best.
The long endless hours devoted to a single pursuit.
The tireless dedication that so few have.

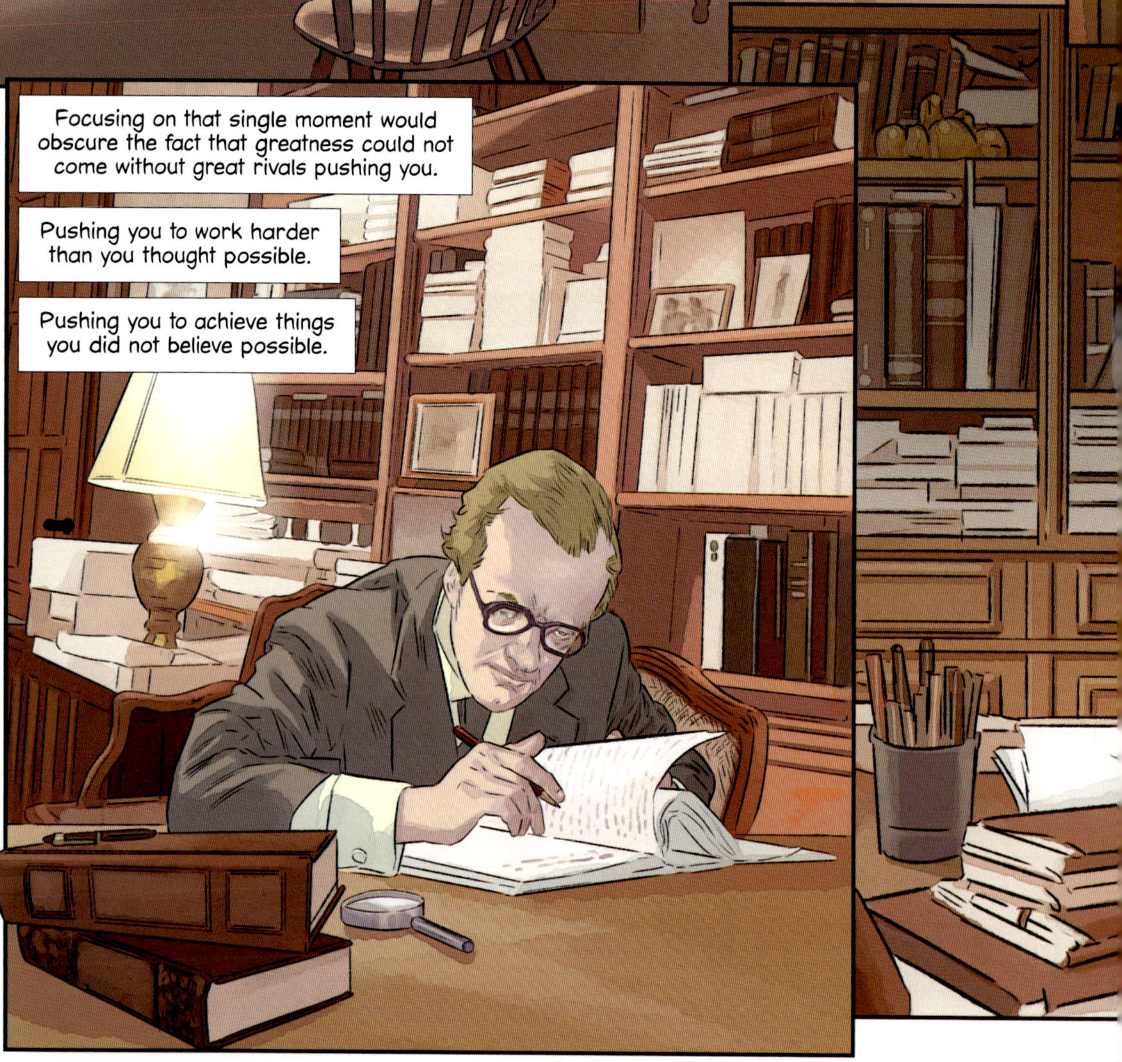
Focusing on that single moment would obscure the fact that greatness could not come without great rivals pushing you.
Pushing you to work harder than you thought possible.
Pushing you to achieve things you did not believe possible.

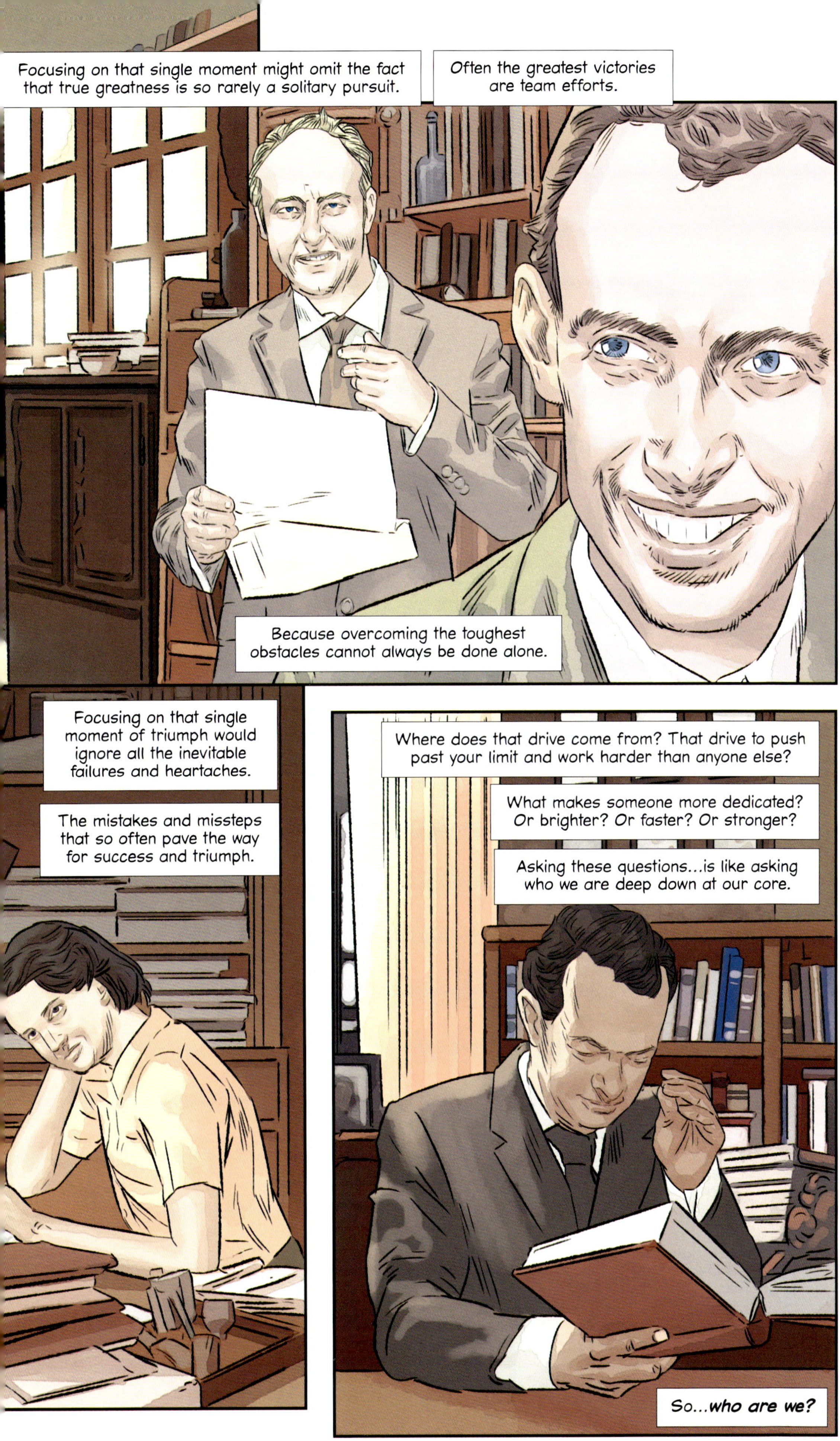

Focusing on that single moment might omit the fact that true greatness is so rarely a solitary pursuit.
Often the greatest victories are team efforts.
Because overcoming the toughest obstacles cannot always be done alone.
Focusing on that single moment of triumph would ignore all the inevitable failures and heartaches.
The mistakes and missteps that so often pave the way for success and triumph.
Where does that drive come from? That drive to push past your limit and work harder than anyone else?
What makes someone more dedicated? Or brighter? Or faster? Or stronger?
Asking these questions...is like asking who we are deep down at our core.
So...*who are we?*

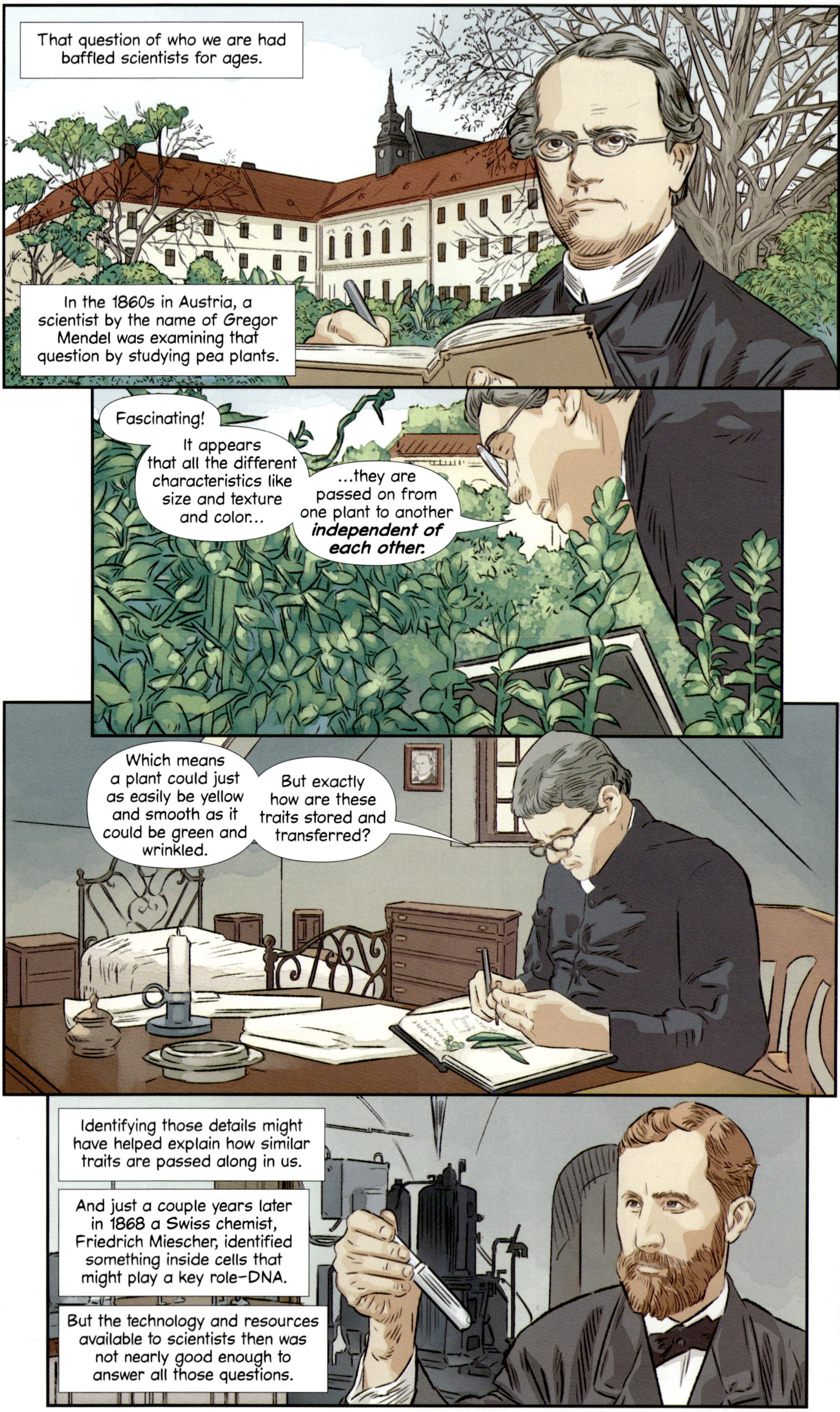

That question of who we are had baffled scientists for ages.
In the 1860s in Austria, a scientist by the name of Gregor Mendel was examining that question by studying pea plants.
Fascinating!
It appears that all the different characteristics like size and texture and color...
...they are passed on from one plant to another ***independent of each other.***
Which means a plant could just as easily be yellow and smooth as it could be green and wrinkled.
But exactly how are these traits stored and transferred?
Identifying those details might have helped explain how similar traits are passed along in us.
And just a couple years later in 1868 a Swiss chemist, Friedrich Miescher, identified something inside cells that might play a key role–DNA.
But the technology and resources available to scientists then was not nearly good enough to answer all those questions.

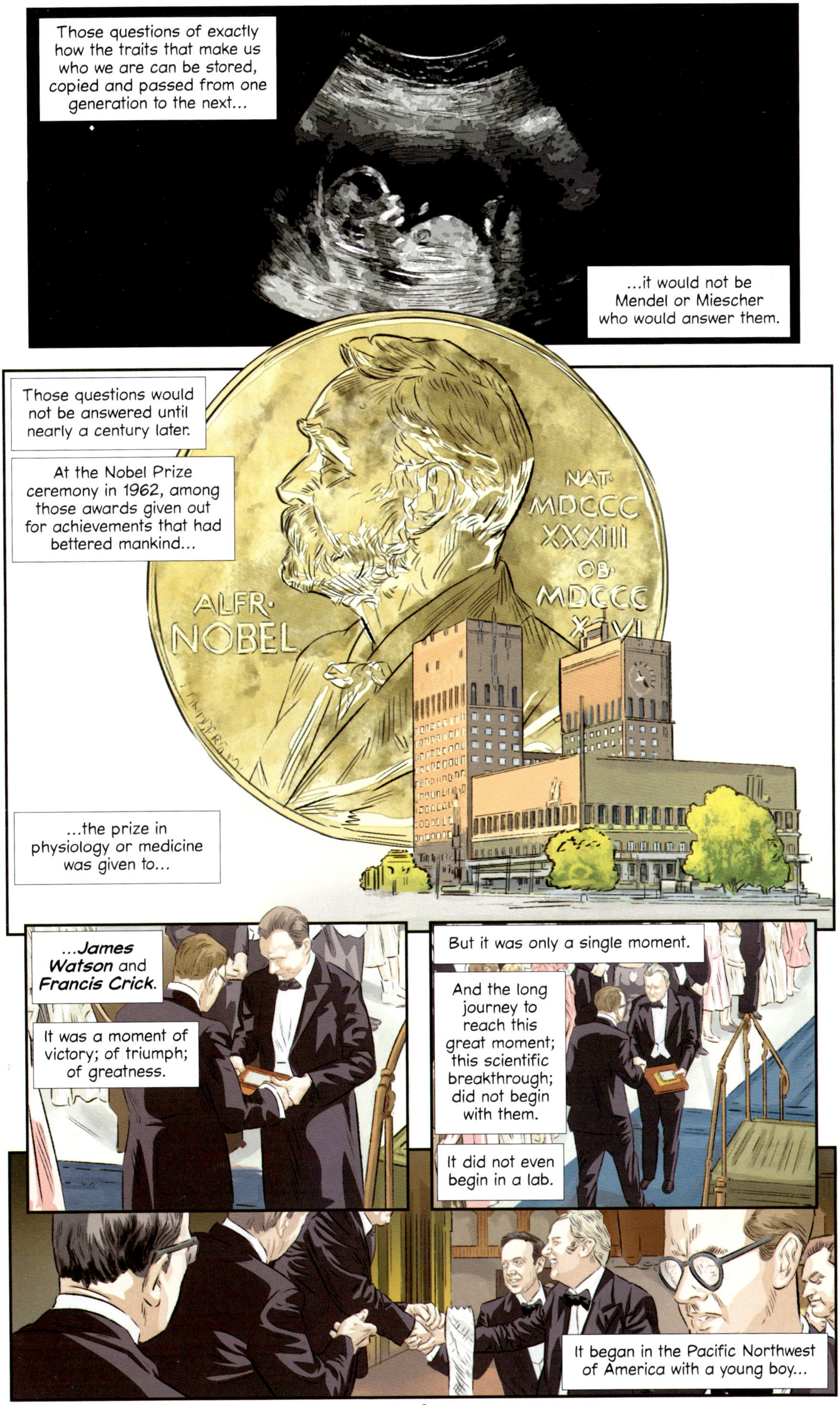
Those questions of exactly how the traits that make us who we are can be stored, copied and passed from one generation to the next...
...it would not be Mendel or Miescher who would answer them.
Those questions would not be answered until nearly a century later.
At the Nobel Prize ceremony in 1962, among those awards given out for achievements that had bettered mankind...
NAT. MDCCC XXXIII OB. MDCCC XCVI
ALFR. NOBEL
...the prize in physiology or medicine was given to...
...James Watson and Francis Crick.
It was a moment of victory; of triumph; of greatness.
But it was only a single moment.
And the long journey to reach this great moment; this scientific breakthrough; did not begin with them.
It did not even begin in a lab.
It began in the Pacific Northwest of America with a young boy...

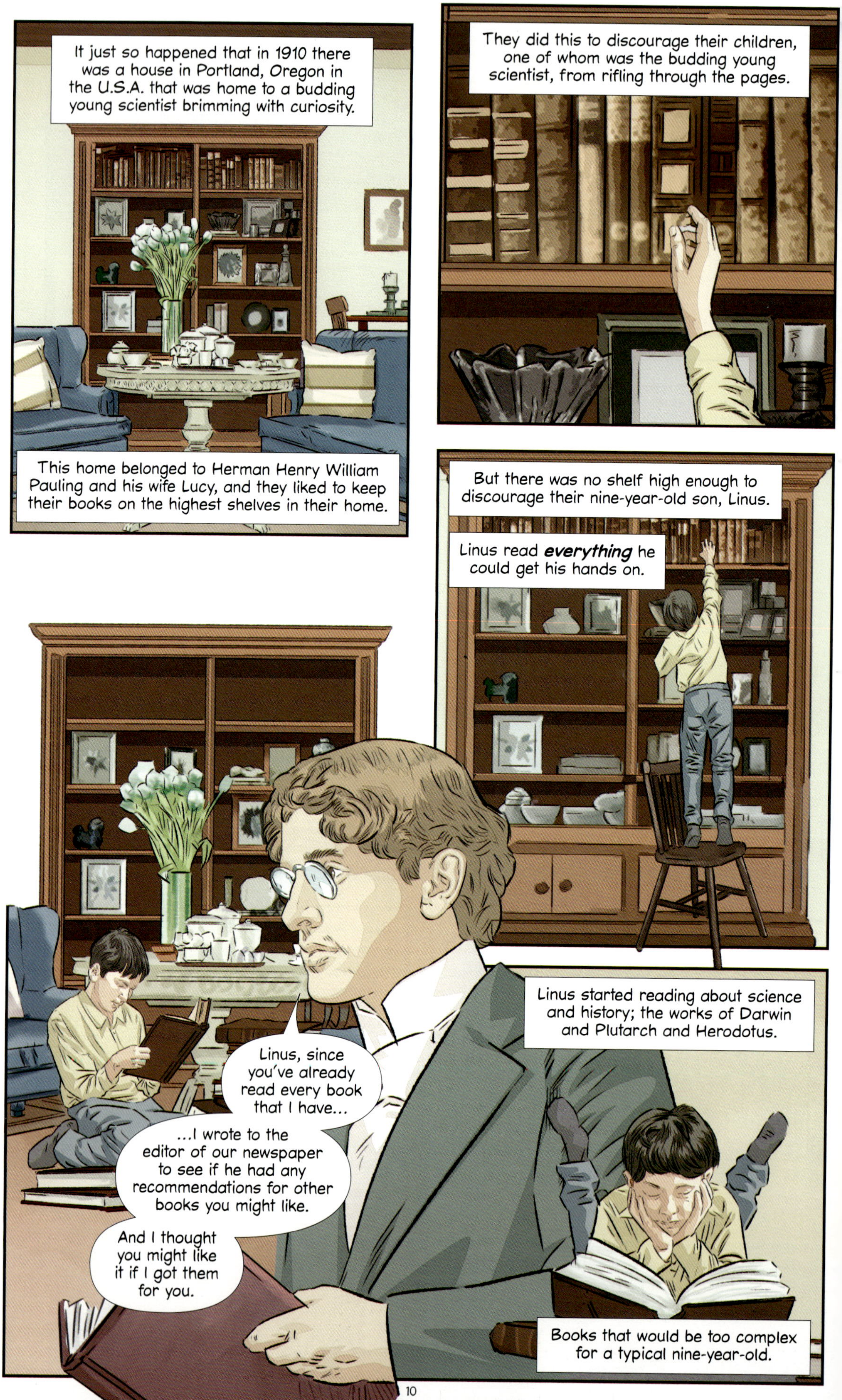
It just so happened that in 1910 there was a house in Portland, Oregon in the U.S.A. that was home to a budding young scientist brimming with curiosity.
This home belonged to Herman Henry William Pauling and his wife Lucy, and they liked to keep their books on the highest shelves in their home.
They did this to discourage their children, one of whom was the budding young scientist, from rifling through the pages.
But there was no shelf high enough to discourage their nine-year-old son, Linus.
Linus read ***everything*** he could get his hands on.
Linus, since you've already read every book that I have...
...I wrote to the editor of our newspaper to see if he had any recommendations for other books you might like.
And I thought you might like it if I got them for you.
Linus started reading about science and history; the works of Darwin and Plutarch and Herodotus.
Books that would be too complex for a typical nine-year-old.

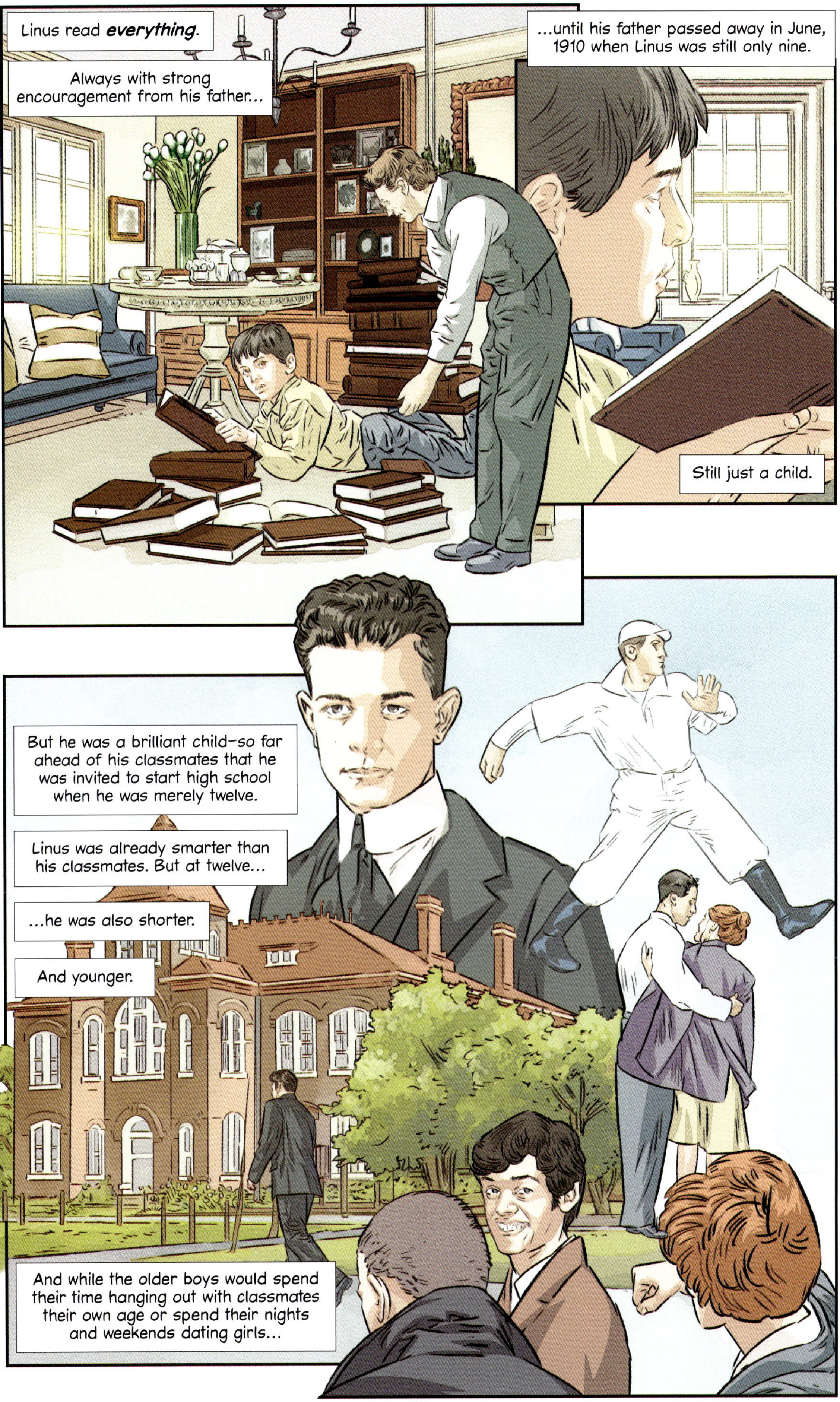
Linus read *everything*.
Always with strong encouragement from his father...
...until his father passed away in June, 1910 when Linus was still only nine.
Still just a child.
But he was a brilliant child–so far ahead of his classmates that he was invited to start high school when he was merely twelve.
Linus was already smarter than his classmates. But at twelve...
...he was also shorter.
And younger.
And while the older boys would spend their time hanging out with classmates their own age or spend their nights and weekends dating girls...

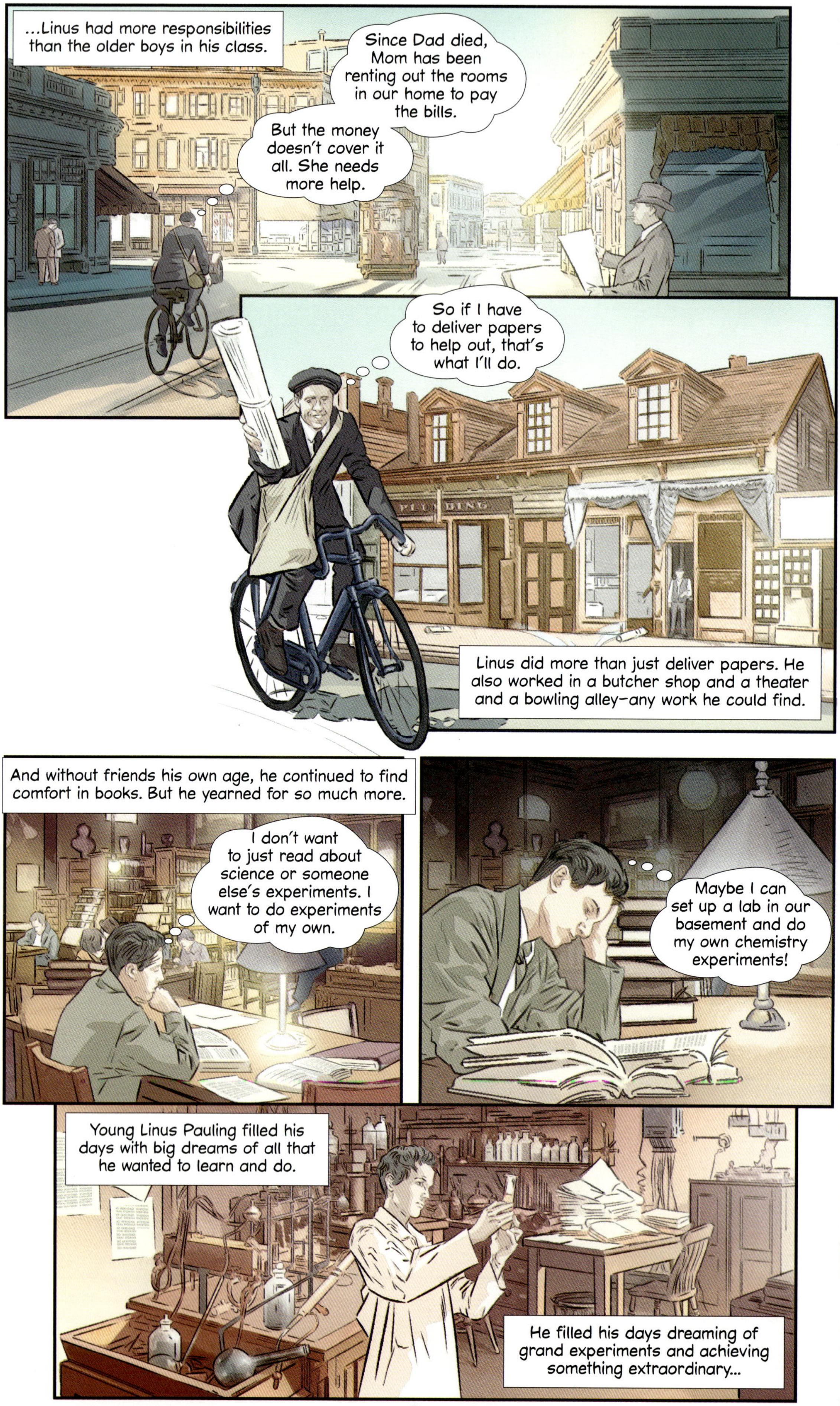
...Linus had more responsibilities than the older boys in his class.
Since Dad died, Mom has been renting out the rooms in our home to pay the bills.
But the money doesn't cover it all. She needs more help.
So if I have to deliver papers to help out, that's what I'll do.
PLUMBING
Linus did more than just deliver papers. He also worked in a butcher shop and a theater and a bowling alley—any work he could find.
And without friends his own age, he continued to find comfort in books. But he yearned for so much more.
I don't want to just read about science or someone else's experiments. I want to do experiments of my own.
Maybe I can set up a lab in our basement and do my own chemistry experiments!
Young Linus Pauling filled his days with big dreams of all that he wanted to learn and do.
He filled his days dreaming of grand experiments and achieving something extraordinary...

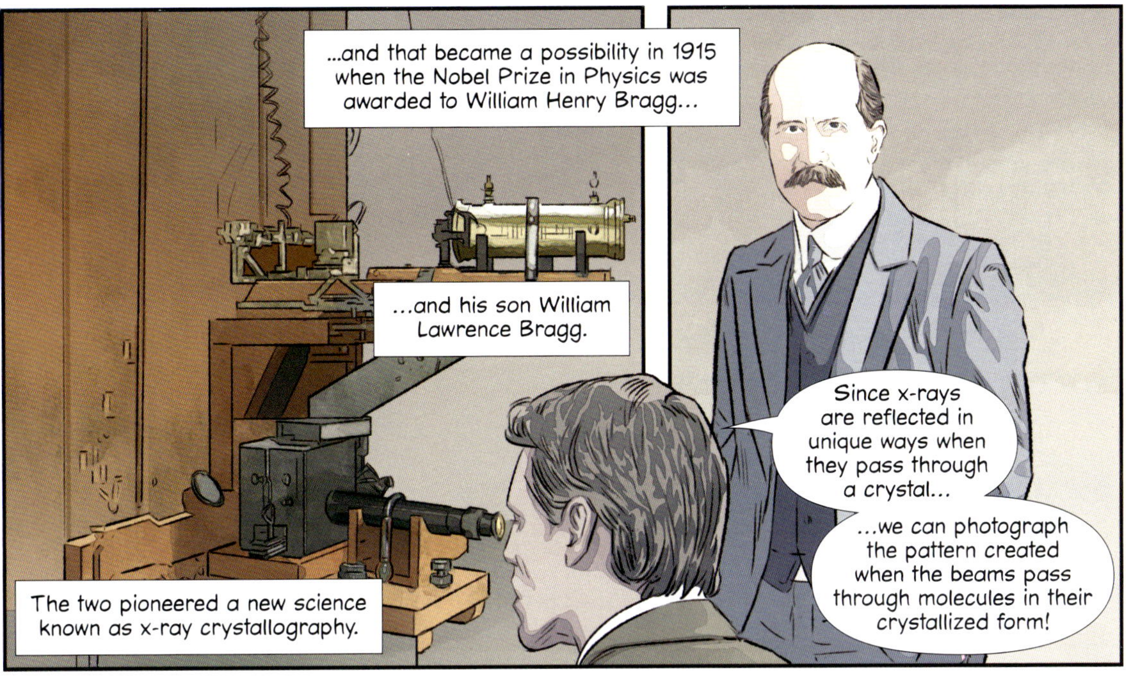
...and that became a possibility in 1915 when the Nobel Prize in Physics was awarded to William Henry Bragg...
...and his son William Lawrence Bragg.
The two pioneered a new science known as x-ray crystallography.
Since x-rays are reflected in unique ways when they pass through a crystal...
...we can photograph the pattern created when the beams pass through molecules in their crystallized form!

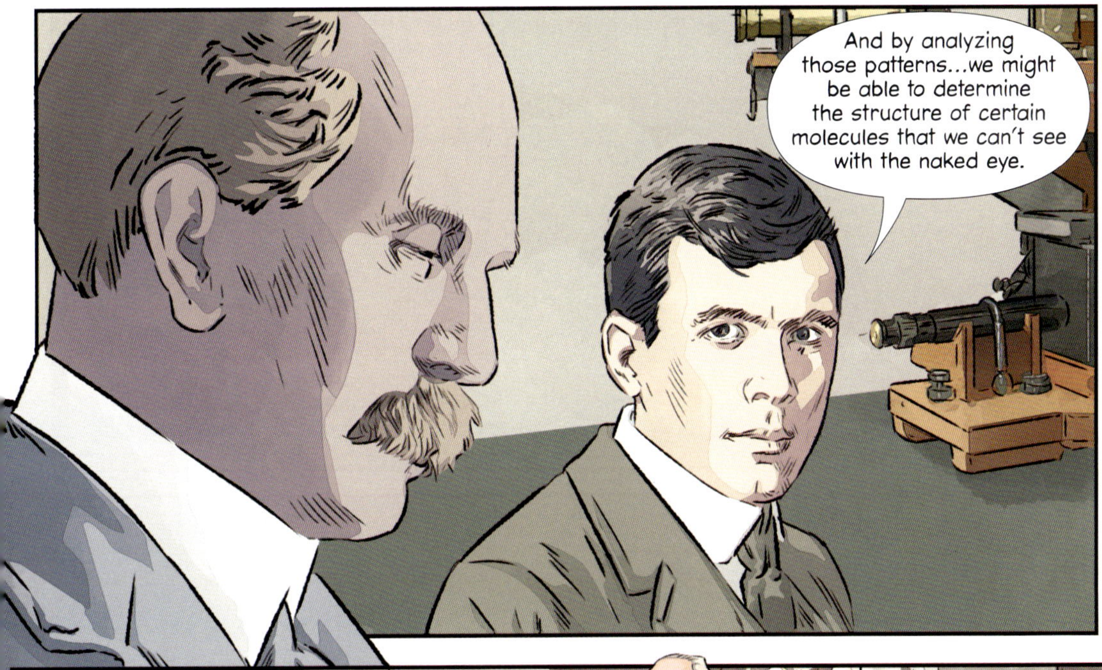
And by analyzing those patterns...we might be able to determine the structure of certain molecules that we can't see with the naked eye.

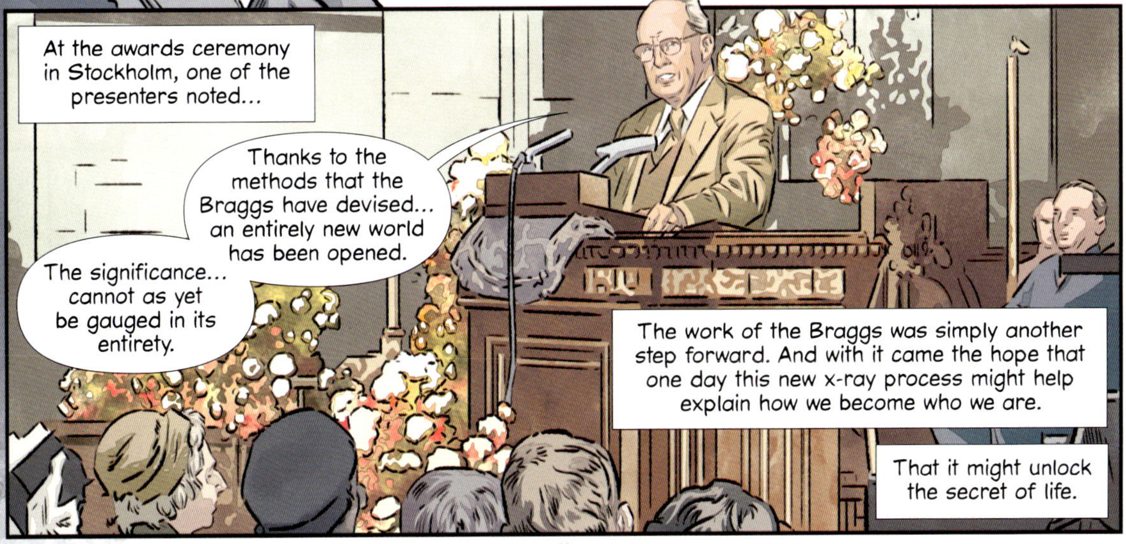
At the awards ceremony in Stockholm, one of the presenters noted...
Thanks to the methods that the Braggs have devised... an entirely new world has been opened.
The significance... cannot as yet be gauged in its entirety.
The work of the Braggs was simply another step forward. And with it came the hope that one day this new x-ray process might help explain how we become who we are.
That it might unlock the secret of life.

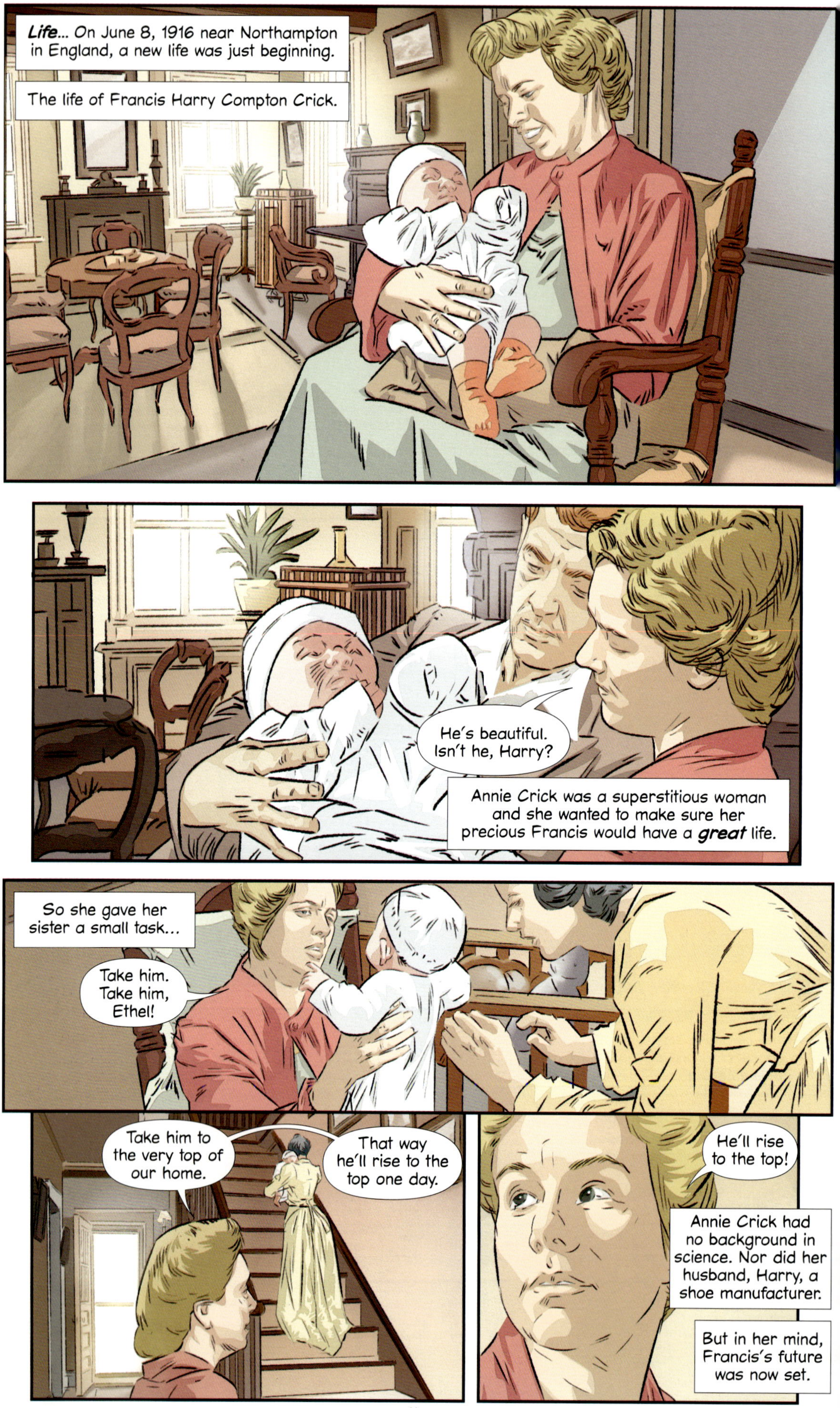
Life... On June 8, 1916 near Northampton in England, a new life was just beginning.
The life of Francis Harry Compton Crick.
He's beautiful. Isn't he, Harry?
Annie Crick was a superstitious woman and she wanted to make sure her precious Francis would have a great life.
So she gave her sister a small task...
Take him. Take him, Ethel!
Take him to the very top of our home.
That way he'll rise to the top one day.
He'll rise to the top!
Annie Crick had no background in science. Nor did her husband, Harry, a shoe manufacturer.
But in her mind, Francis's future was now set.

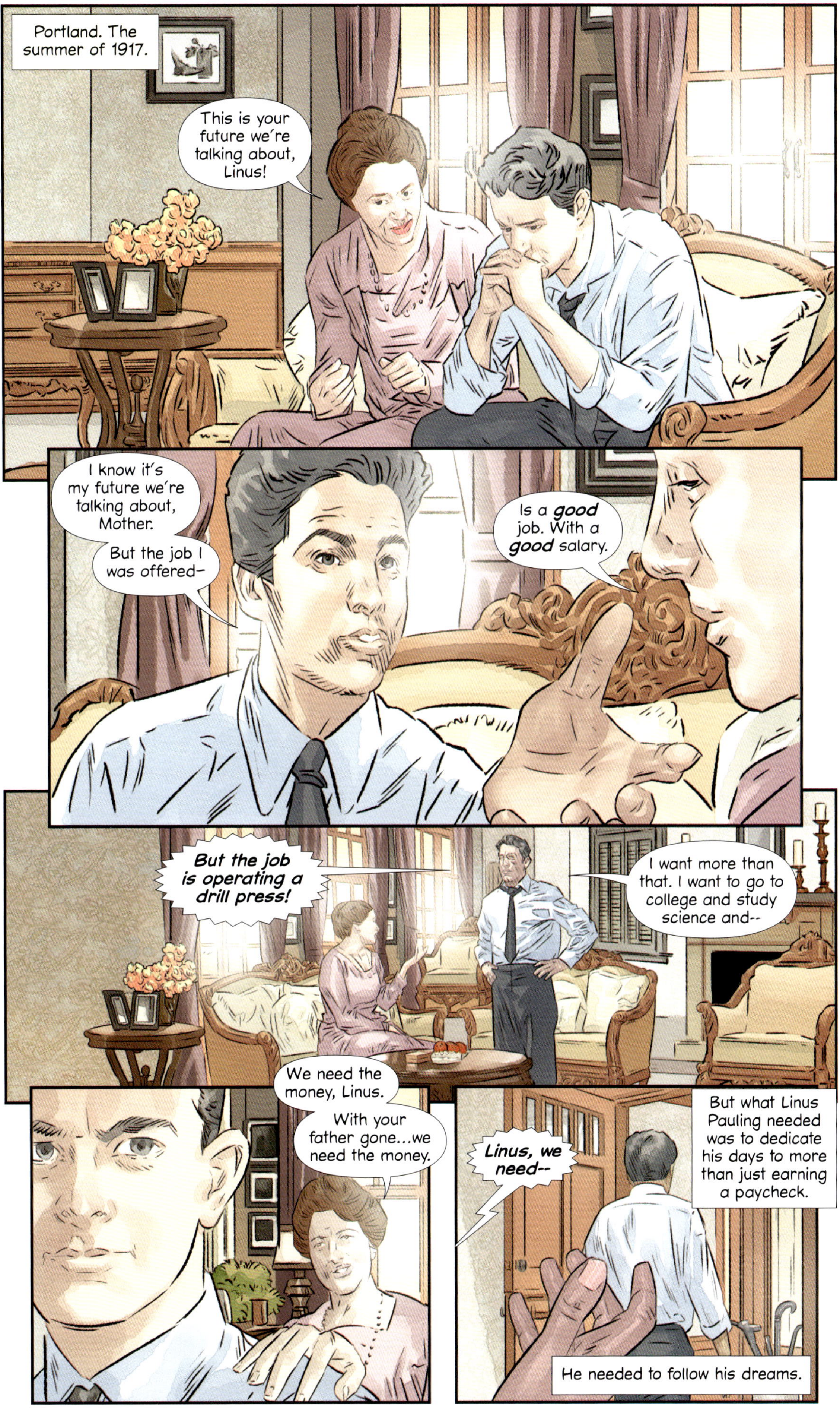

Portland. The summer of 1917.
This is your future we're talking about, Linus!
I know it's my future we're talking about, Mother.
But the job I was offered–
Is a *good* job. With a *good* salary.
But the job is operating a drill press!
I want more than that. I want to go to college and study science and--
We need the money, Linus.
With your father gone...we need the money.
Linus, we need--
But what Linus Pauling needed was to dedicate his days to more than just earning a paycheck.
He needed to follow his dreams.

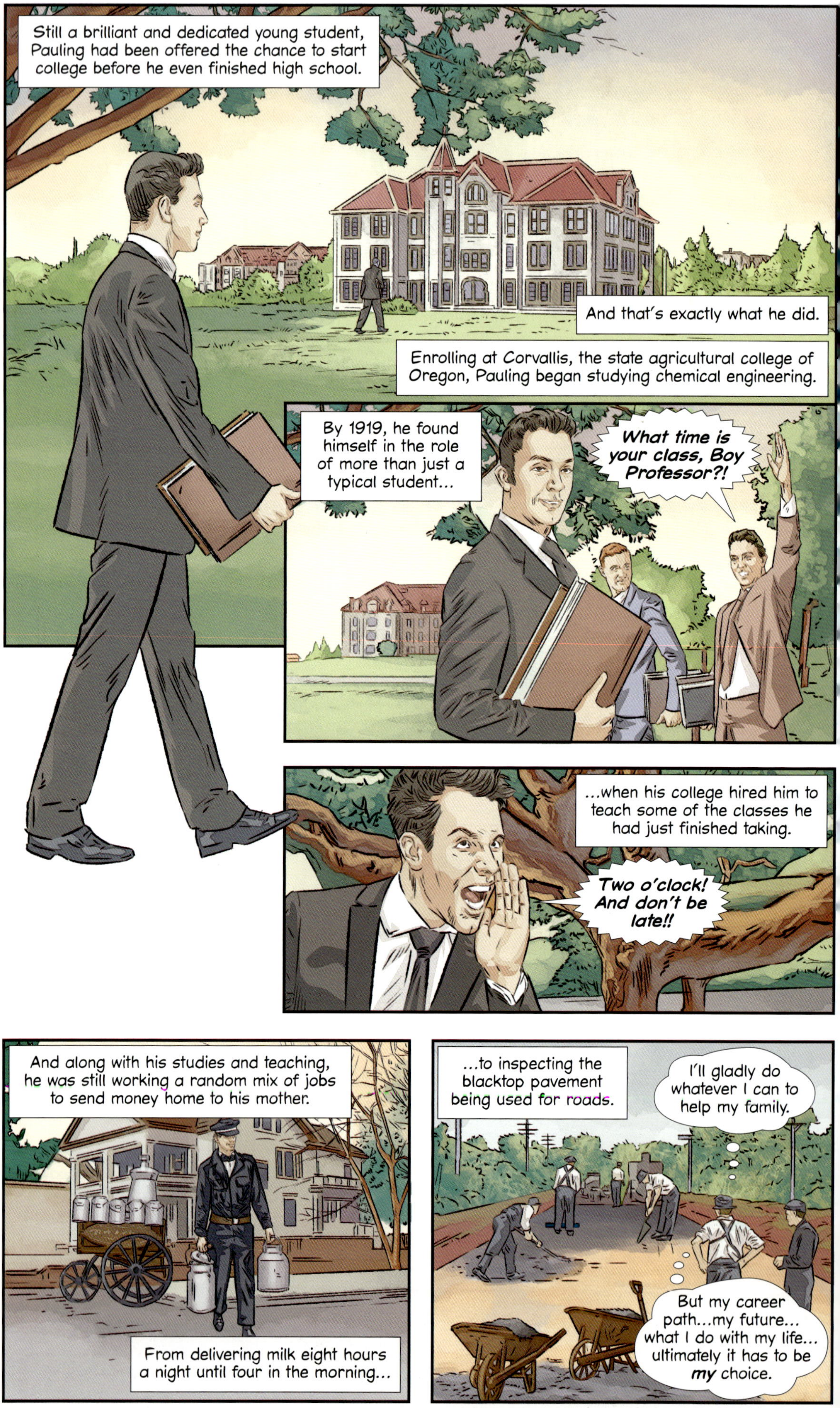

Still a brilliant and dedicated young student, Pauling had been offered the chance to start college before he even finished high school.
And that's exactly what he did.
Enrolling at Corvallis, the state agricultural college of Oregon, Pauling began studying chemical engineering.
By 1919, he found himself in the role of more than just a typical student...
What time is your class, Boy Professor?!
...when his college hired him to teach some of the classes he had just finished taking.
Two o'clock! And don't be late!!
And along with his studies and teaching, he was still working a random mix of jobs to send money home to his mother.
From delivering milk eight hours a night until four in the morning...
...to inspecting the blacktop pavement being used for roads.
I'll gladly do whatever I can to help my family.
But my career path...my future... what I do with my life... ultimately it has to be *my* choice.

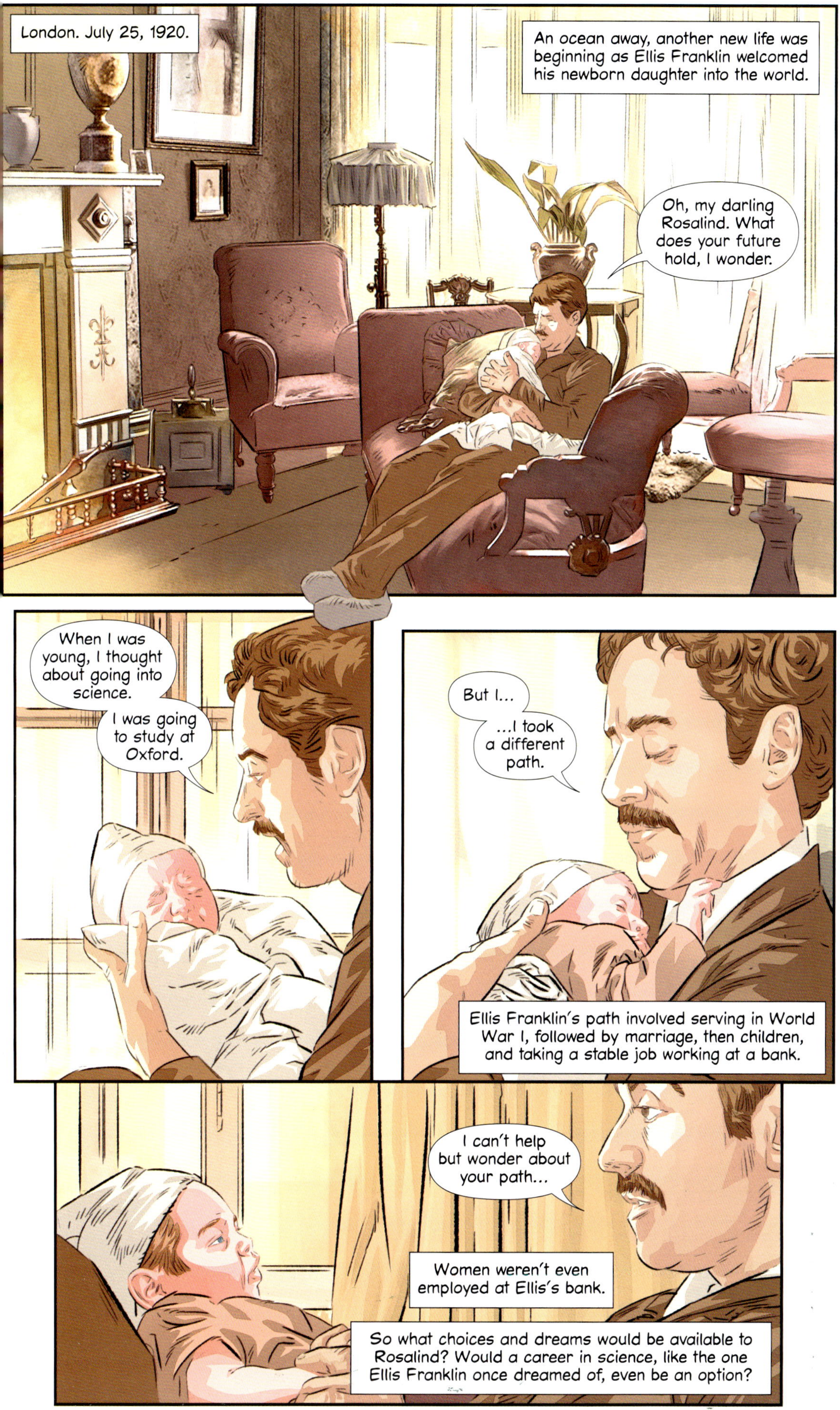

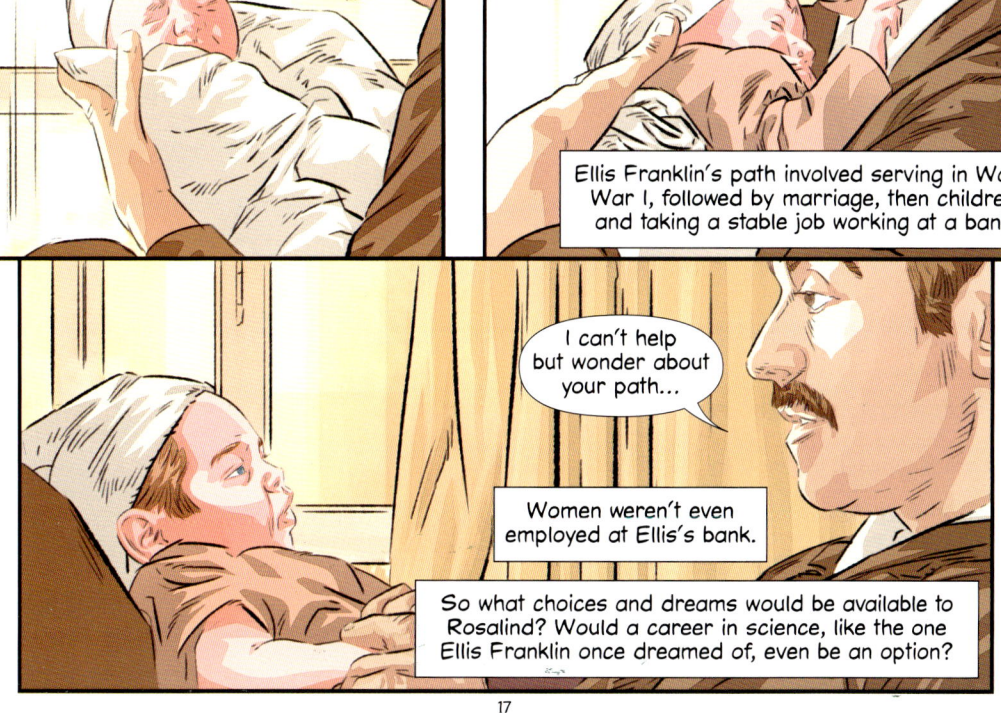

London. July 25, 1920.

An ocean away, another new life was beginning as Ellis Franklin welcomed his newborn daughter into the world.

Oh, my darling Rosalind. What does your future hold, I wonder.

When I was young, I thought about going into science. I was going to study at Oxford.

But I... ...I took a different path.

Ellis Franklin's path involved serving in World War I, followed by marriage, then children, and taking a stable job working at a bank.

I can't help but wonder about your path...

Women weren't even employed at Ellis's bank.

So what choices and dreams would be available to Rosalind? Would a career in science, like the one Ellis Franklin once dreamed of, even be an option?

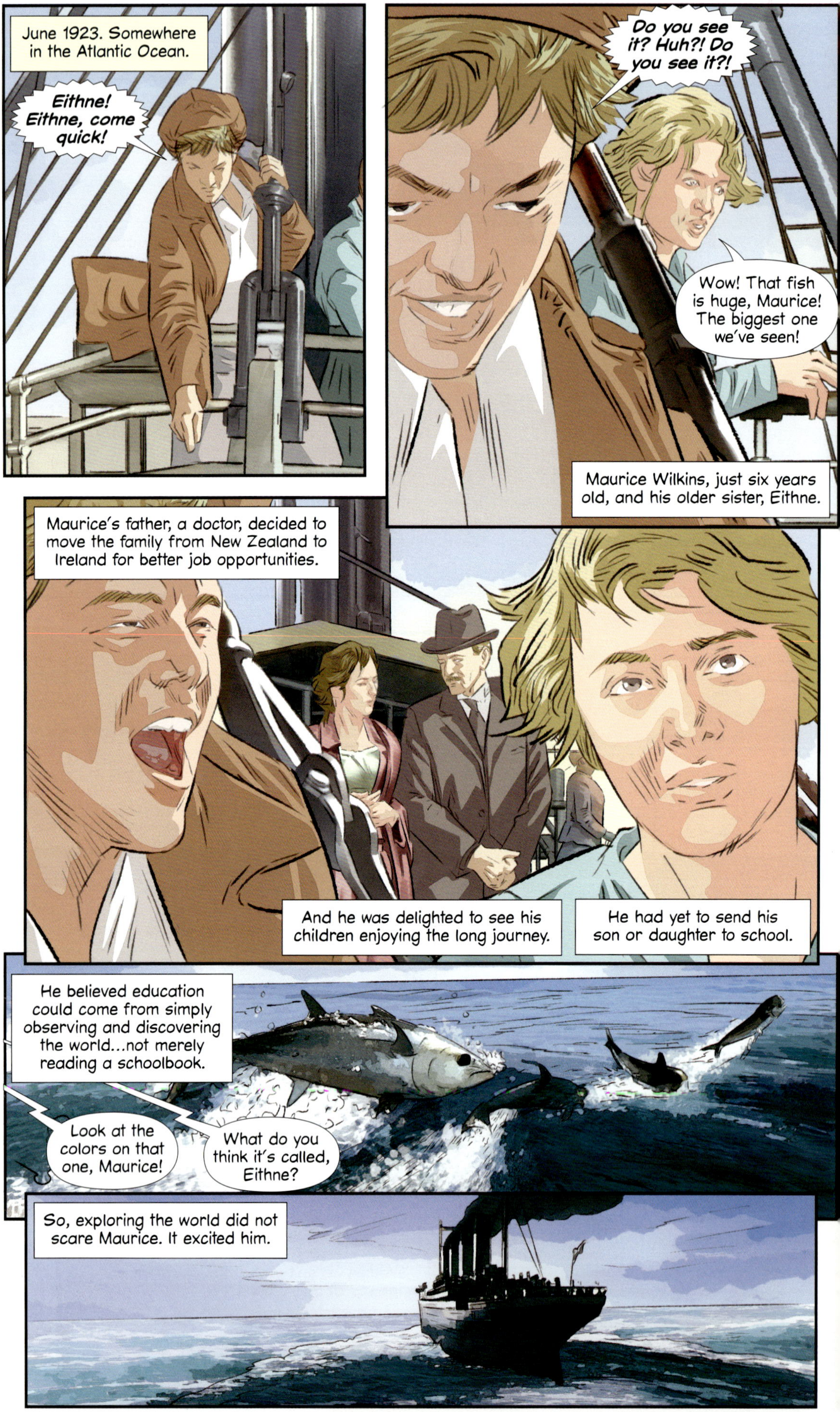

June 1923. Somewhere in the Atlantic Ocean.
Eithne! Eithne, come quick!
Do you see it? Huh?! Do you see it?!
Wow! That fish is huge, Maurice! The biggest one we've seen!
Maurice Wilkins, just six years old, and his older sister, Eithne.
Maurice's father, a doctor, decided to move the family from New Zealand to Ireland for better job opportunities.
And he was delighted to see his children enjoying the long journey.
He had yet to send his son or daughter to school.
He believed education could come from simply observing and discovering the world...not merely reading a schoolbook.
Look at the colors on that one, Maurice!
What do you think it's called, Eithne?
So, exploring the world did not scare Maurice. It excited him.

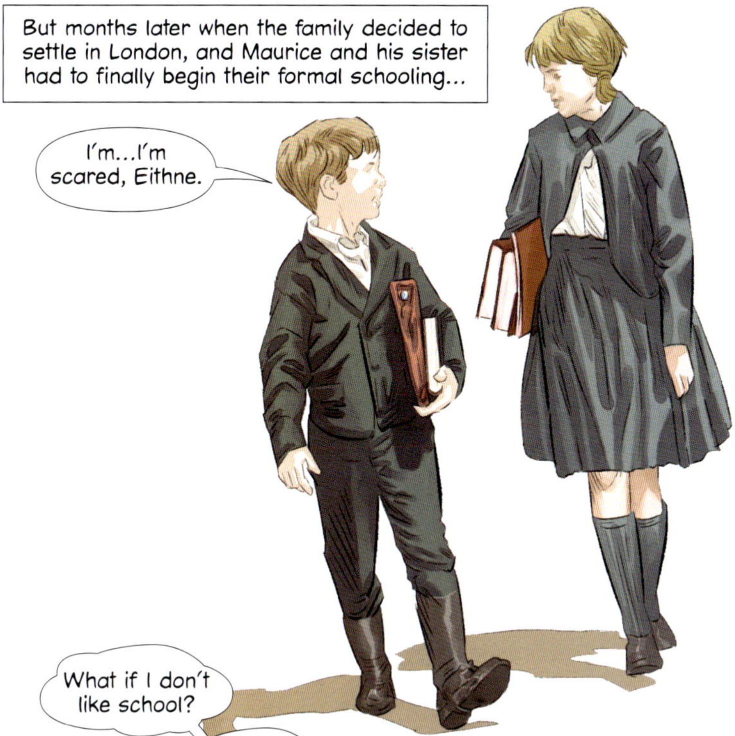
But months later when the family decided to settle in London, and Maurice and his sister had to finally begin their formal schooling...
I'm...I'm scared, Eithne.
What if I don't like school?

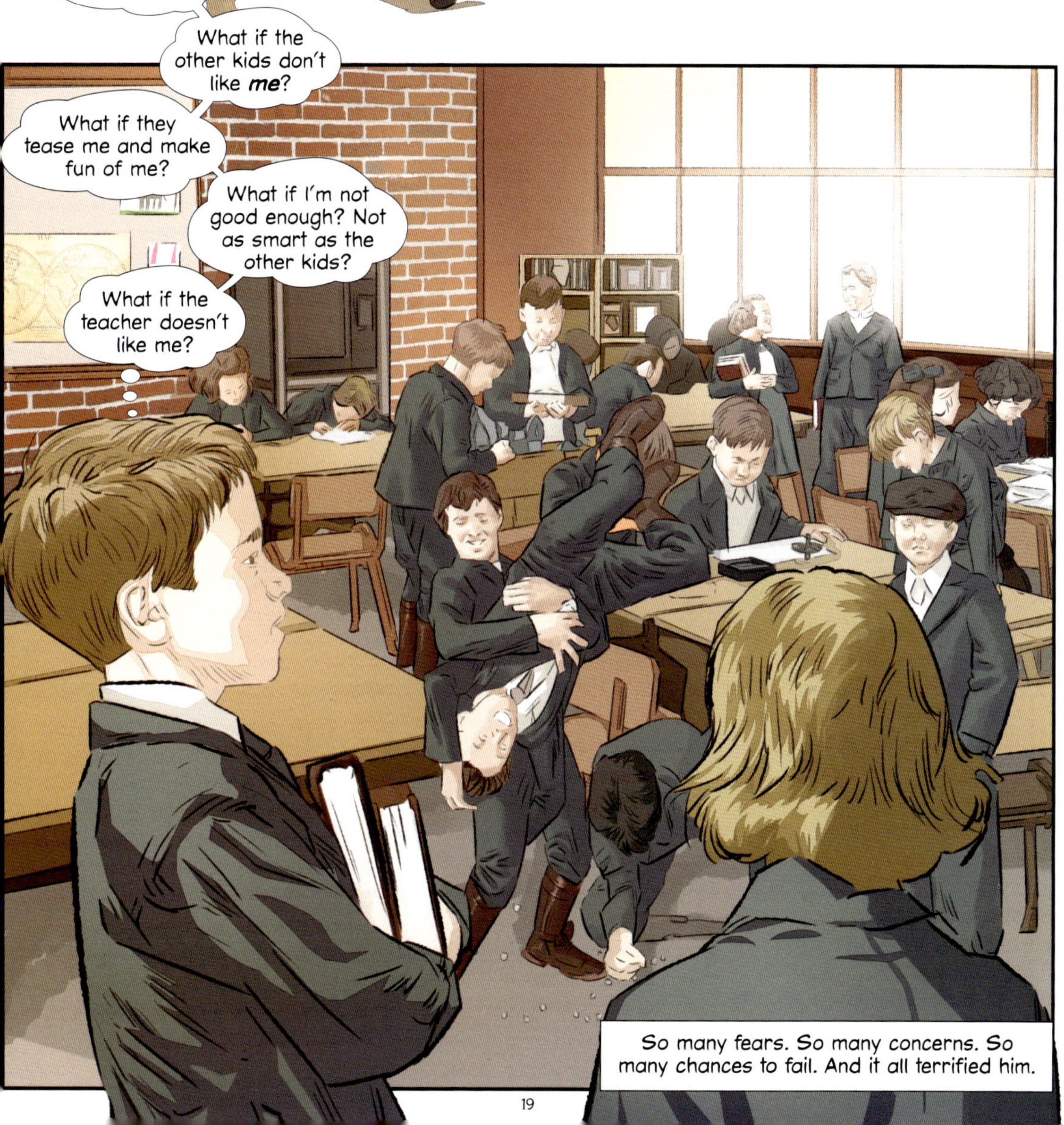
What if the other kids don't like *me*?
What if they tease me and make fun of me?
What if I'm not good enough? Not as smart as the other kids?
What if the teacher doesn't like me?
So many fears. So many concerns. So many chances to fail. And it all terrified him.

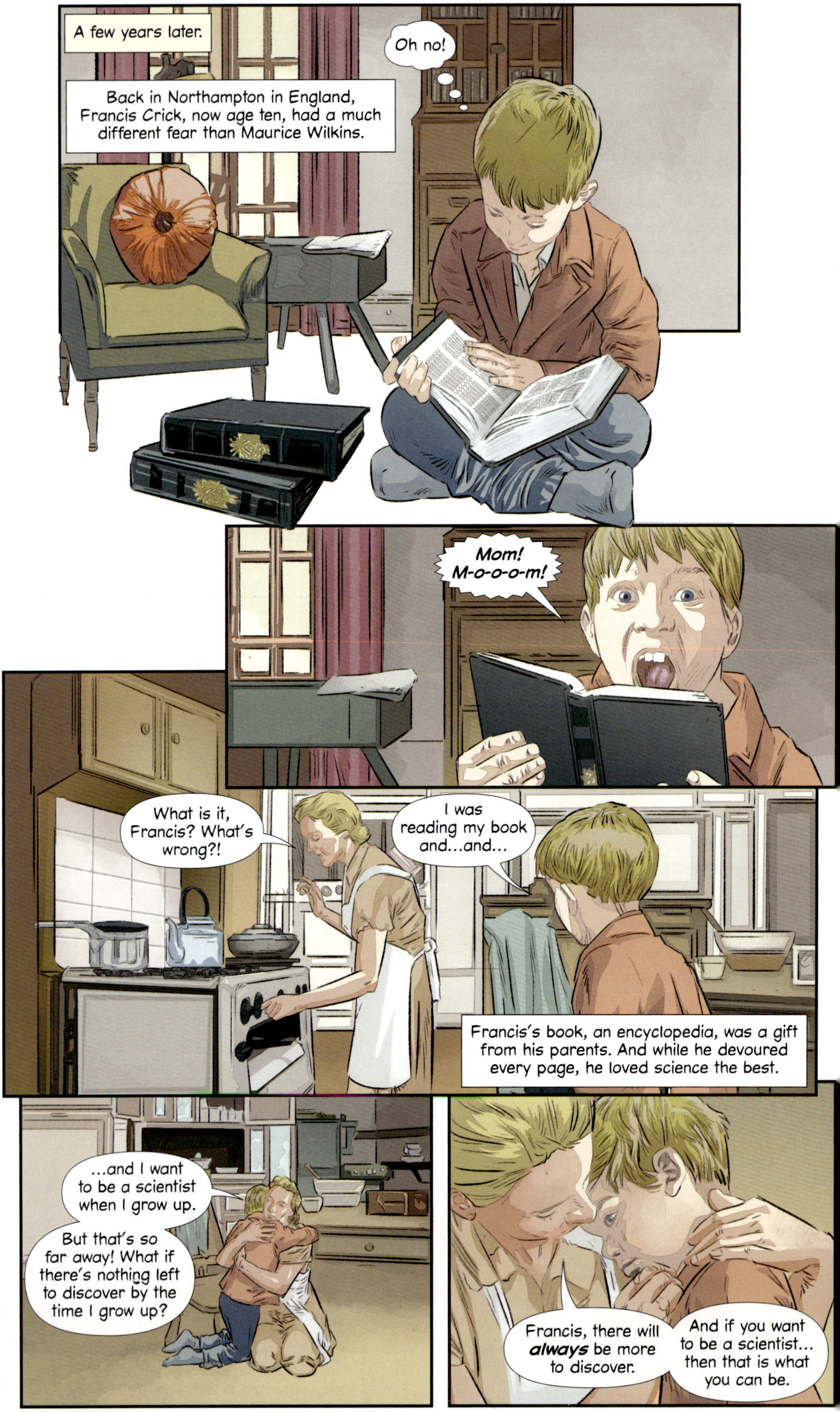

A few years later.
Back in Northampton in England, Francis Crick, now age ten, had a much different fear than Maurice Wilkins.
Oh no!
Mom! M-o-o-o-m!
What is it, Francis? What's wrong?!
I was reading my book and...and...
Francis's book, an encyclopedia, was a gift from his parents. And while he devoured every page, he loved science the best.
...and I want to be a scientist when I grow up.
But that's so far away! What if there's nothing left to discover by the time I grow up?
Francis, there will *always* be more to discover.
And if you want to be a scientist... then that is what you can be.

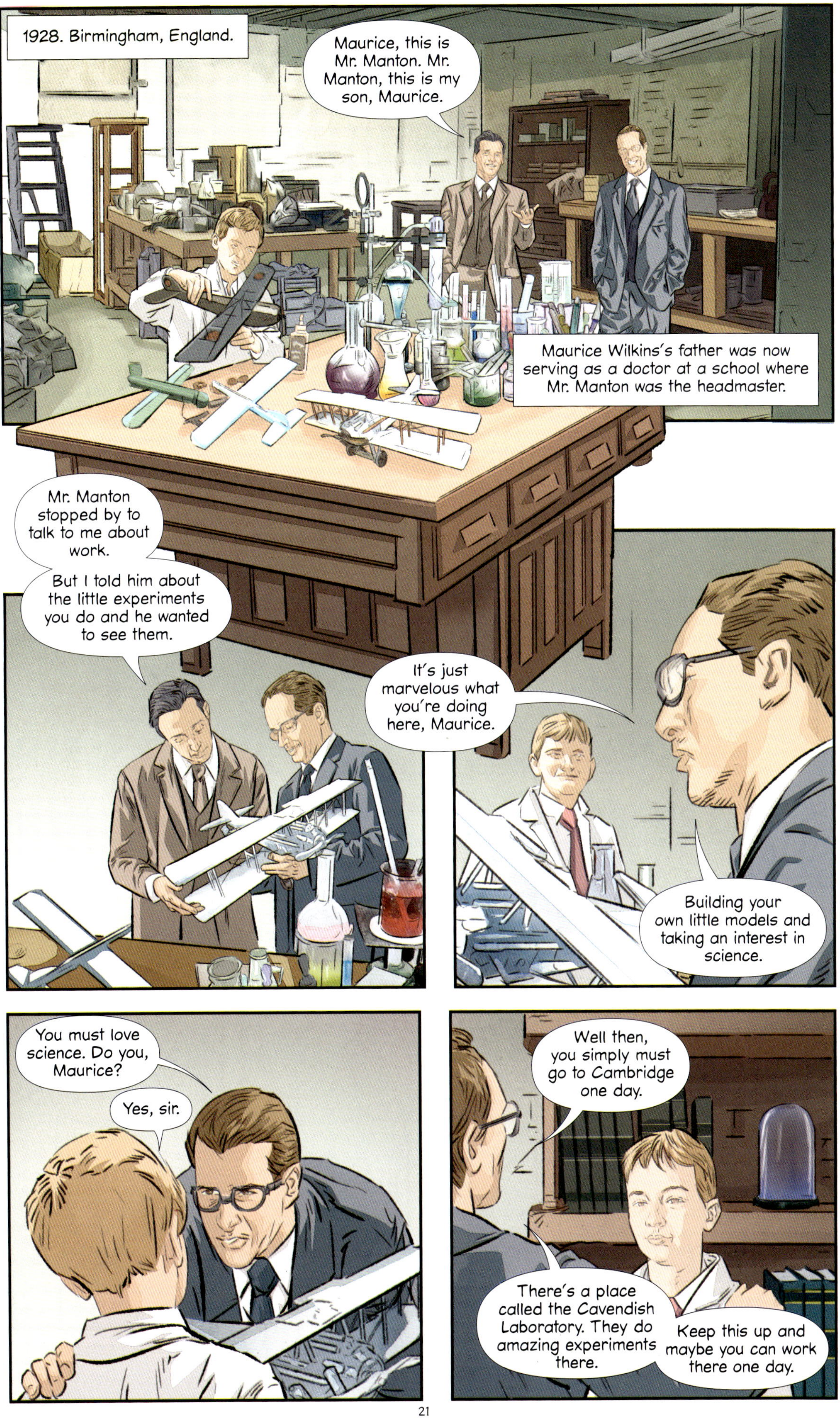
1928. Birmingham, England.
Maurice, this is Mr. Manton. Mr. Manton, this is my son, Maurice.
Maurice Wilkins's father was now serving as a doctor at a school where Mr. Manton was the headmaster.
Mr. Manton stopped by to talk to me about work.
But I told him about the little experiments you do and he wanted to see them.
It's just marvelous what you're doing here, Maurice.
Building your own little models and taking an interest in science.
You must love science. Do you, Maurice?
Yes, sir.
Well then, you simply must go to Cambridge one day.
There's a place called the Cavendish Laboratory. They do amazing experiments there.
Keep this up and maybe you can work there one day.

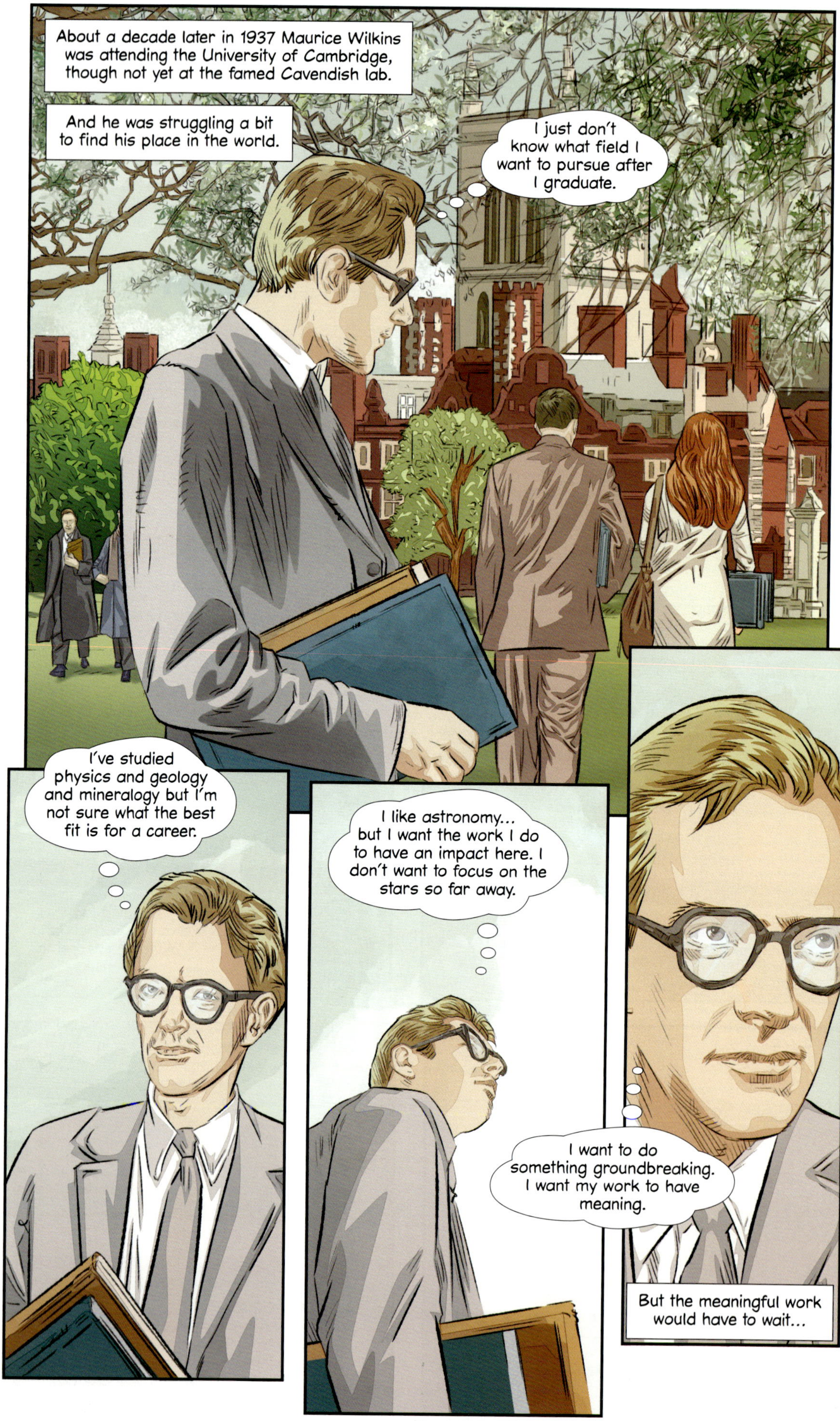
About a decade later in 1937 Maurice Wilkins was attending the University of Cambridge, though not yet at the famed Cavendish lab.
And he was struggling a bit to find his place in the world.
I just don't know what field I want to pursue after I graduate.
I've studied physics and geology and mineralogy but I'm not sure what the best fit is for a career.
I like astronomy... but I want the work I do to have an impact here. I don't want to focus on the stars so far away.
I want to do something groundbreaking. I want my work to have meaning.
But the meaningful work would have to wait...

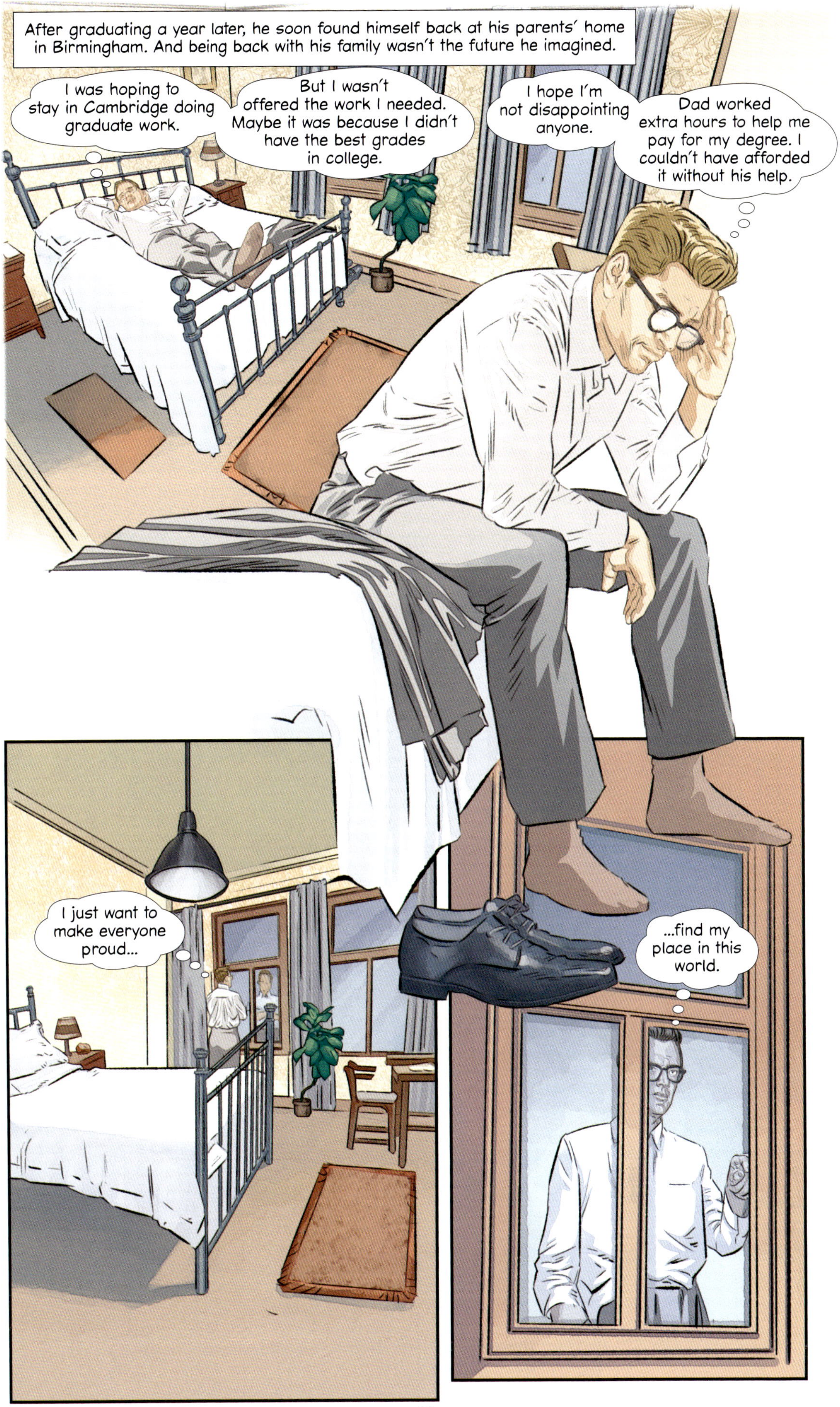
After graduating a year later, he soon found himself back at his parents' home in Birmingham. And being back with his family wasn't the future he imagined.
I was hoping to stay in Cambridge doing graduate work.
But I wasn't offered the work I needed. Maybe it was because I didn't have the best grades in college.
I hope I'm not disappointing anyone.
Dad worked extra hours to help me pay for my degree. I couldn't have afforded it without his help.
I just want to make everyone proud...
...find my place in this world.

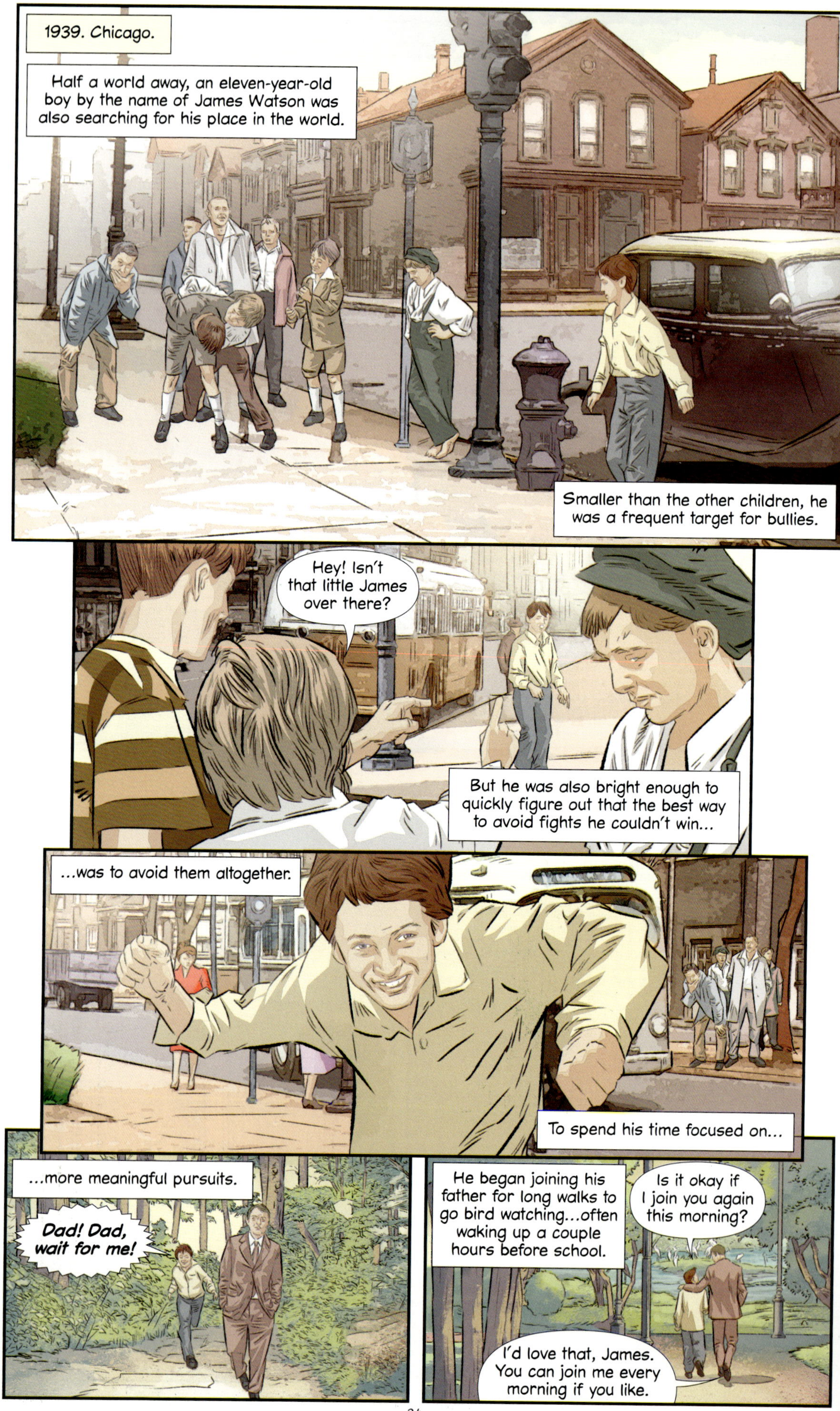
1939. Chicago.
Half a world away, an eleven-year-old boy by the name of James Watson was also searching for his place in the world.
Smaller than the other children, he was a frequent target for bullies.
Hey! Isn't that little James over there?
But he was also bright enough to quickly figure out that the best way to avoid fights he couldn't win...
...was to avoid them altogether.
To spend his time focused on...
...more meaningful pursuits.
Dad! Dad, wait for me!
He began joining his father for long walks to go bird watching...often waking up a couple hours before school.
Is it okay if I join you again this morning?
I'd love that, James. You can join me every morning if you like.

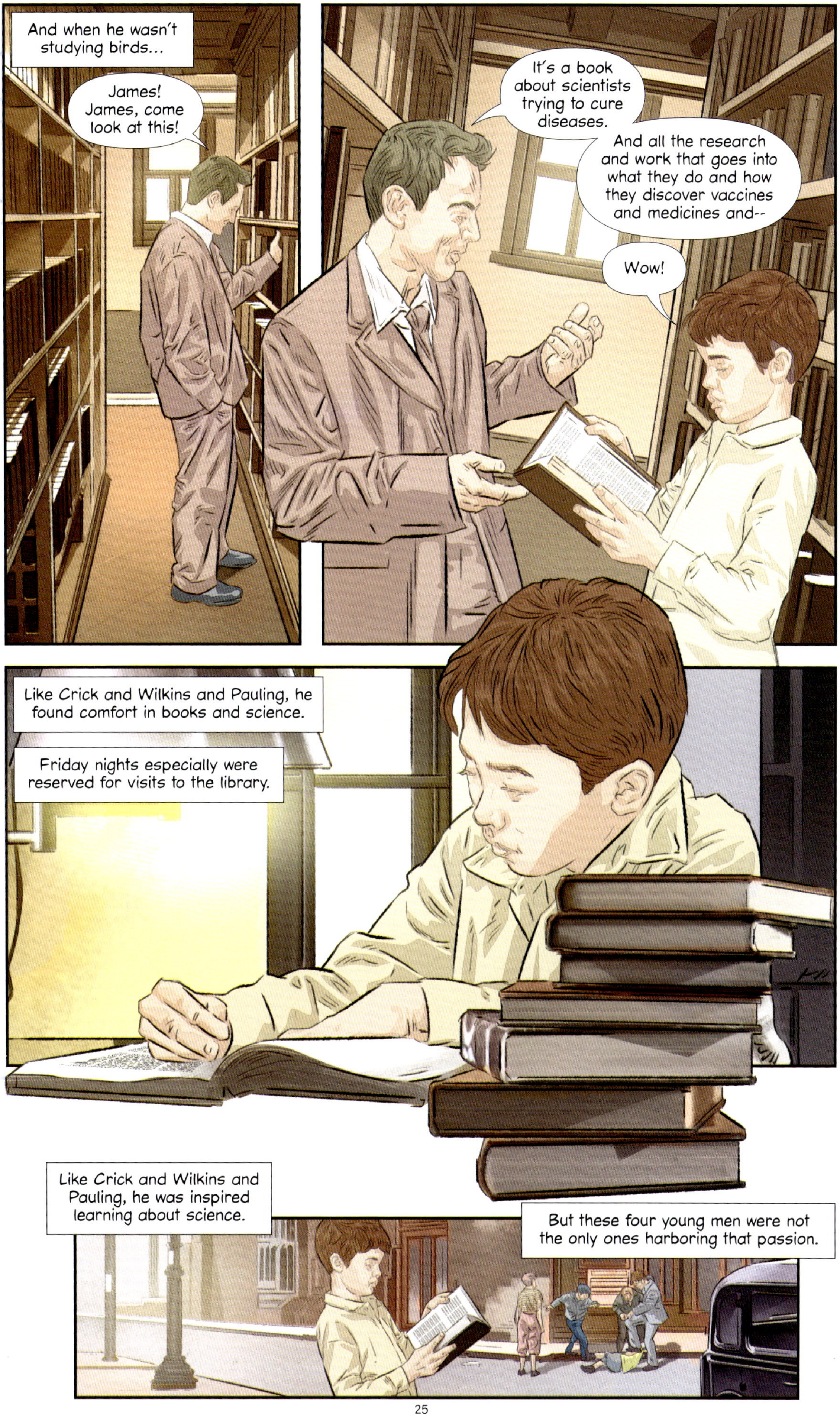
And when he wasn't studying birds...
James! James, come look at this!
It's a book about scientists trying to cure diseases.
And all the research and work that goes into what they do and how they discover vaccines and medicines and--
Wow!
Like Crick and Wilkins and Pauling, he found comfort in books and science.
Friday nights especially were reserved for visits to the library.
Like Crick and Wilkins and Pauling, he was inspired learning about science.
But these four young men were not the only ones harboring that passion.

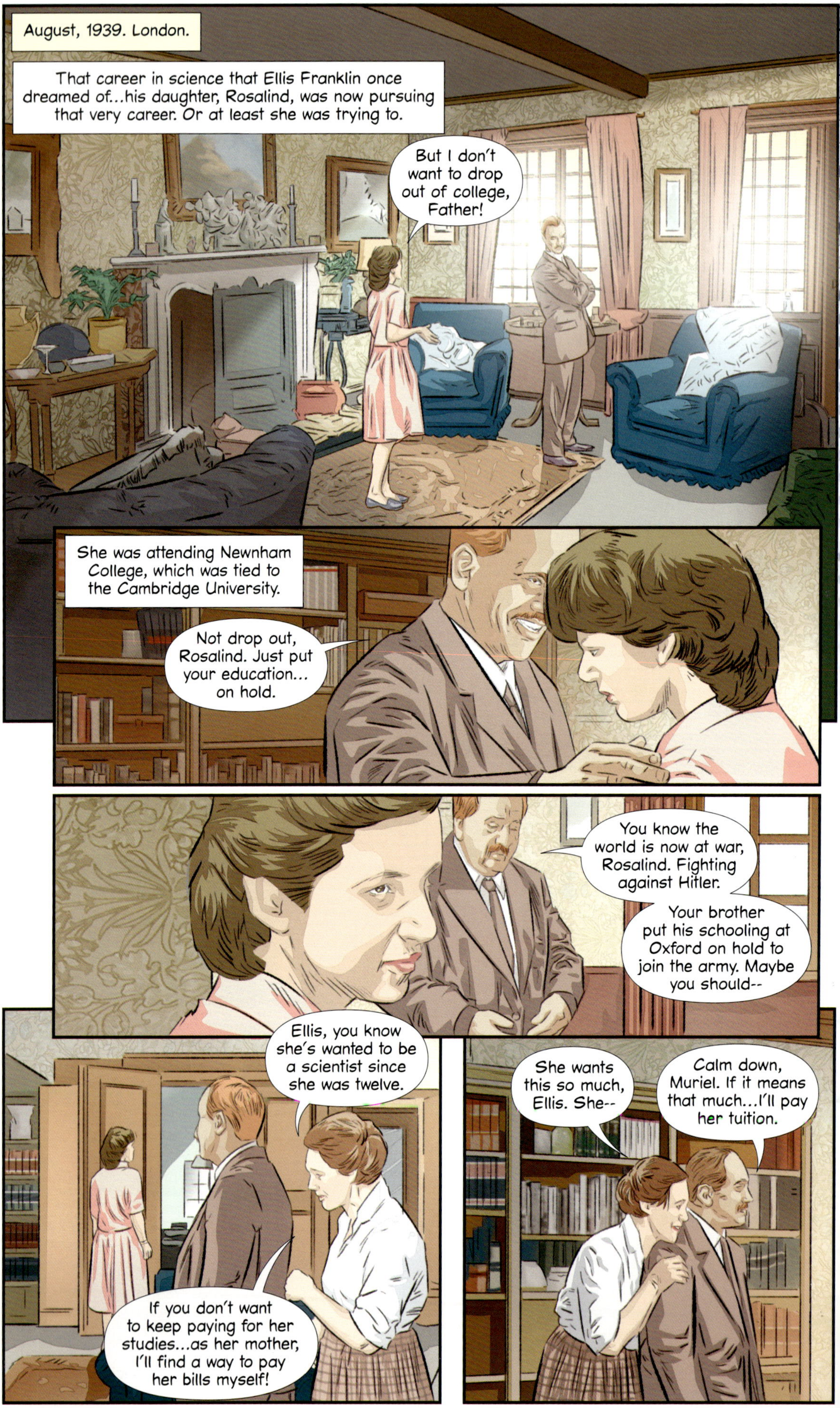

August, 1939. London.
That career in science that Ellis Franklin once dreamed of...his daughter, Rosalind, was now pursuing that very career. Or at least she was trying to.
But I don't want to drop out of college, Father!
She was attending Newnham College, which was tied to the Cambridge University.
Not drop out, Rosalind. Just put your education... on hold.
You know the world is now at war, Rosalind. Fighting against Hitler.
Your brother put his schooling at Oxford on hold to join the army. Maybe you should--
Ellis, you know she's wanted to be a scientist since she was twelve.
If you don't want to keep paying for her studies...as her mother, I'll find a way to pay her bills myself!
She wants this so much, Ellis. She--
Calm down, Muriel. If it means that much...I'll pay her tuition.

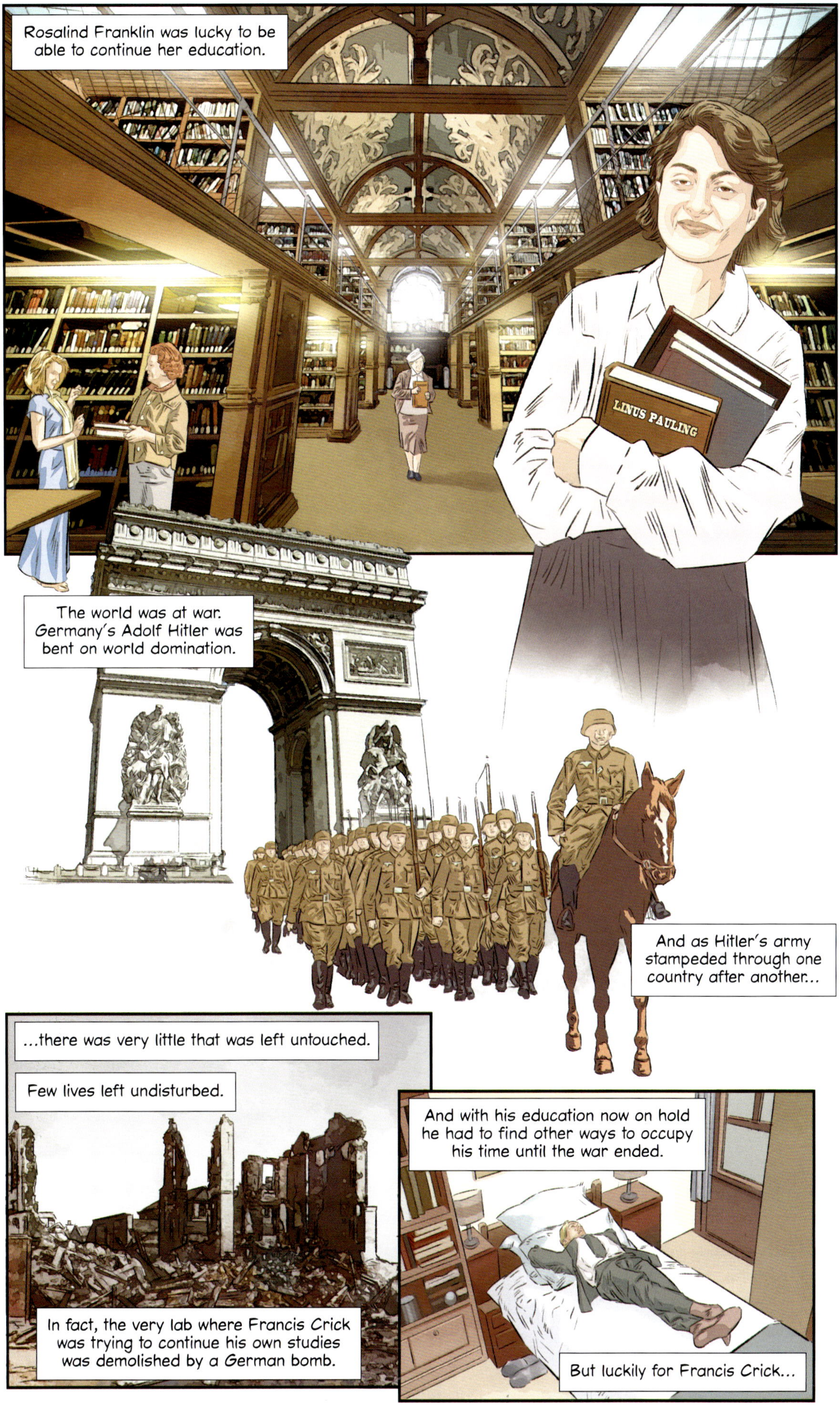
Rosalind Franklin was lucky to be able to continue her education.
LINUS PAULING
The world was at war. Germany's Adolf Hitler was bent on world domination.
And as Hitler's army stampeded through one country after another...
...there was very little that was left untouched.
Few lives left undisturbed.
In fact, the very lab where Francis Crick was trying to continue his own studies was demolished by a German bomb.
And with his education now on hold he had to find other ways to occupy his time until the war ended.
But luckily for Francis Crick...

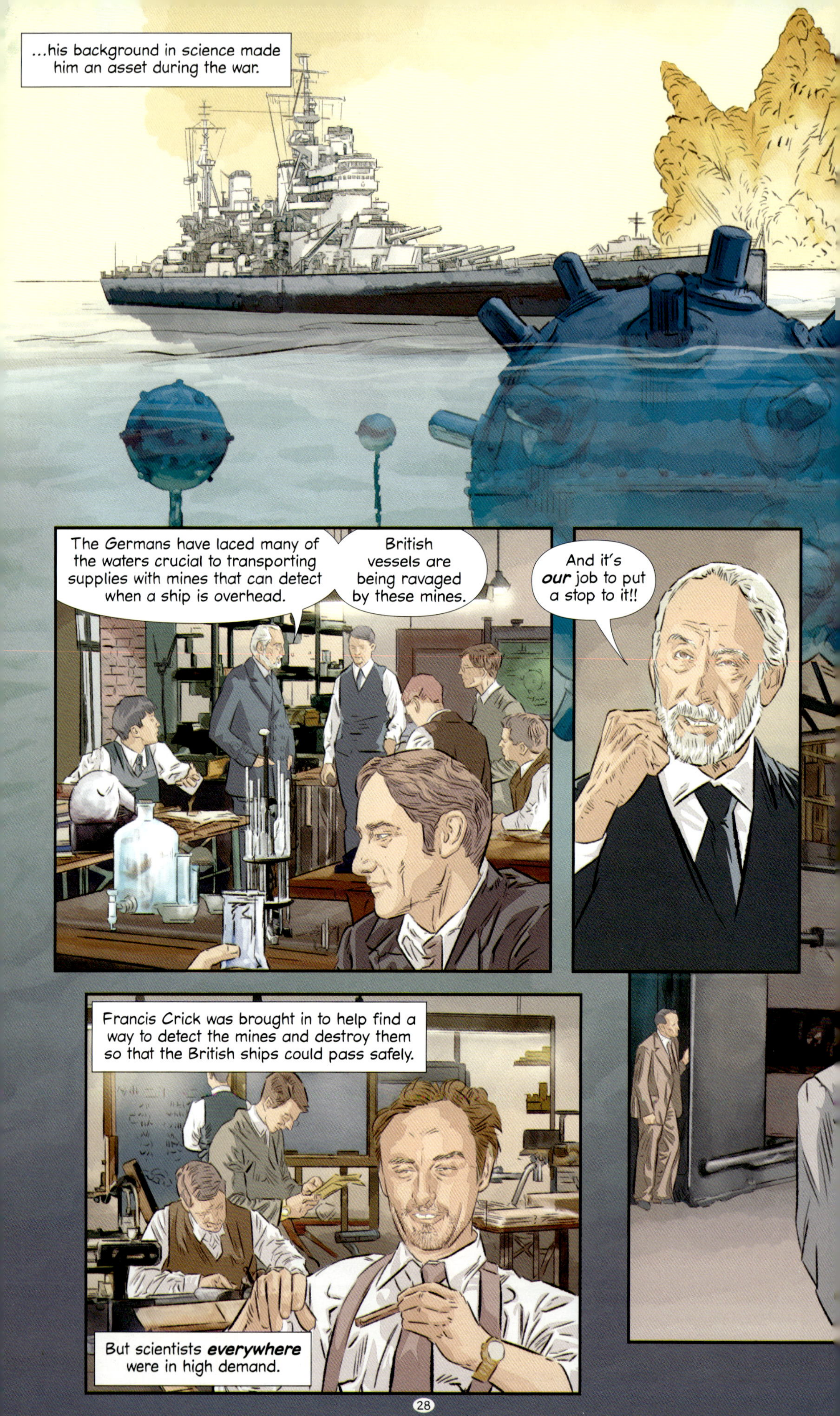
...his background in science made him an asset during the war.
The Germans have laced many of the waters crucial to transporting supplies with mines that can detect when a ship is overhead.
British vessels are being ravaged by these mines.
And it's ***our*** job to put a stop to it!!
Francis Crick was brought in to help find a way to detect the mines and destroy them so that the British ships could pass safely.
But scientists ***everywhere*** were in high demand.

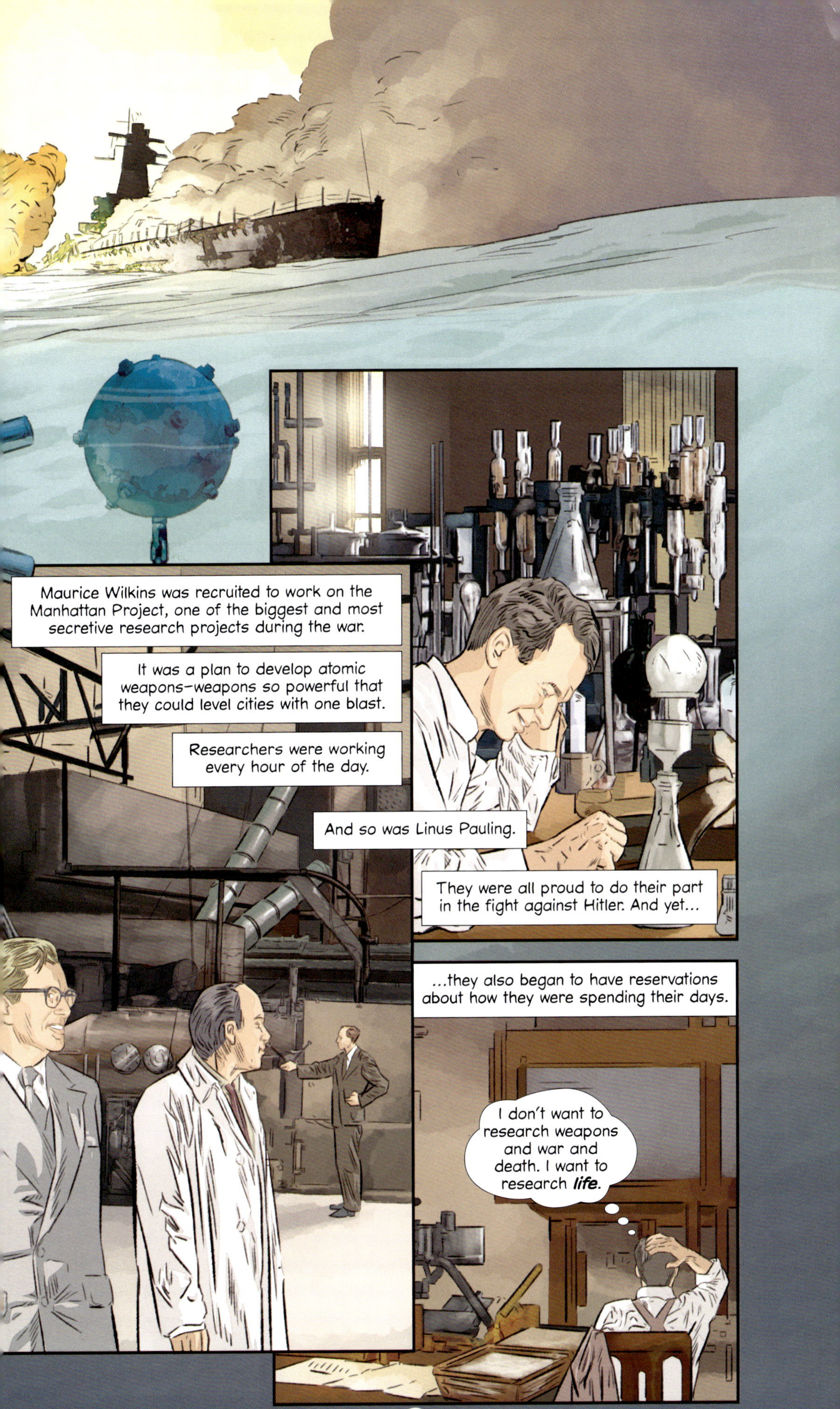
Maurice Wilkins was recruited to work on the Manhattan Project, one of the biggest and most secretive research projects during the war.
It was a plan to develop atomic weapons–weapons so powerful that they could level cities with one blast.
Researchers were working every hour of the day.
And so was Linus Pauling.
They were all proud to do their part in the fight against Hitler. And yet...
...they also began to have reservations about how they were spending their days.
I don't want to research weapons and war and death. I want to research ***life***.

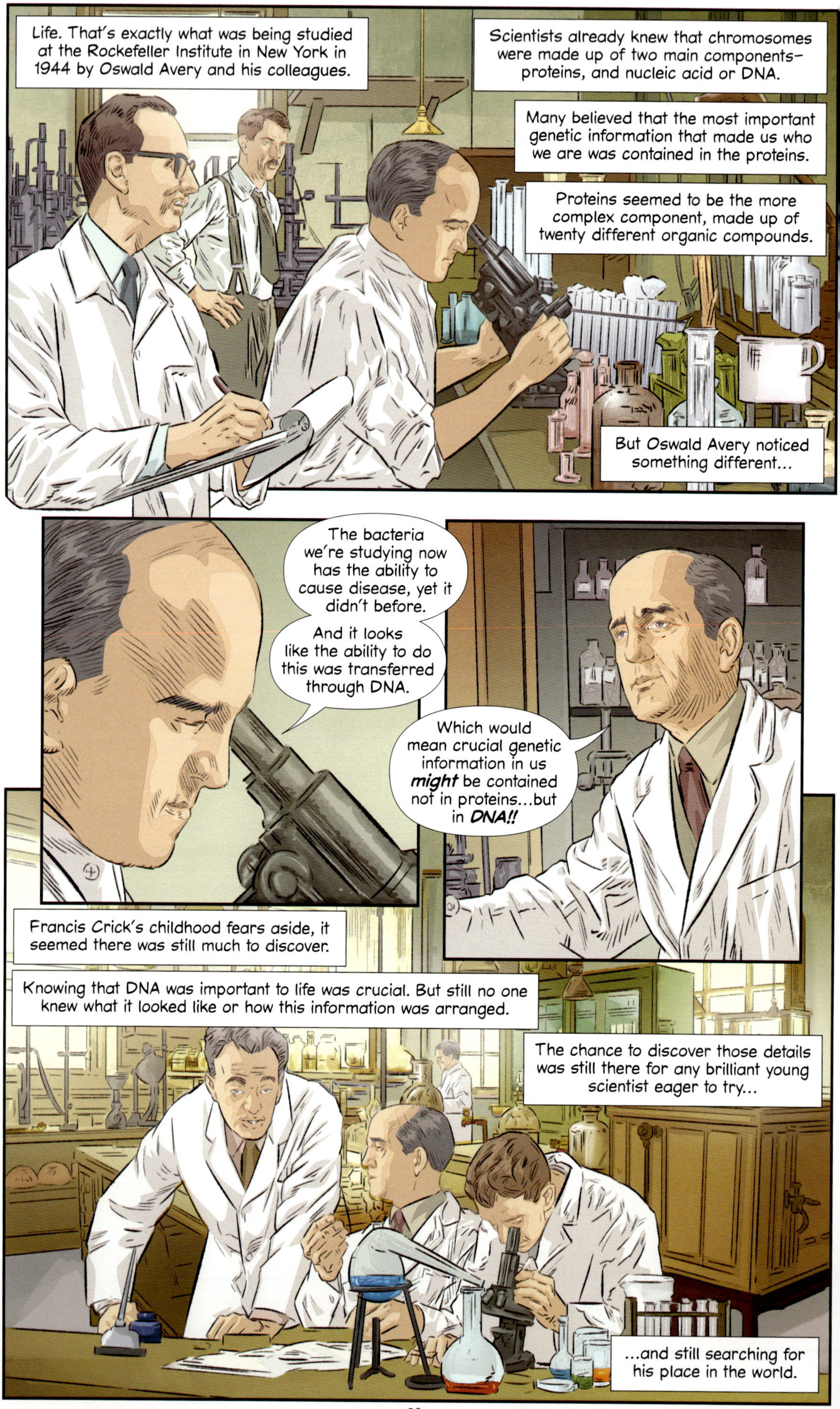
Life. That's exactly what was being studied at the Rockefeller Institute in New York in 1944 by Oswald Avery and his colleagues.
Scientists already knew that chromosomes were made up of two main components–proteins, and nucleic acid or DNA.
Many believed that the most important genetic information that made us who we are was contained in the proteins.
Proteins seemed to be the more complex component, made up of twenty different organic compounds.
But Oswald Avery noticed something different...
The bacteria we're studying now has the ability to cause disease, yet it didn't before.
And it looks like the ability to do this was transferred through DNA.
Which would mean crucial genetic information in us *might* be contained not in proteins...but in *DNA!!*
Francis Crick's childhood fears aside, it seemed there was still much to discover.
Knowing that DNA was important to life was crucial. But still no one knew what it looked like or how this information was arranged.
The chance to discover those details was still there for any brilliant young scientist eager to try...
...and still searching for his place in the world.

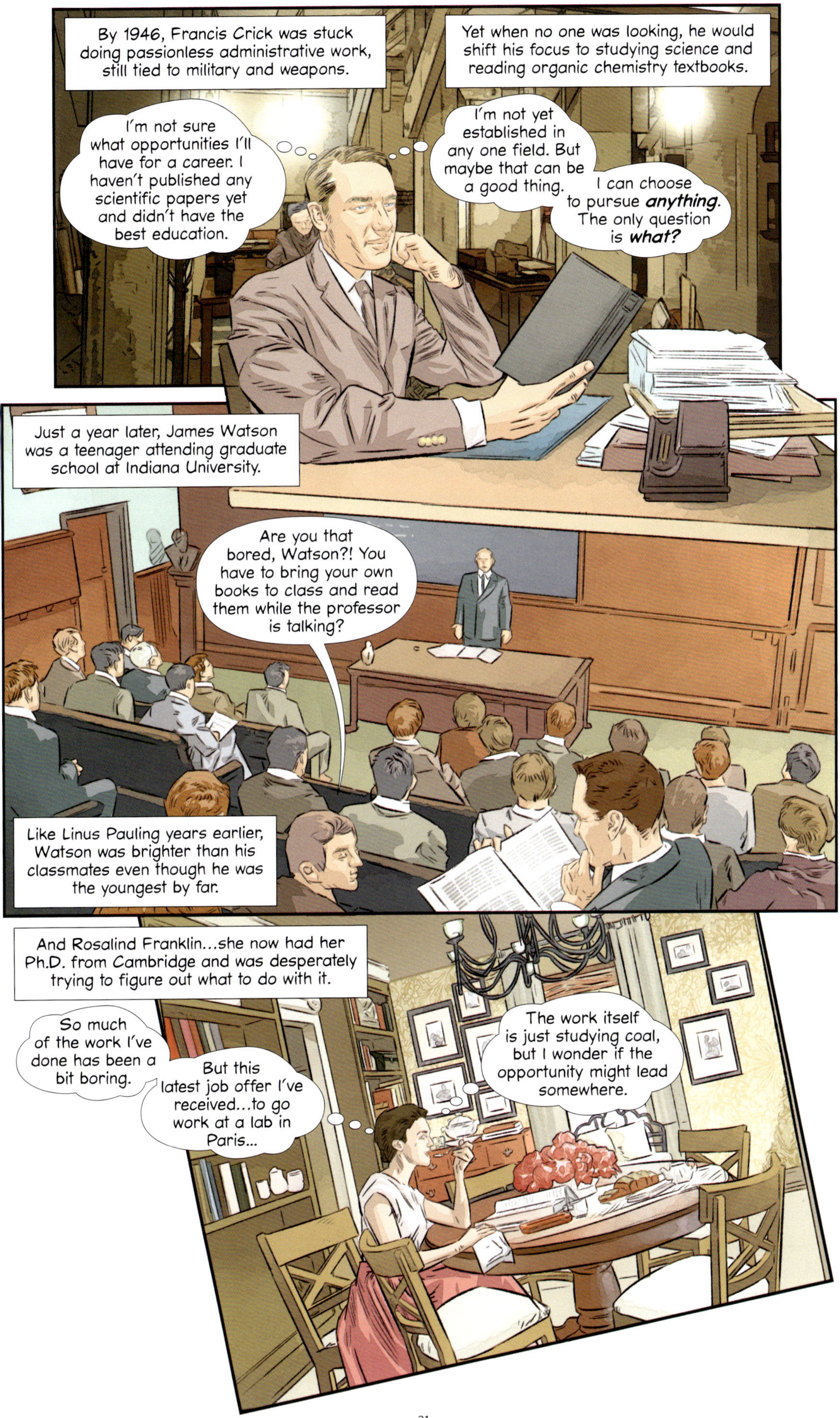
By 1946, Francis Crick was stuck doing passionless administrative work, still tied to military and weapons.
Yet when no one was looking, he would shift his focus to studying science and reading organic chemistry textbooks.
I'm not sure what opportunities I'll have for a career. I haven't published any scientific papers yet and didn't have the best education.
I'm not yet established in any one field. But maybe that can be a good thing.
I can choose to pursue ***anything.*** The only question is ***what?***
Just a year later, James Watson was a teenager attending graduate school at Indiana University.
Are you that bored, Watson?! You have to bring your own books to class and read them while the professor is talking?
Like Linus Pauling years earlier, Watson was brighter than his classmates even though he was the youngest by far.
And Rosalind Franklin...she now had her Ph.D. from Cambridge and was desperately trying to figure out what to do with it.
So much of the work I've done has been a bit boring.
But this latest job offer I've received...to go work at a lab in Paris...
The work itself is just studying coal, but I wonder if the opportunity might lead somewhere.

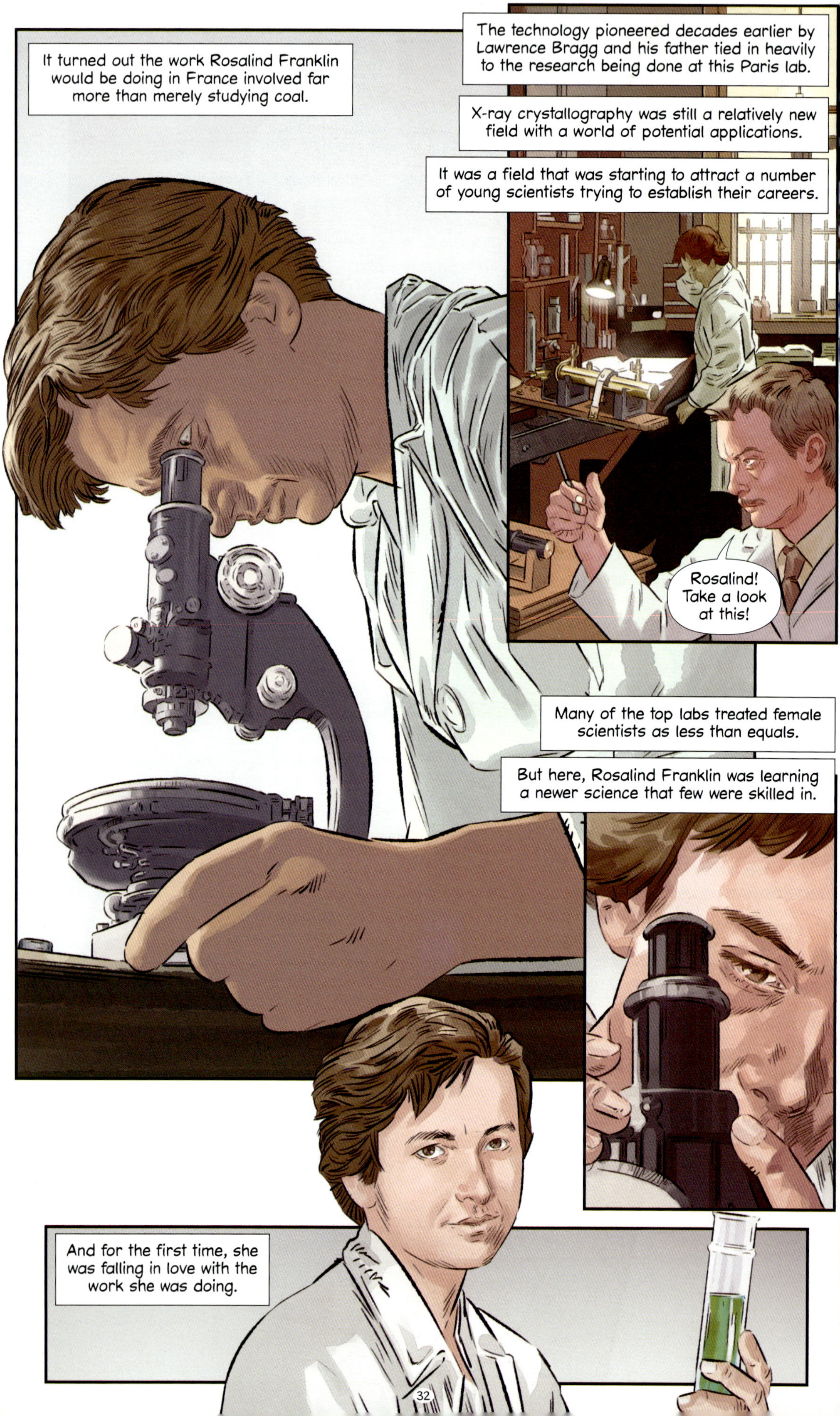
It turned out the work Rosalind Franklin would be doing in France involved far more than merely studying coal.
The technology pioneered decades earlier by Lawrence Bragg and his father tied in heavily to the research being done at this Paris lab.
X-ray crystallography was still a relatively new field with a world of potential applications.
It was a field that was starting to attract a number of young scientists trying to establish their careers.
Rosalind! Take a look at this!
Many of the top labs treated female scientists as less than equals.
But here, Rosalind Franklin was learning a newer science that few were skilled in.
And for the first time, she was falling in love with the work she was doing.

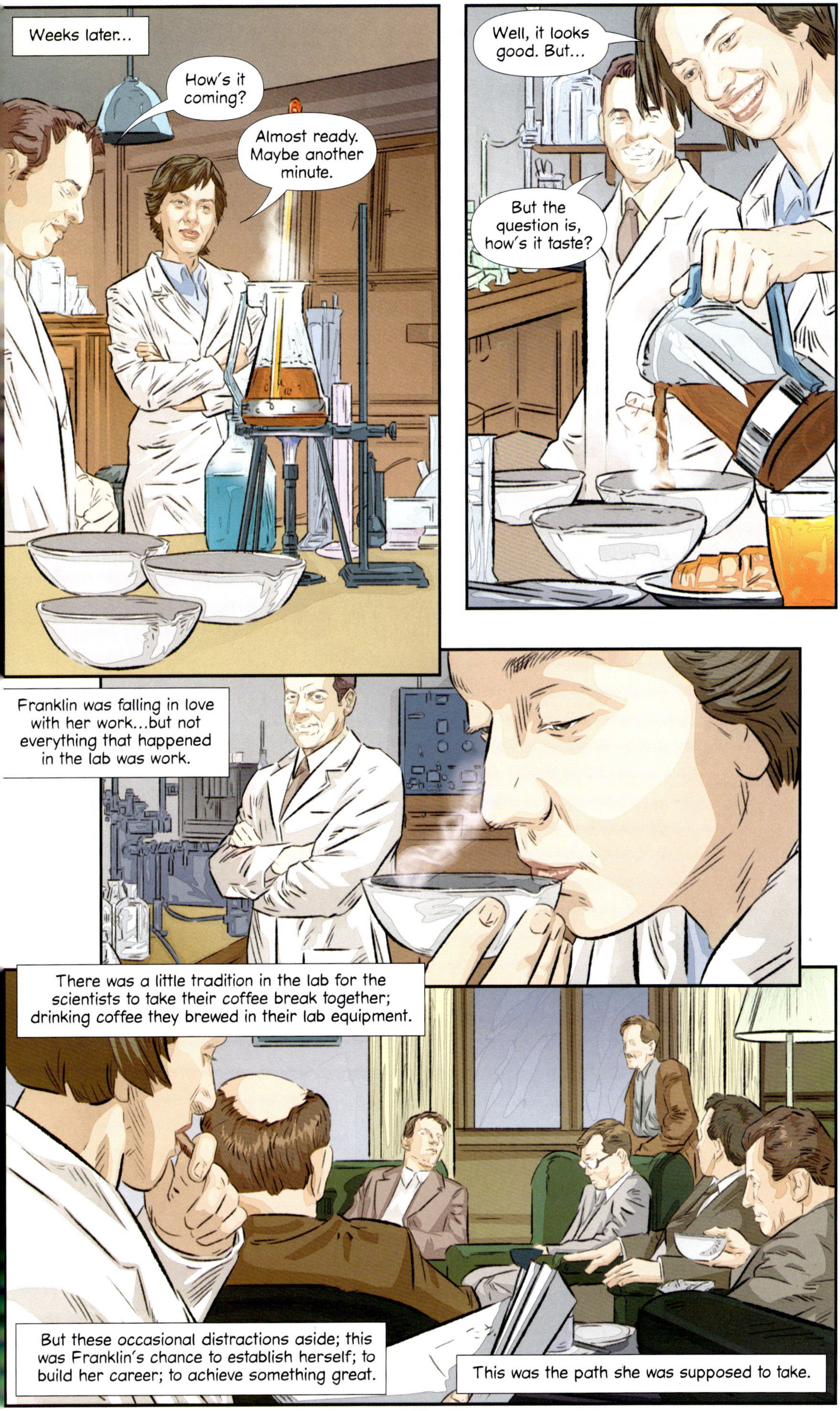
Weeks later...
How's it coming?
Almost ready. Maybe another minute.
Well, it looks good. But...
But the question is, how's it taste?
Franklin was falling in love with her work...but not everything that happened in the lab was work.
There was a little tradition in the lab for the scientists to take their coffee break together; drinking coffee they brewed in their lab equipment.
But these occasional distractions aside; this was Franklin's chance to establish herself; to build her career; to achieve something great.
This was the path she was supposed to take.

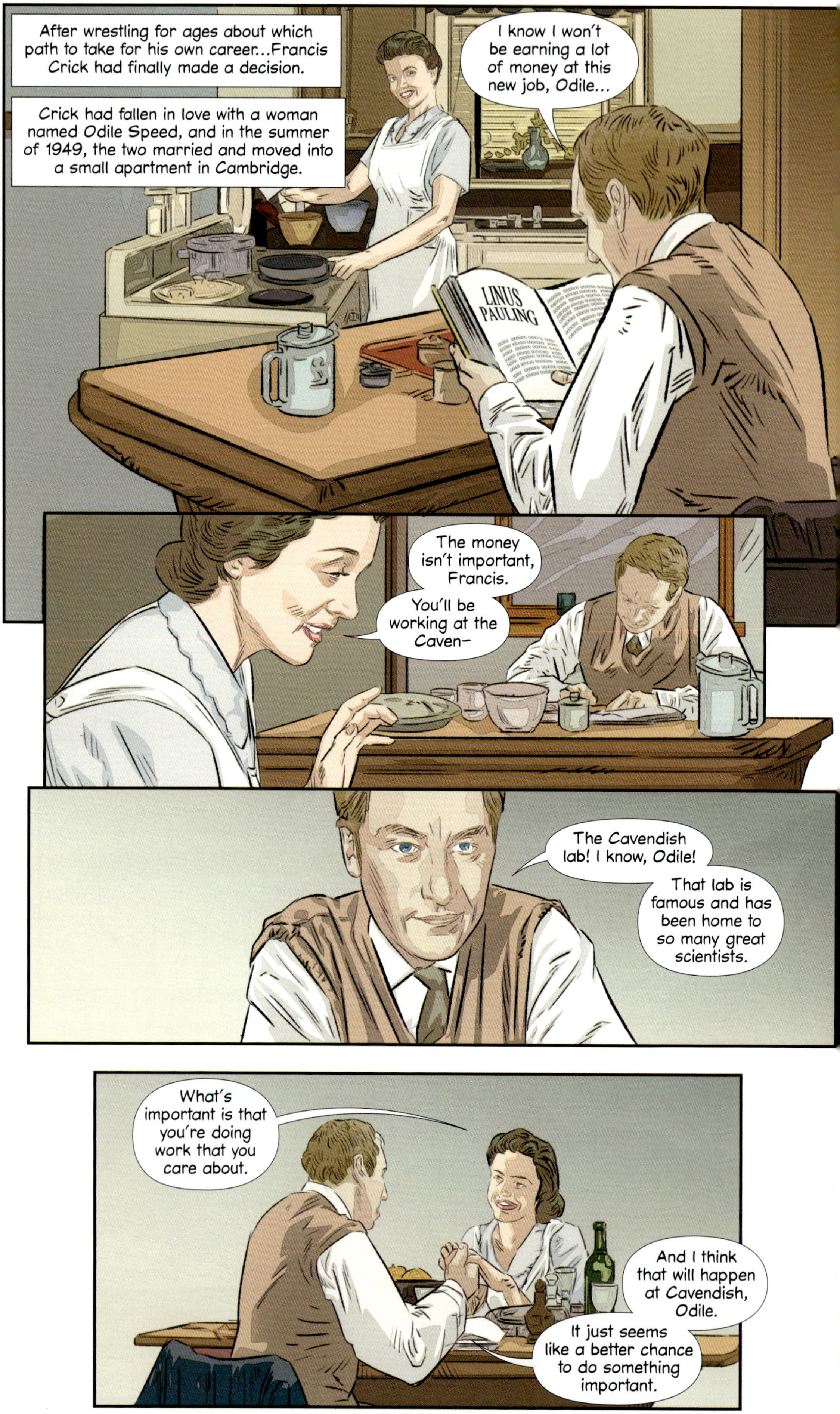

After wrestling for ages about which path to take for his own career...Francis Crick had finally made a decision.
Crick had fallen in love with a woman named Odile Speed, and in the summer of 1949, the two married and moved into a small apartment in Cambridge.
I know I won't be earning a lot of money at this new job, Odile...
LINUS PAULING
The money isn't important, Francis.
You'll be working at the Caven–
The Cavendish lab! I know, Odile!
That lab is famous and has been home to so many great scientists.
What's important is that you're doing work that you care about.
And I think that will happen at Cavendish, Odile.
It just seems like a better chance to do something important.

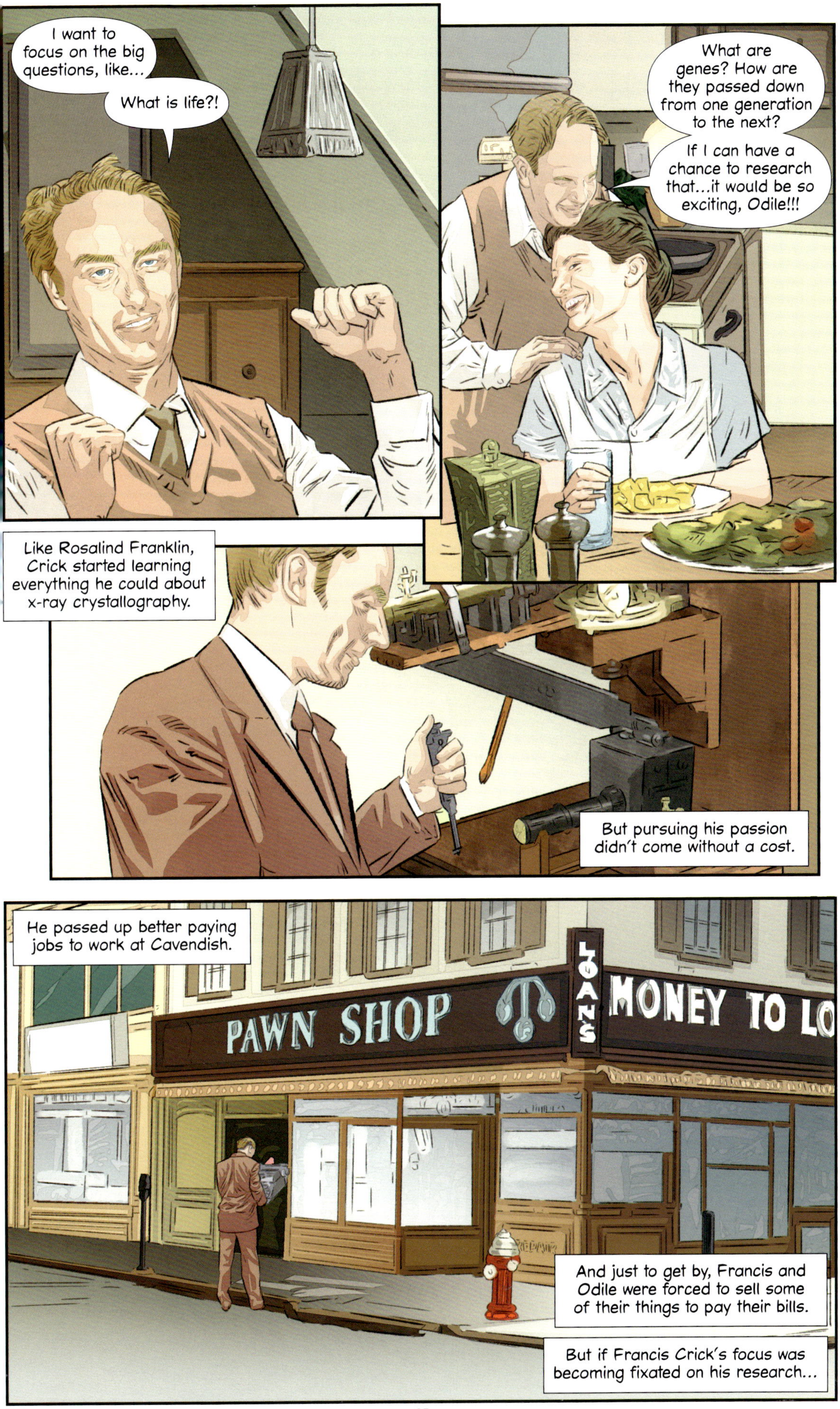
I want to focus on the big questions, like...
What is life?!
What are genes? How are they passed down from one generation to the next?
If I can have a chance to research that...it would be so exciting, Odile!!!
Like Rosalind Franklin, Crick started learning everything he could about x-ray crystallography.
But pursuing his passion didn't come without a cost.
He passed up better paying jobs to work at Cavendish.
PAWN SHOP
LOANS
MONEY TO LO
And just to get by, Francis and Odile were forced to sell some of their things to pay their bills.
But if Francis Crick's focus was becoming fixated on his research...

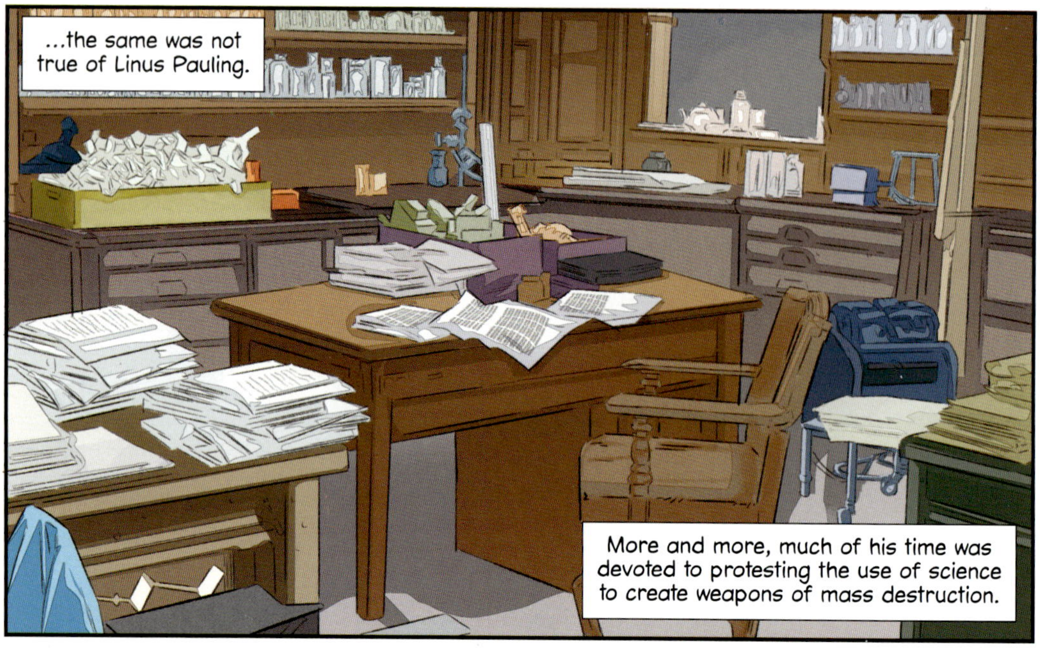
...the same was not true of Linus Pauling.
More and more, much of his time was devoted to protesting the use of science to create weapons of mass destruction.

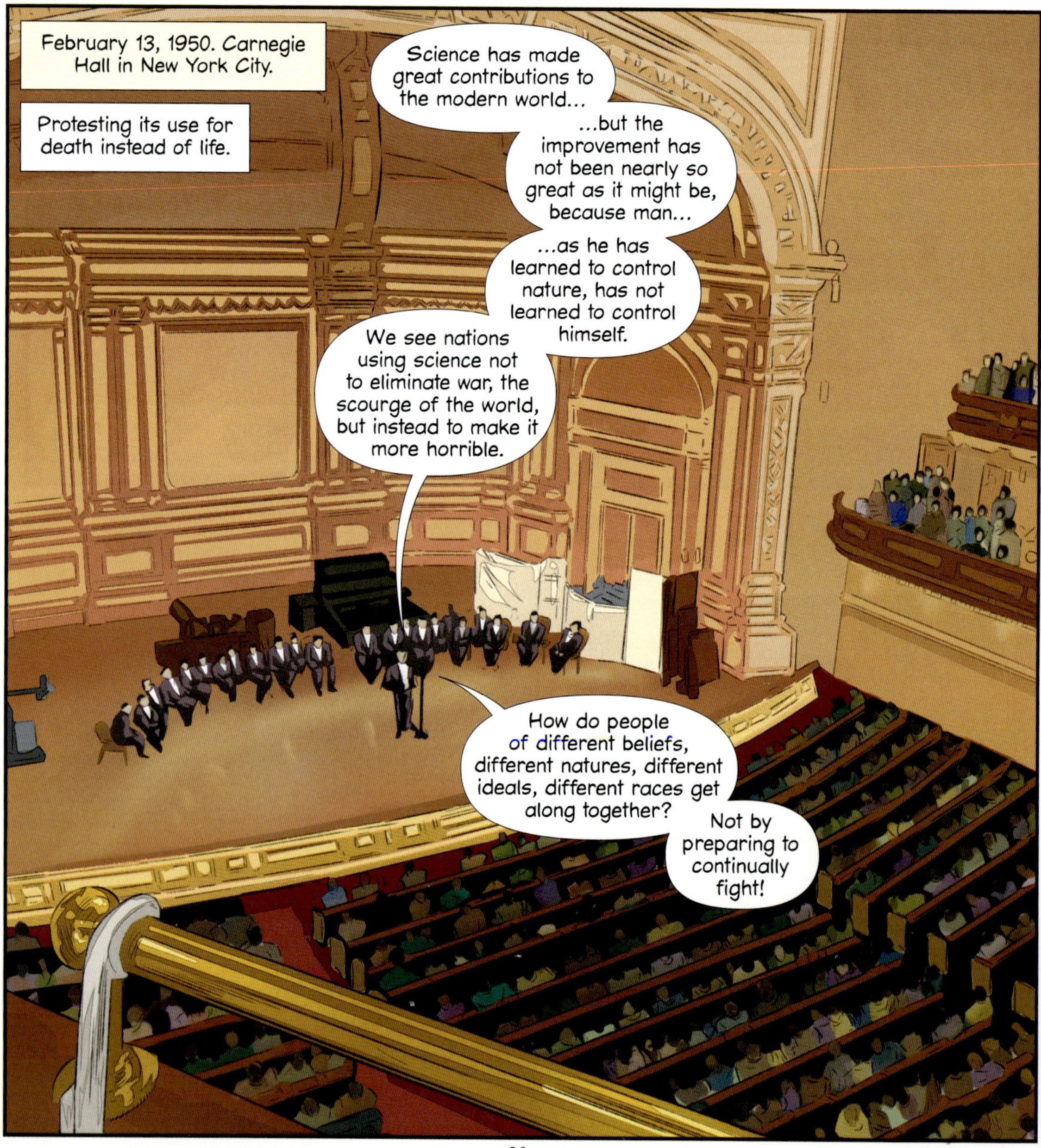
February 13, 1950. Carnegie Hall in New York City.
Protesting its use for death instead of life.
Science has made great contributions to the modern world...
...but the improvement has not been nearly so great as it might be, because man...
...as he has learned to control nature, has not learned to control himself.
We see nations using science not to eliminate war, the scourge of the world, but instead to make it more horrible.
How do people of different beliefs, different natures, different ideals, different races get along together?
Not by preparing to continually fight!

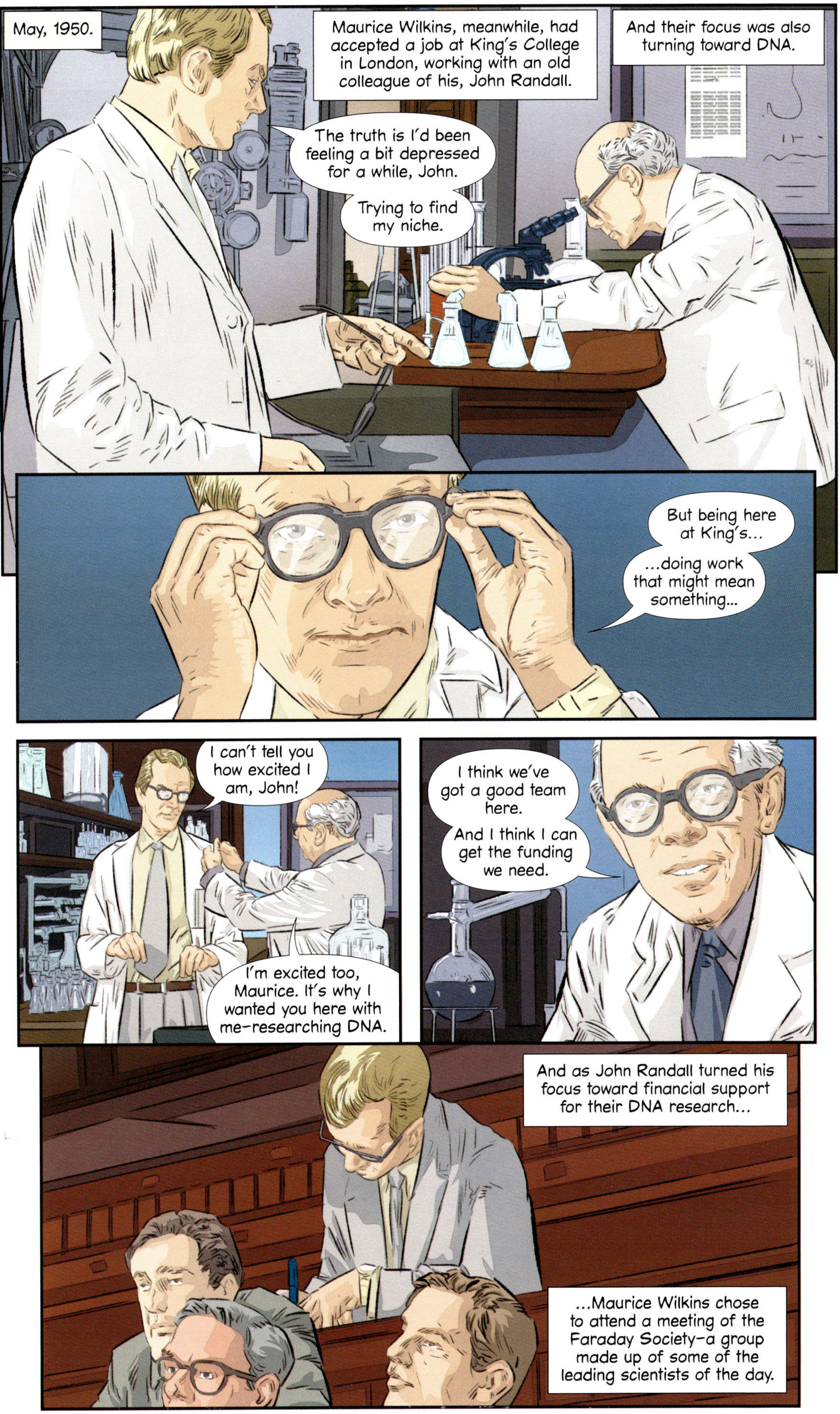
May, 1950.
Maurice Wilkins, meanwhile, had accepted a job at King's College in London, working with an old colleague of his, John Randall.
And their focus was also turning toward DNA.
The truth is I'd been feeling a bit depressed for a while, John.
Trying to find my niche.
But being here at King's...
...doing work that might mean something...
I can't tell you how excited I am, John!
I'm excited too, Maurice. It's why I wanted you here with me—researching DNA.
I think we've got a good team here.
And I think I can get the funding we need.
And as John Randall turned his focus toward financial support for their DNA research...
...Maurice Wilkins chose to attend a meeting of the Faraday Society—a group made up of some of the leading scientists of the day.

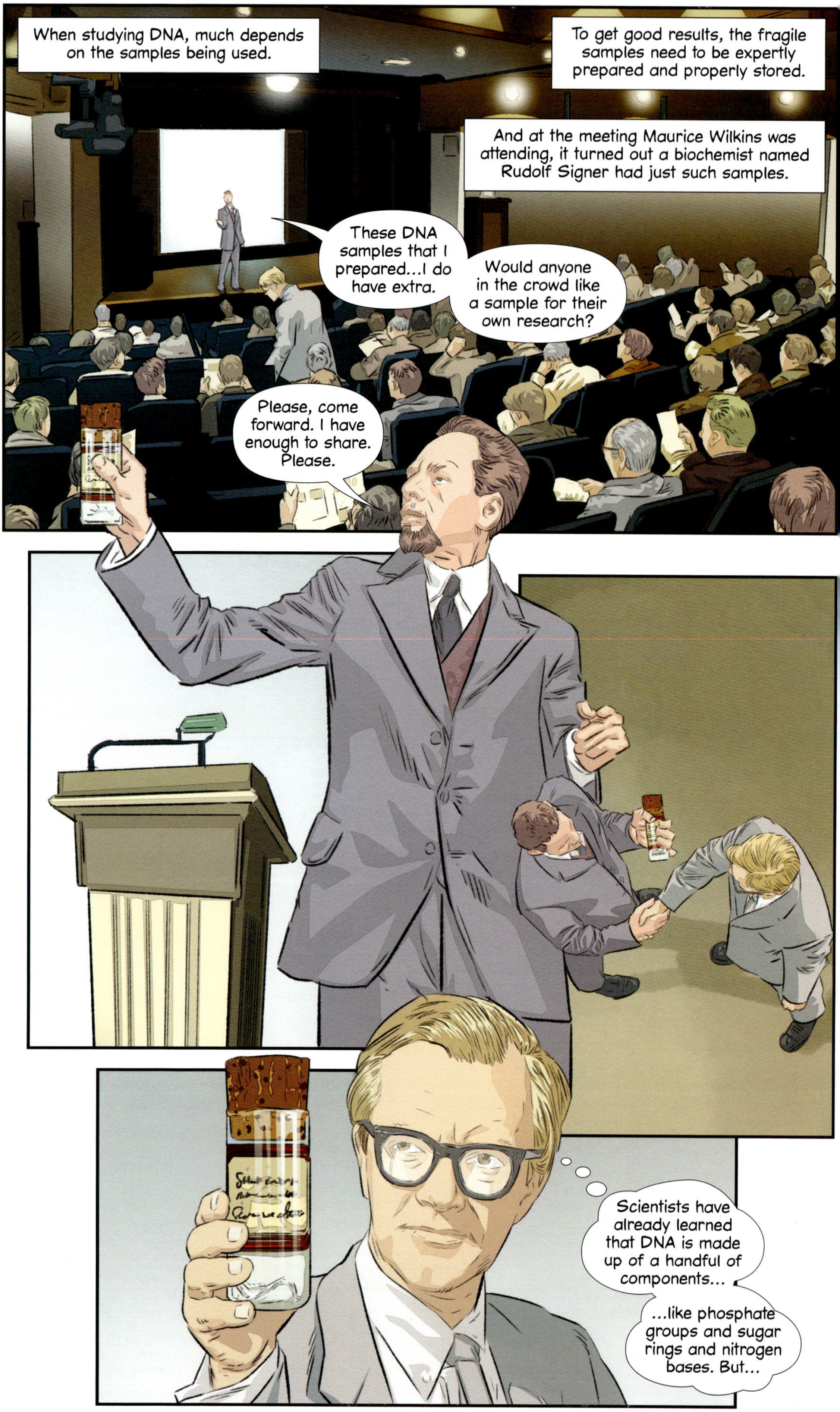
When studying DNA, much depends on the samples being used.
To get good results, the fragile samples need to be expertly prepared and properly stored.
And at the meeting Maurice Wilkins was attending, it turned out a biochemist named Rudolf Signer had just such samples.
These DNA samples that I prepared...I do have extra.
Would anyone in the crowd like a sample for their own research?
Please, come forward. I have enough to share. Please.
Scientists have already learned that DNA is made up of a handful of components...
...like phosphate groups and sugar rings and nitrogen bases. But...

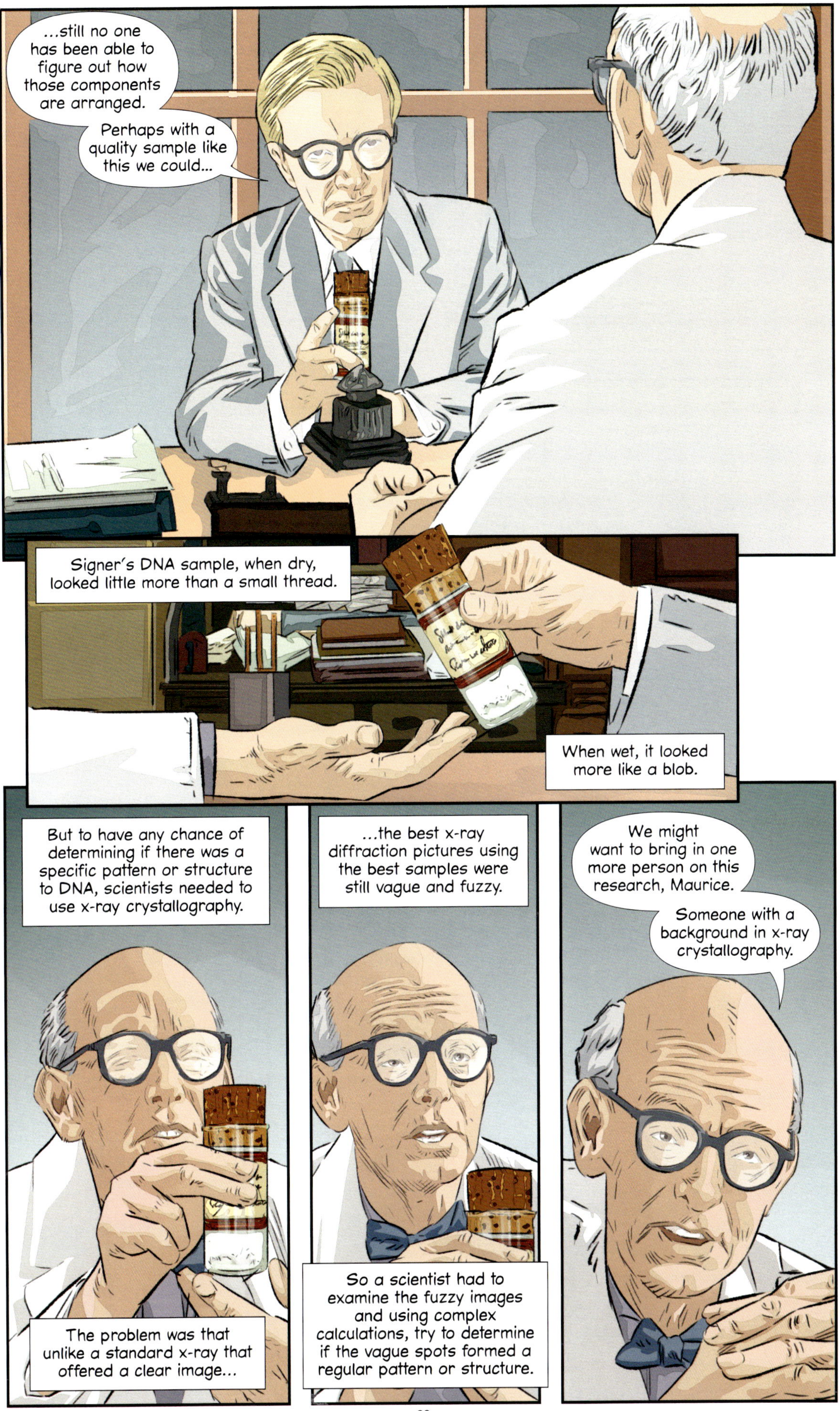
...still no one has been able to figure out how those components are arranged.
Perhaps with a quality sample like this we could...
Signer's DNA sample, when dry, looked little more than a small thread.
When wet, it looked more like a blob.
But to have any chance of determining if there was a specific pattern or structure to DNA, scientists needed to use x-ray crystallography.
The problem was that unlike a standard x-ray that offered a clear image...
...the best x-ray diffraction pictures using the best samples were still vague and fuzzy.
So a scientist had to examine the fuzzy images and using complex calculations, try to determine if the vague spots formed a regular pattern or structure.
We might want to bring in one more person on this research, Maurice.
Someone with a background in x-ray crystallography.

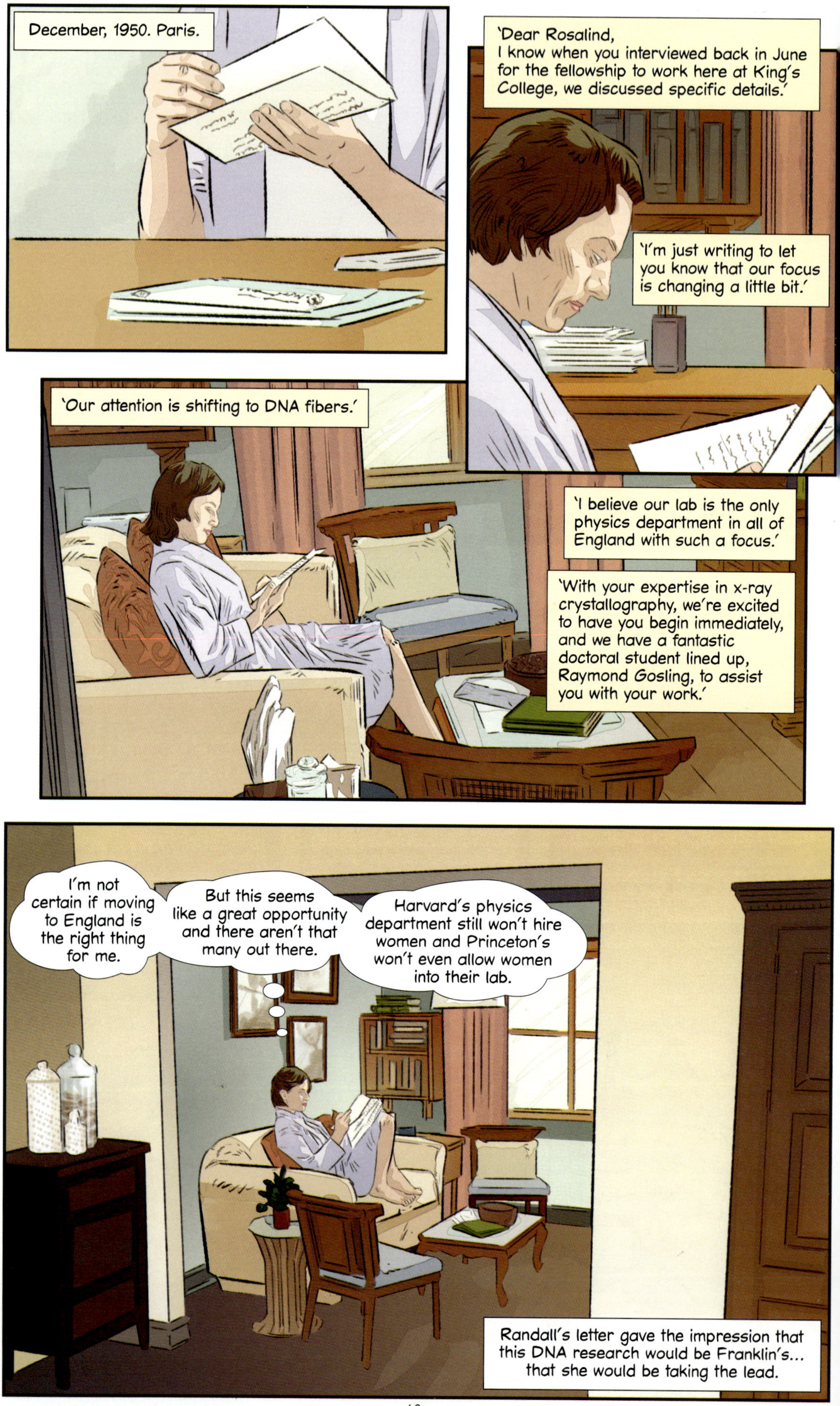
December, 1950. Paris.
'Dear Rosalind,
I know when you interviewed back in June for the fellowship to work here at King's College, we discussed specific details.'
'I'm just writing to let you know that our focus is changing a little bit.'
'Our attention is shifting to DNA fibers.'
'I believe our lab is the only physics department in all of England with such a focus.'
'With your expertise in x-ray crystallography, we're excited to have you begin immediately, and we have a fantastic doctoral student lined up, Raymond Gosling, to assist you with your work.'
I'm not certain if moving to England is the right thing for me.
But this seems like a great opportunity and there aren't that many out there.
Harvard's physics department still won't hire women and Princeton's won't even allow women into their lab.
Randall's letter gave the impression that this DNA research would be Franklin's... that she would be taking the lead.

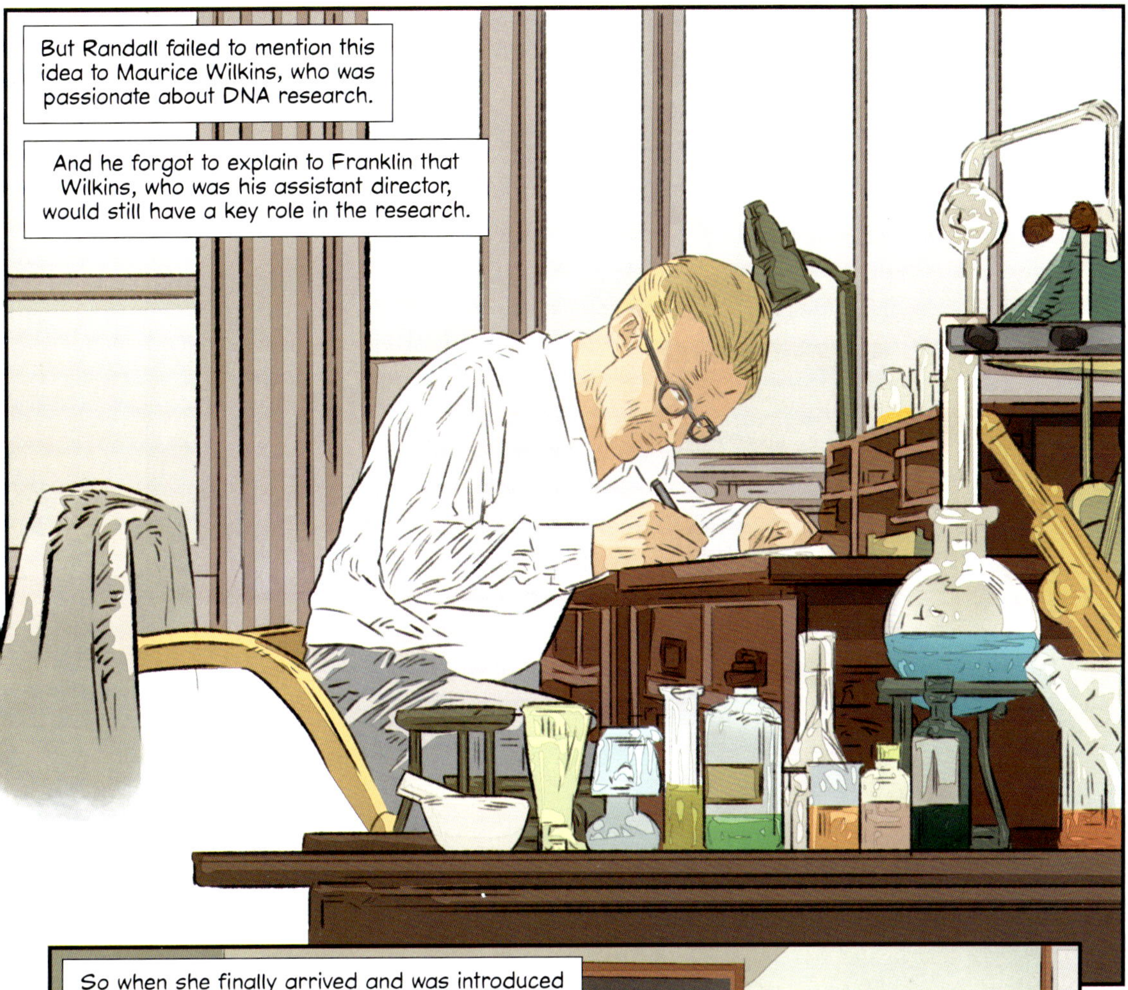
But Randall failed to mention this idea to Maurice Wilkins, who was passionate about DNA research.
And he forgot to explain to Franklin that Wilkins, who was his assistant director, would still have a key role in the research.

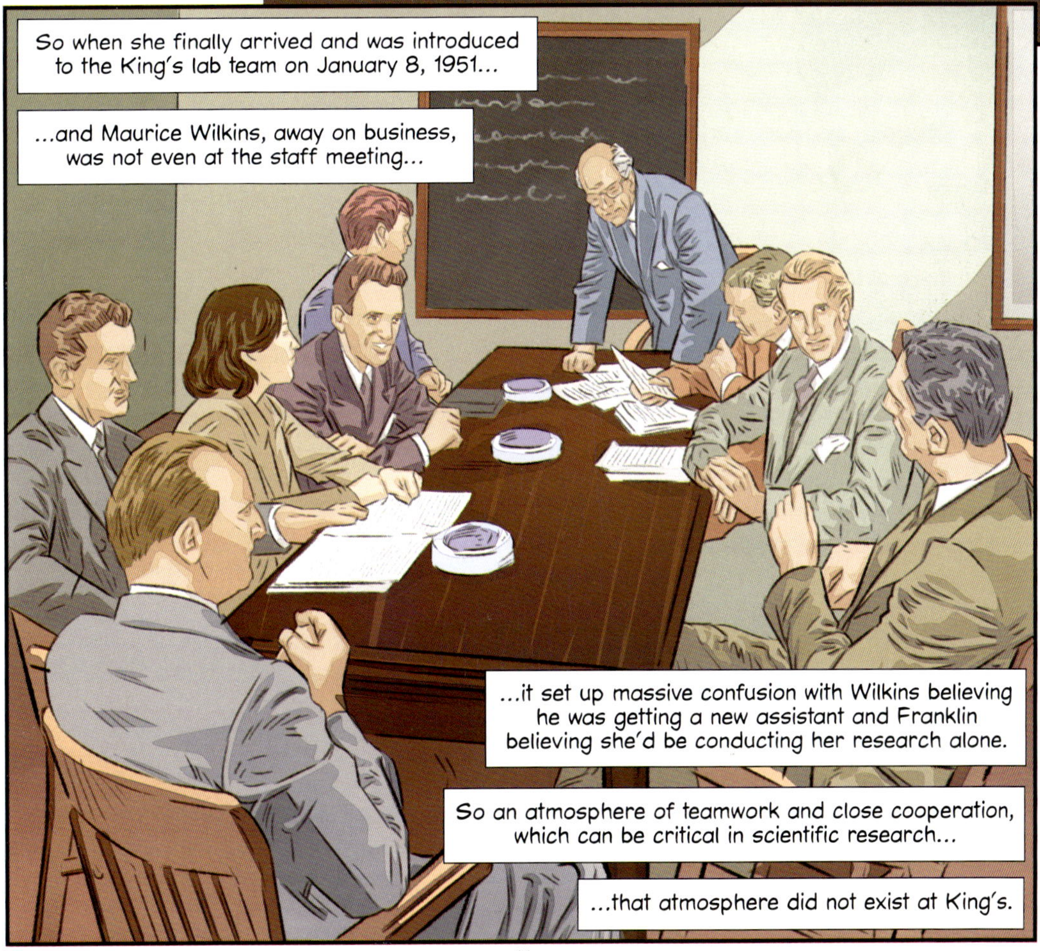
So when she finally arrived and was introduced to the King's lab team on January 8, 1951...
...and Maurice Wilkins, away on business, was not even at the staff meeting...
...it set up massive confusion with Wilkins believing he was getting a new assistant and Franklin believing she'd be conducting her research alone.
So an atmosphere of teamwork and close cooperation, which can be critical in scientific research...
...that atmosphere did not exist at King's.

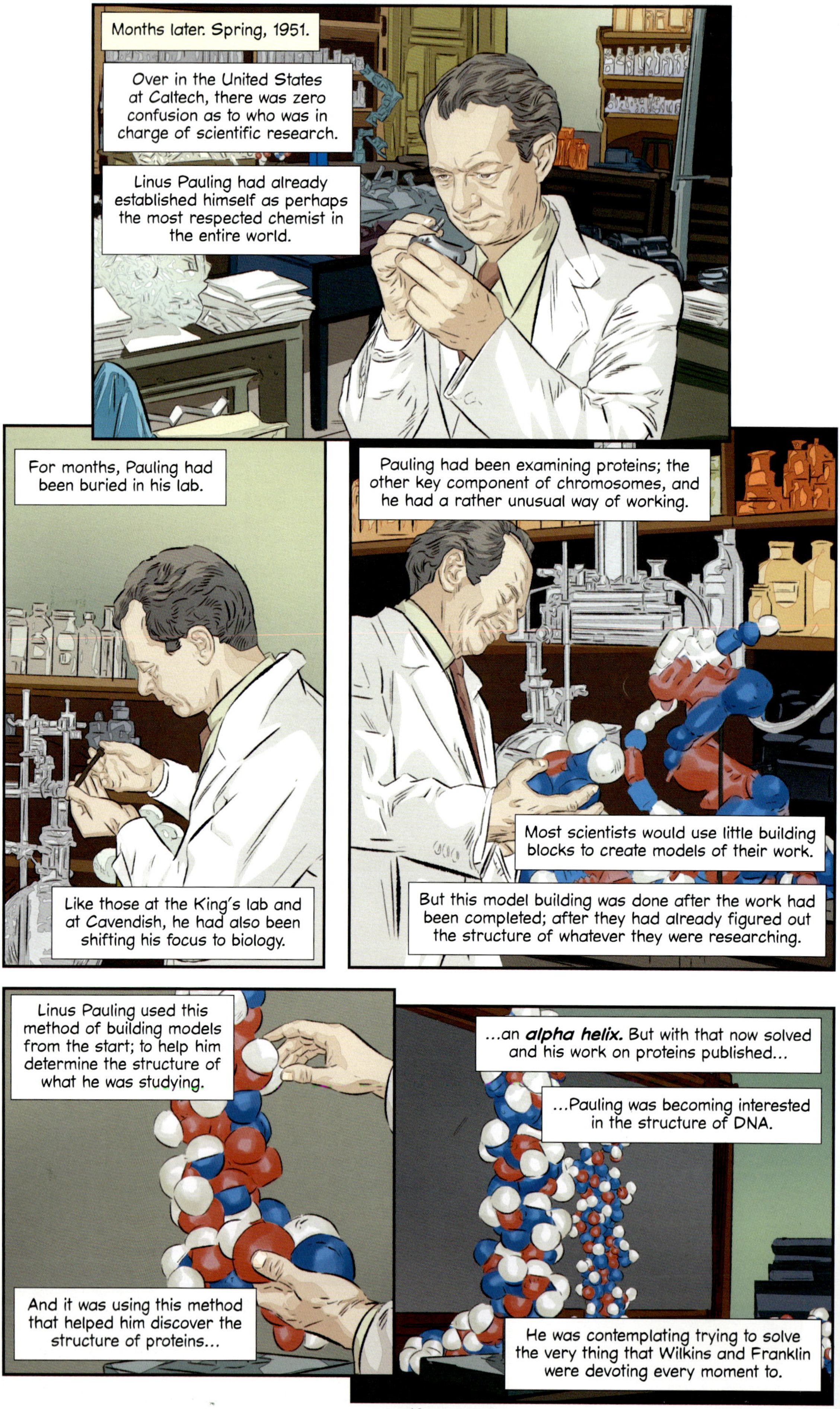
Months later. Spring, 1951.
Over in the United States at Caltech, there was zero confusion as to who was in charge of scientific research.
Linus Pauling had already established himself as perhaps the most respected chemist in the entire world.
For months, Pauling had been buried in his lab.
Like those at the King's lab and at Cavendish, he had also been shifting his focus to biology.
Pauling had been examining proteins; the other key component of chromosomes, and he had a rather unusual way of working.
Most scientists would use little building blocks to create models of their work.
But this model building was done after the work had been completed; after they had already figured out the structure of whatever they were researching.
Linus Pauling used this method of building models from the start; to help him determine the structure of what he was studying.
And it was using this method that helped him discover the structure of proteins...
...an ***alpha helix.*** But with that now solved and his work on proteins published...
...Pauling was becoming interested in the structure of DNA.
He was contemplating trying to solve the very thing that Wilkins and Franklin were devoting every moment to.

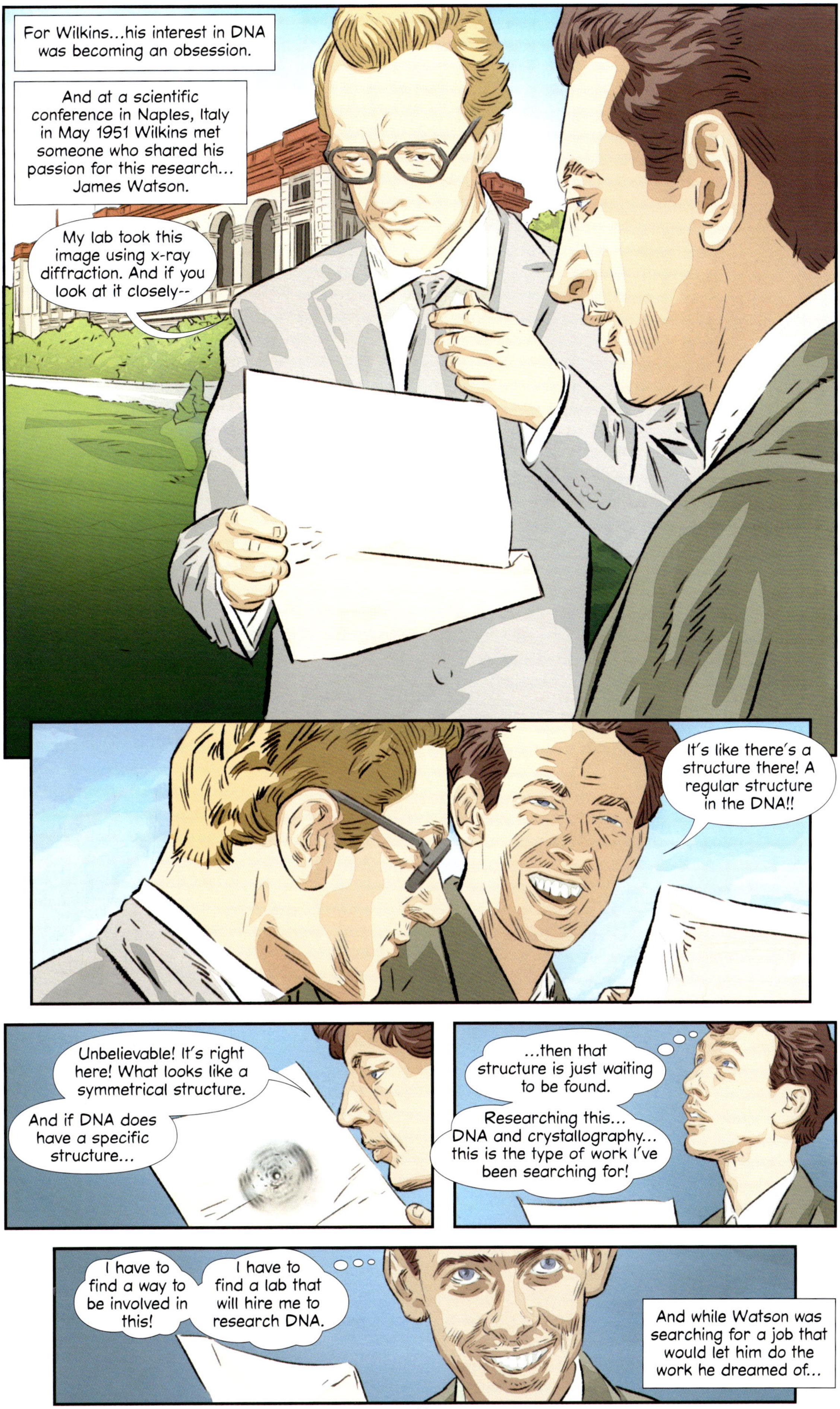
For Wilkins...his interest in DNA was becoming an obsession.
And at a scientific conference in Naples, Italy in May 1951 Wilkins met someone who shared his passion for this research... James Watson.
My lab took this image using x-ray diffraction. And if you look at it closely--
It's like there's a structure there! A regular structure in the DNA!!
Unbelievable! It's right here! What looks like a symmetrical structure.
And if DNA does have a specific structure...
...then that structure is just waiting to be found.
Researching this... DNA and crystallography... this is the type of work I've been searching for!
I have to find a way to be involved in this!
I have to find a lab that will hire me to research DNA.
And while Watson was searching for a job that would let him do the work he dreamed of...

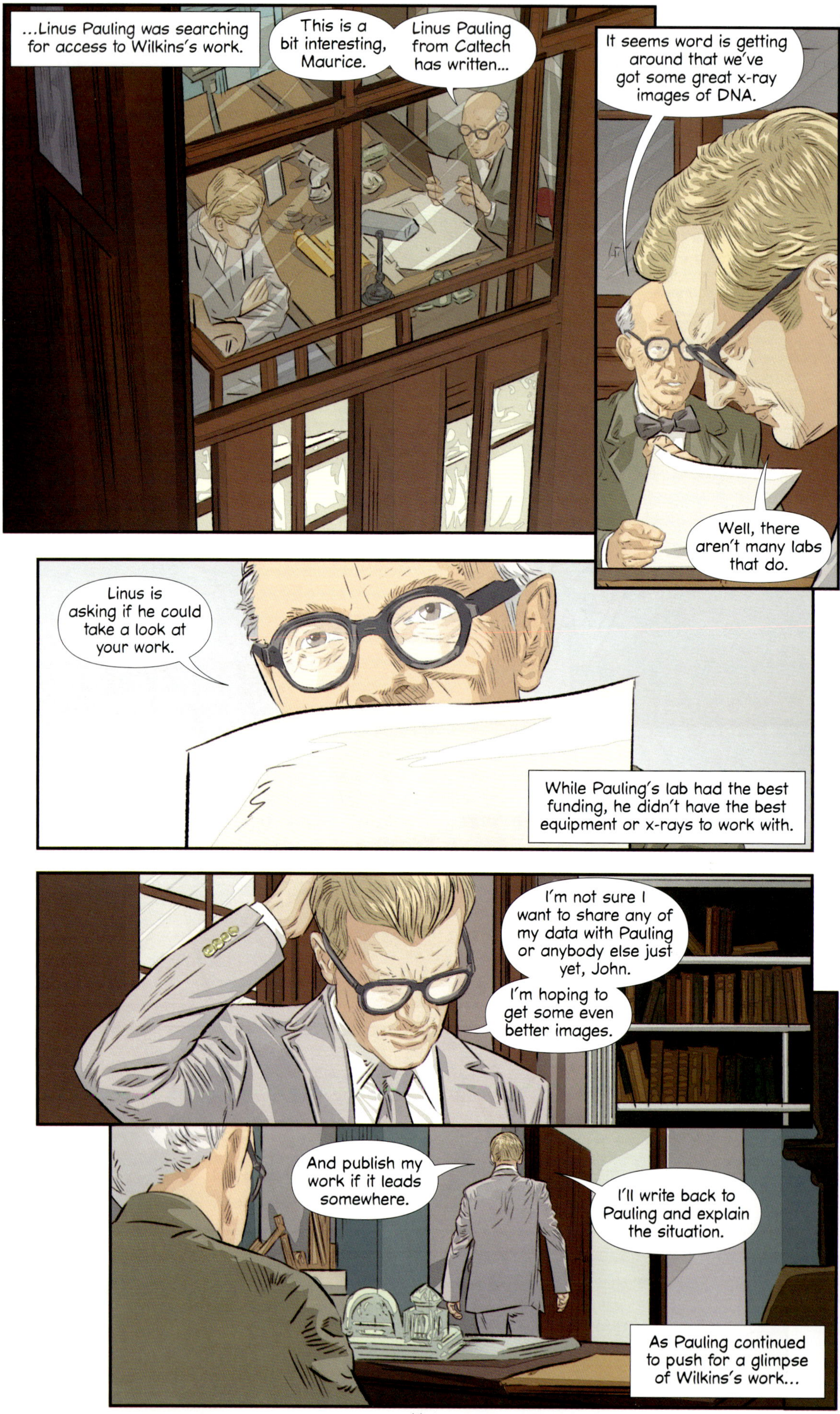
...Linus Pauling was searching for access to Wilkins's work.
This is a bit interesting, Maurice.
Linus Pauling from Caltech has written...
It seems word is getting around that we've got some great x-ray images of DNA.
Well, there aren't many labs that do.
Linus is asking if he could take a look at your work.
While Pauling's lab had the best funding, he didn't have the best equipment or x-rays to work with.
I'm not sure I want to share any of my data with Pauling or anybody else just yet, John.
I'm hoping to get some even better images.
And publish my work if it leads somewhere.
I'll write back to Pauling and explain the situation.
As Pauling continued to push for a glimpse of Wilkins's work...

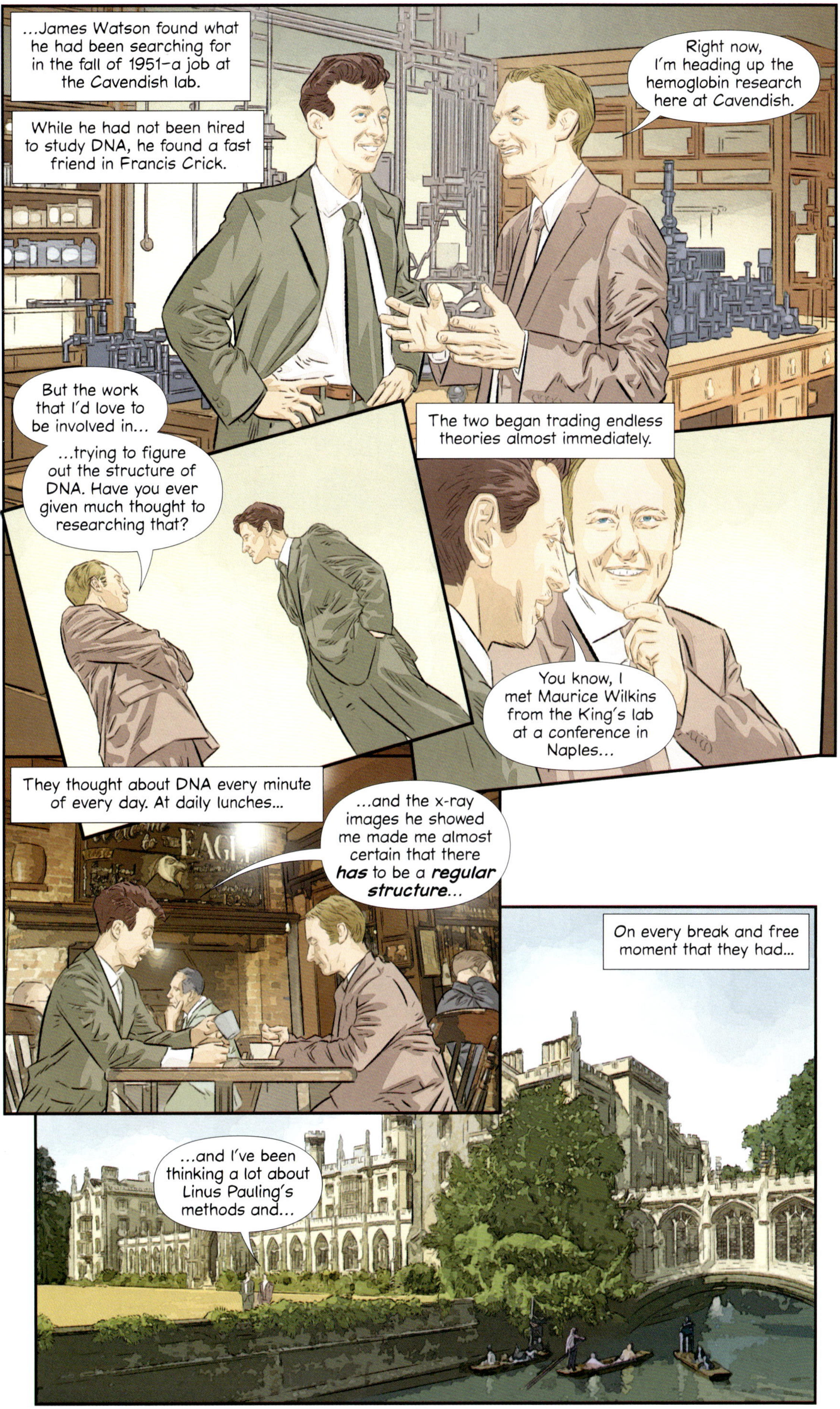
...James Watson found what he had been searching for in the fall of 1951—a job at the Cavendish lab.
While he had not been hired to study DNA, he found a fast friend in Francis Crick.
Right now, I'm heading up the hemoglobin research here at Cavendish.
But the work that I'd love to be involved in...
...trying to figure out the structure of DNA. Have you ever given much thought to researching that?
The two began trading endless theories almost immediately.
You know, I met Maurice Wilkins from the King's lab at a conference in Naples...
They thought about DNA every minute of every day. At daily lunches...
...and the x-ray images he showed me made me almost certain that there ***has*** to be a ***regular structure***...
On every break and free moment that they had...
...and I've been thinking a lot about Linus Pauling's methods and...

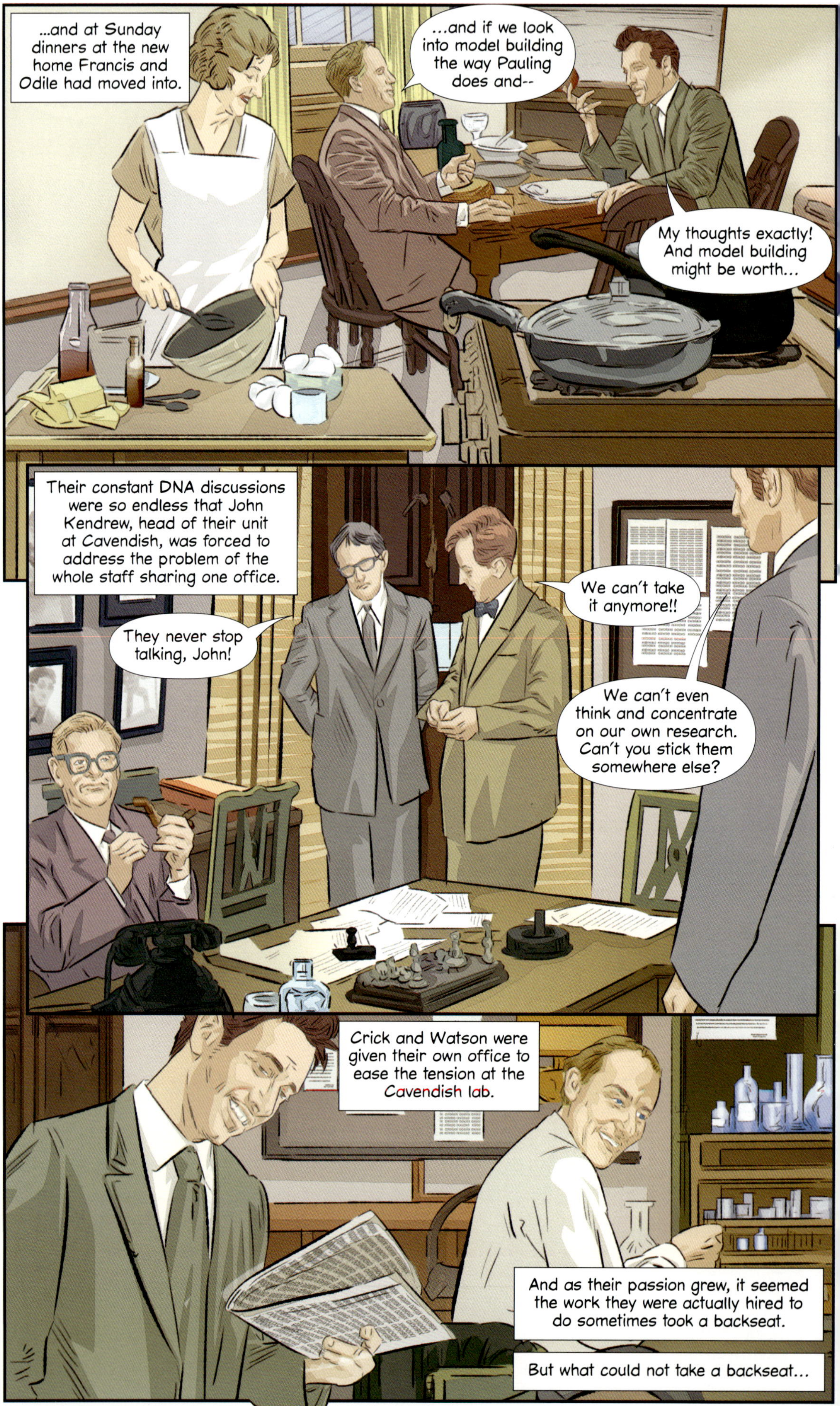
...and at Sunday dinners at the new home Francis and Odile had moved into.
...and if we look into model building the way Pauling does and--
My thoughts exactly! And model building might be worth...
Their constant DNA discussions were so endless that John Kendrew, head of their unit at Cavendish, was forced to address the problem of the whole staff sharing one office.
They never stop talking, John!
We can't take it anymore!!
We can't even think and concentrate on our own research. Can't you stick them somewhere else?
Crick and Watson were given their own office to ease the tension at the Cavendish lab.
And as their passion grew, it seemed the work they were actually hired to do sometimes took a backseat.
But what could not take a backseat...

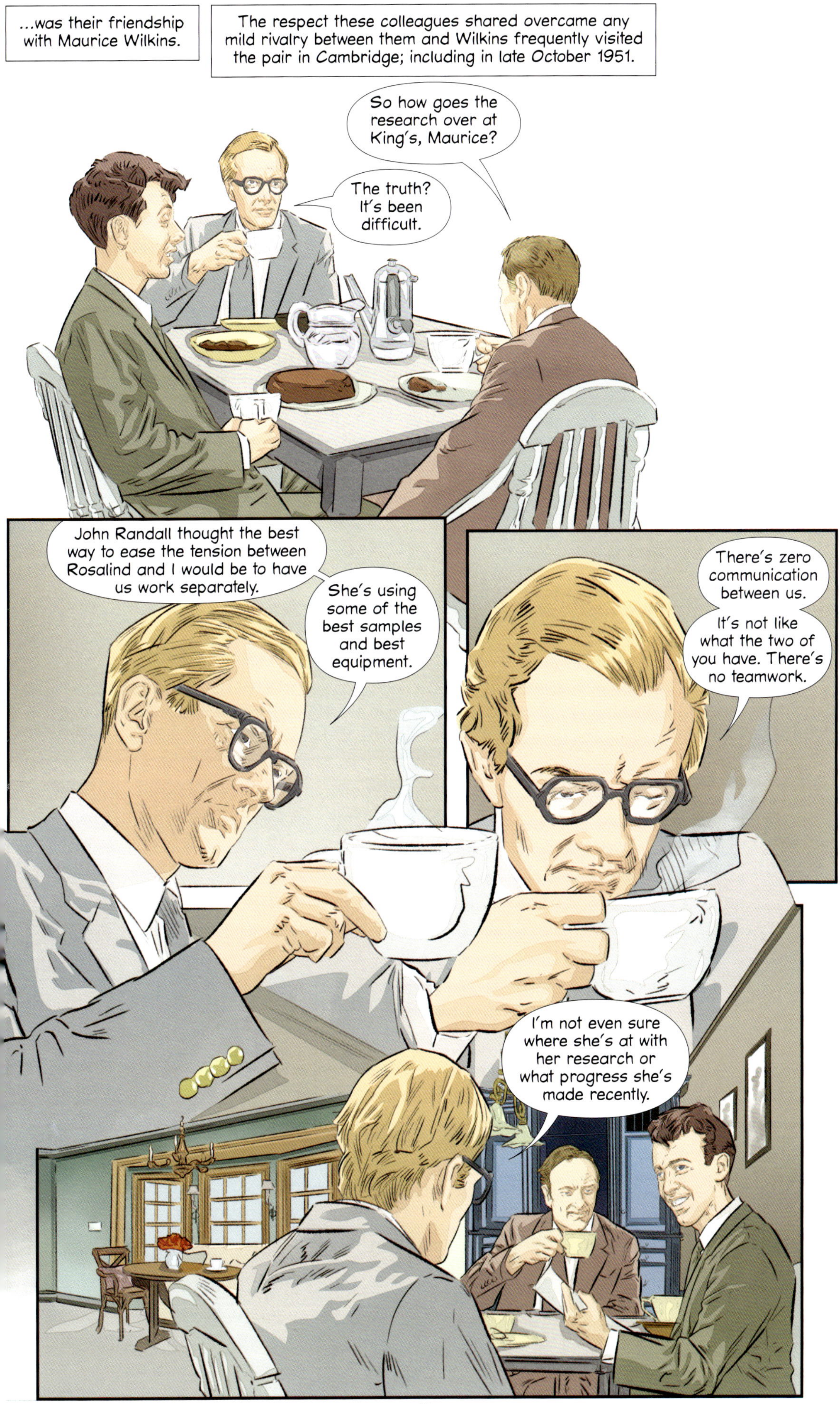

...was their friendship with Maurice Wilkins.
The respect these colleagues shared overcame any mild rivalry between them and Wilkins frequently visited the pair in Cambridge; including in late October 1951.
So how goes the research over at King's, Maurice?
The truth? It's been difficult.
John Randall thought the best way to ease the tension between Rosalind and I would be to have us work separately.
She's using some of the best samples and best equipment.
There's zero communication between us.
It's not like what the two of you have. There's no teamwork.
I'm not even sure where she's at with her research or what progress she's made recently.

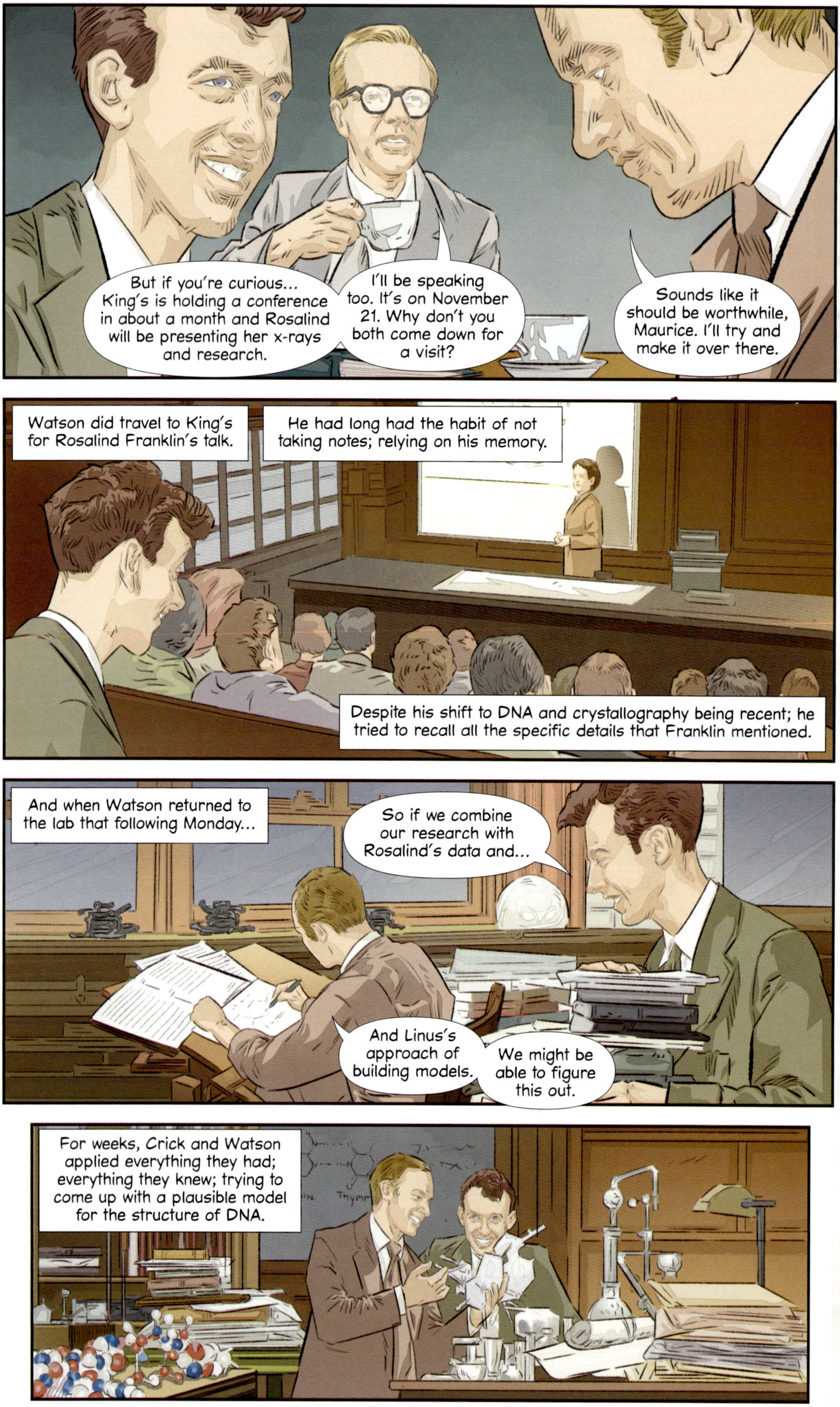
But if you're curious... King's is holding a conference in about a month and Rosalind will be presenting her x-rays and research.
I'll be speaking too. It's on November 21. Why don't you both come down for a visit?
Sounds like it should be worthwhile, Maurice. I'll try and make it over there.
Watson did travel to King's for Rosalind Franklin's talk.
He had long had the habit of not taking notes; relying on his memory.
Despite his shift to DNA and crystallography being recent; he tried to recall all the specific details that Franklin mentioned.
And when Watson returned to the lab that following Monday...
So if we combine our research with Rosalind's data and...
And Linus's approach of building models.
We might be able to figure this out.
For weeks, Crick and Watson applied everything they had; everything they knew; trying to come up with a plausible model for the structure of DNA.

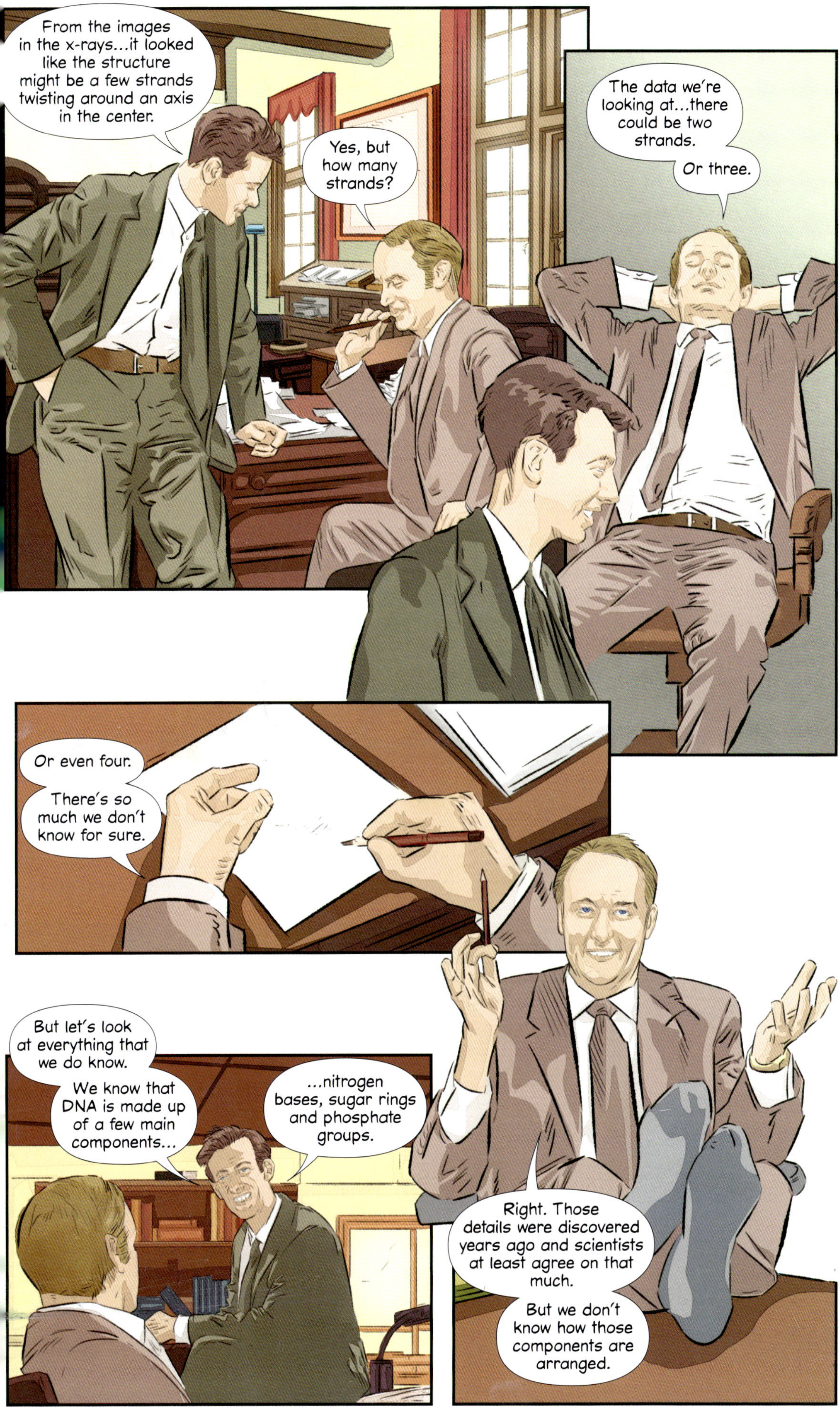
From the images in the x-rays...it looked like the structure might be a few strands twisting around an axis in the center.
Yes, but how many strands?
The data we're looking at...there could be two strands.
Or three.
Or even four.
There's so much we don't know for sure.
But let's look at everything that we do know.
We know that DNA is made up of a few main components...
...nitrogen bases, sugar rings and phosphate groups.
Right. Those details were discovered years ago and scientists at least agree on that much.
But we don't know how those components are arranged.

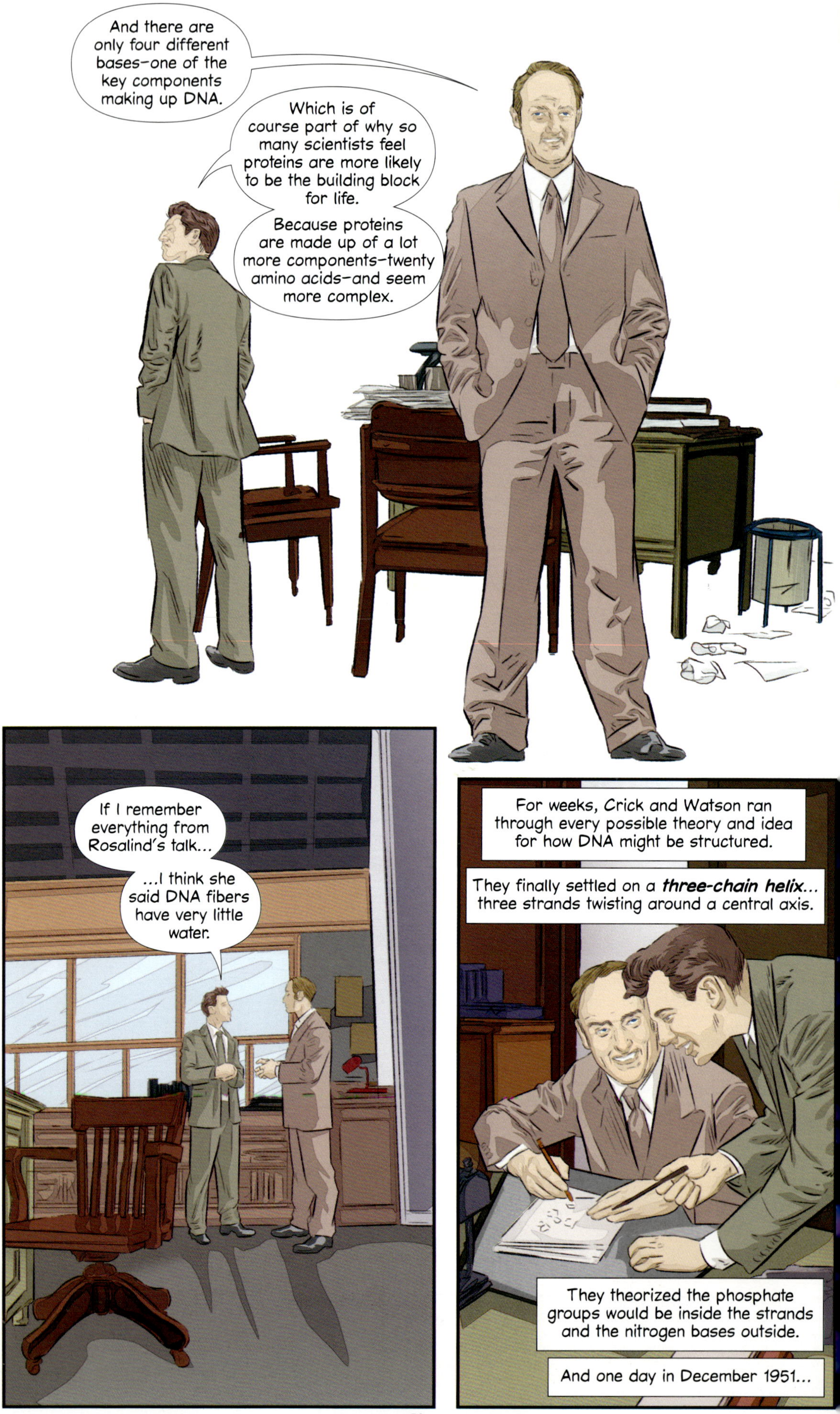
And there are only four different bases–one of the key components making up DNA.
Which is of course part of why so many scientists feel proteins are more likely to be the building block for life.
Because proteins are made up of a lot more components–twenty amino acids–and seem more complex.
If I remember everything from Rosalind's talk...
...I think she said DNA fibers have very little water.
For weeks, Crick and Watson ran through every possible theory and idea for how DNA might be structured.
They finally settled on a ***three-chain helix***... three strands twisting around a central axis.
They theorized the phosphate groups would be inside the strands and the nitrogen bases outside.
And one day in December 1951...

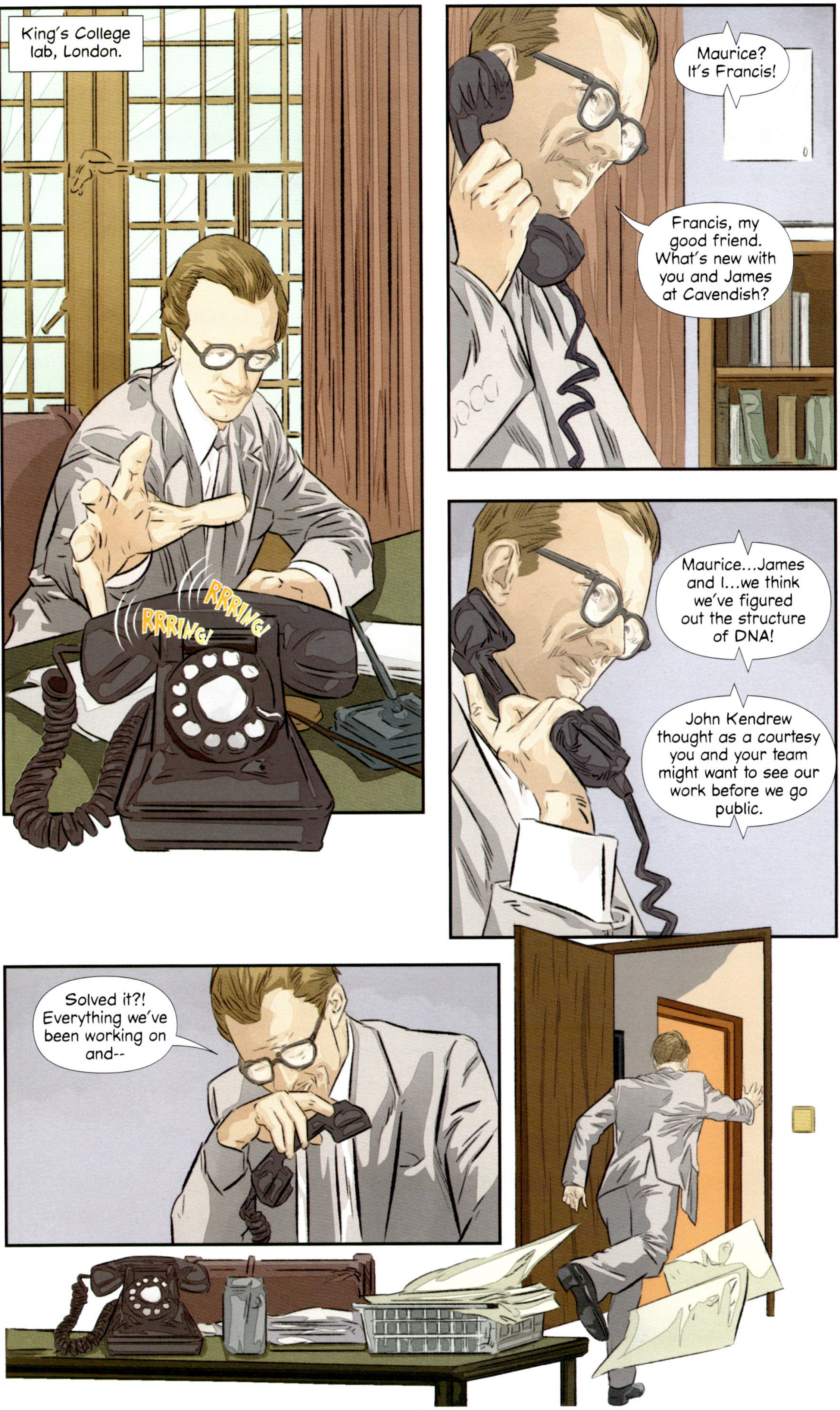
King's College lab, London.
RRRING!
RRRING!
Maurice? It's Francis!
Francis, my good friend. What's new with you and James at Cavendish?
Maurice...James and I...we think we've figured out the structure of DNA!
John Kendrew thought as a courtesy you and your team might want to see our work before we go public.
Solved it?! Everything we've been working on and--

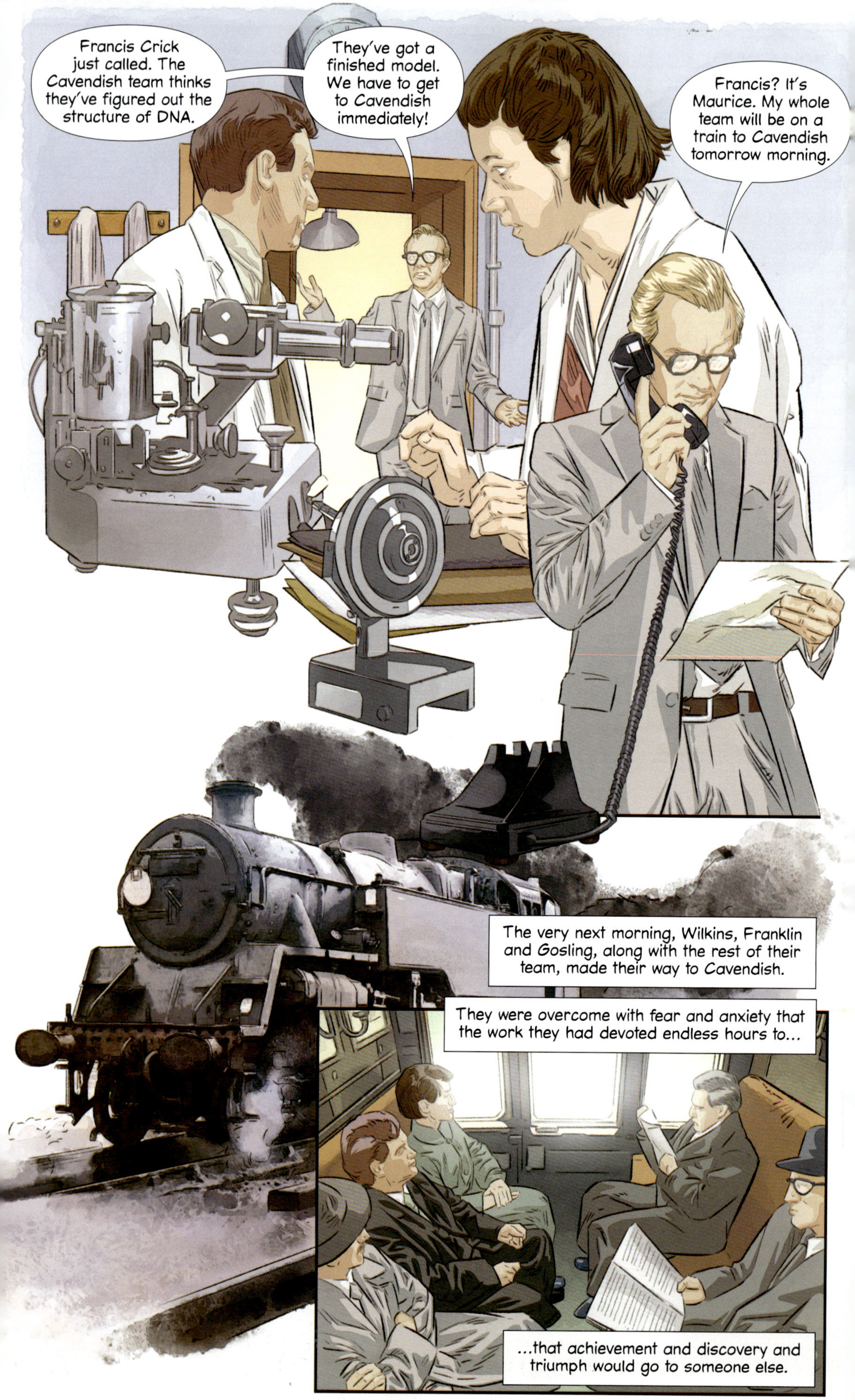
Francis Crick just called. The Cavendish team thinks they've figured out the structure of DNA.
They've got a finished model. We have to get to Cavendish immediately!
Francis? It's Maurice. My whole team will be on a train to Cavendish tomorrow morning.
The very next morning, Wilkins, Franklin and Gosling, along with the rest of their team, made their way to Cavendish.
They were overcome with fear and anxiety that the work they had devoted endless hours to...
...that achievement and discovery and triumph would go to someone else.

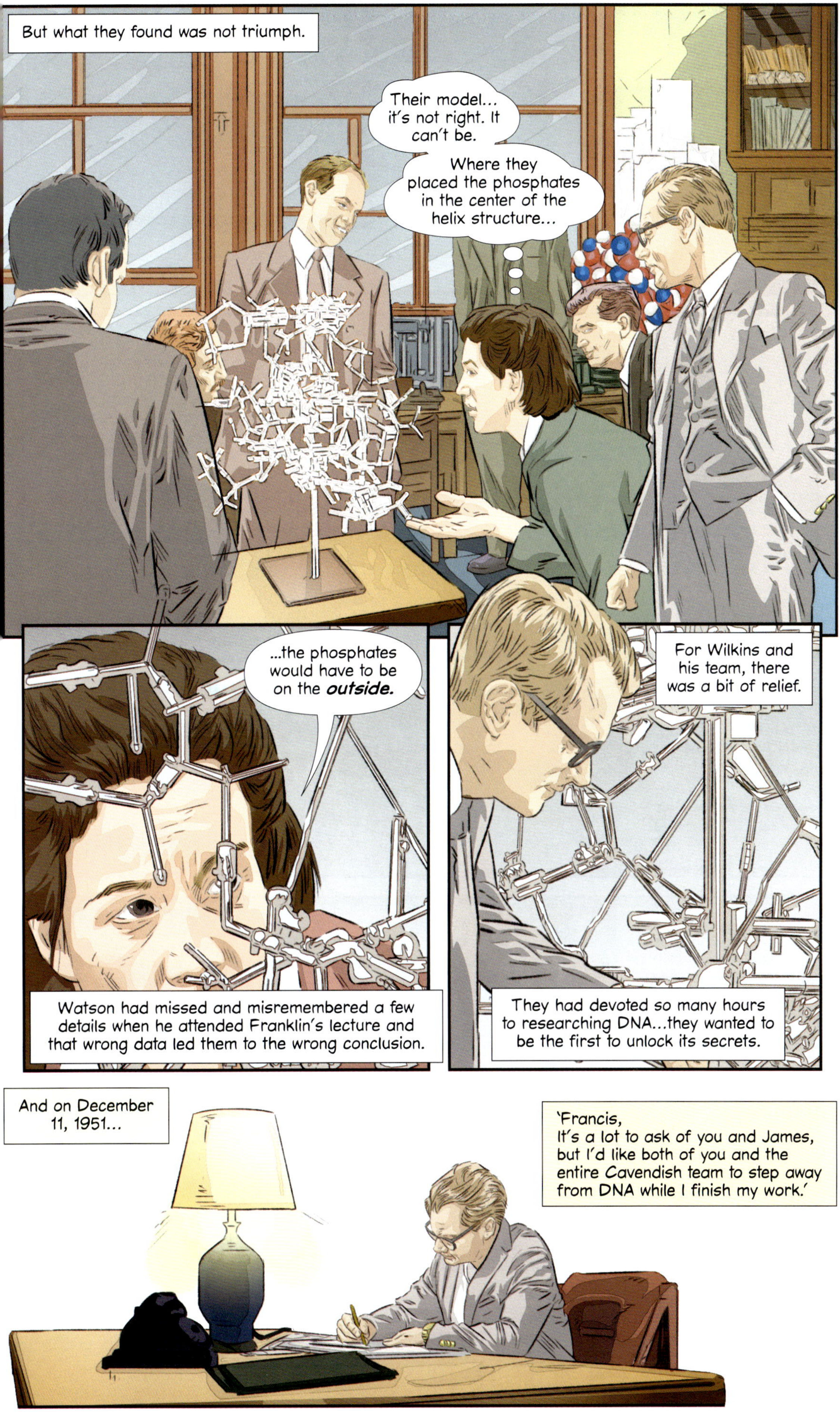
But what they found was not triumph.
Their model... it's not right. It can't be.
Where they placed the phosphates in the center of the helix structure...
...the phosphates would have to be on the *outside.*
Watson had missed and misremembered a few details when he attended Franklin's lecture and that wrong data led them to the wrong conclusion.
For Wilkins and his team, there was a bit of relief.
They had devoted so many hours to researching DNA...they wanted to be the first to unlock its secrets.
And on December 11, 1951...
'Francis,
It's a lot to ask of you and James, but I'd like both of you and the entire Cavendish team to step away from DNA while I finish my work.'

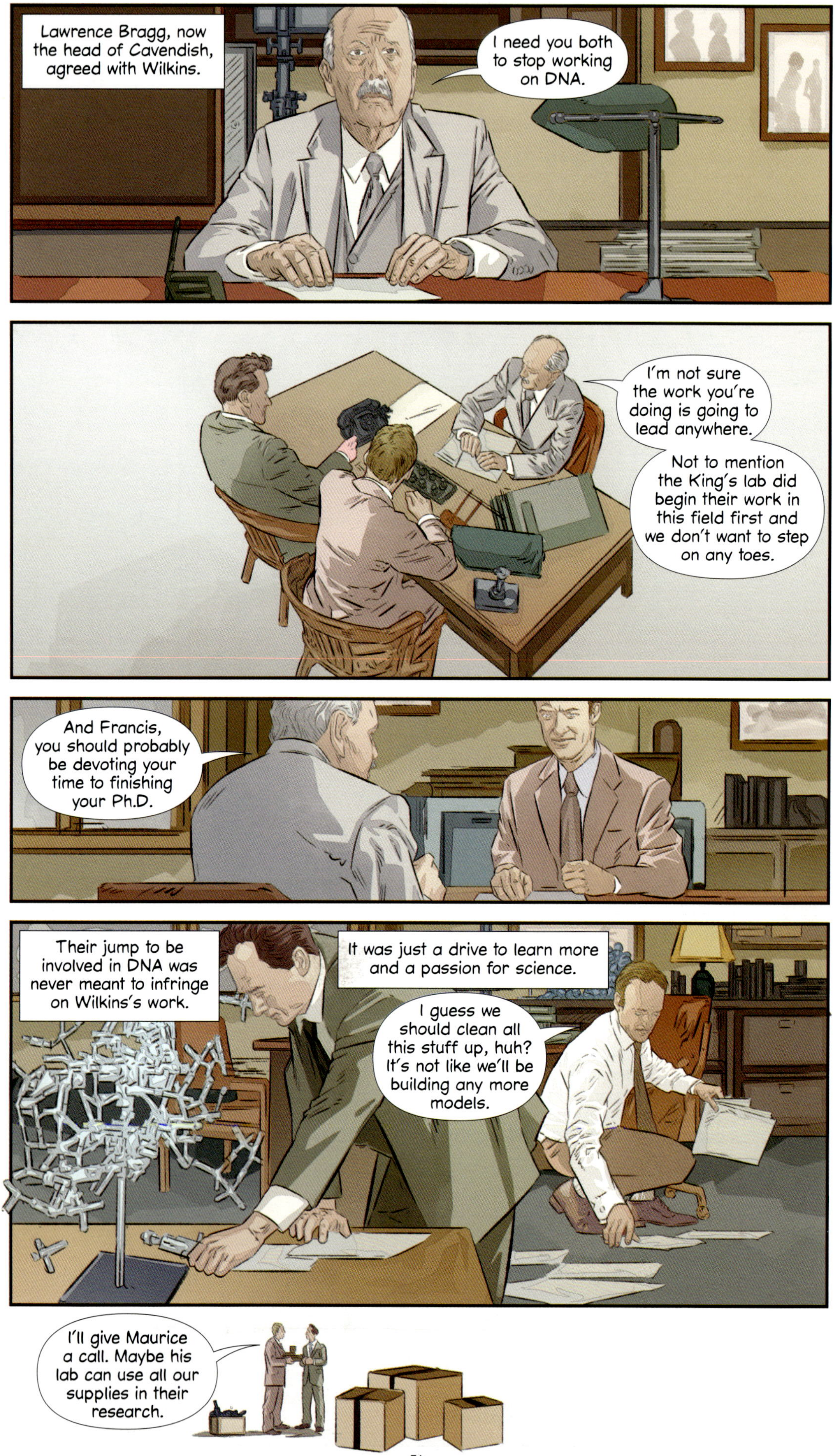
Lawrence Bragg, now the head of Cavendish, agreed with Wilkins.
I need you both to stop working on DNA.
I'm not sure the work you're doing is going to lead anywhere.
Not to mention the King's lab did begin their work in this field first and we don't want to step on any toes.
And Francis, you should probably be devoting your time to finishing your Ph.D.
Their jump to be involved in DNA was never meant to infringe on Wilkins's work.
It was just a drive to learn more and a passion for science.
I guess we should clean all this stuff up, huh? It's not like we'll be building any more models.
I'll give Maurice a call. Maybe his lab can use all our supplies in their research.

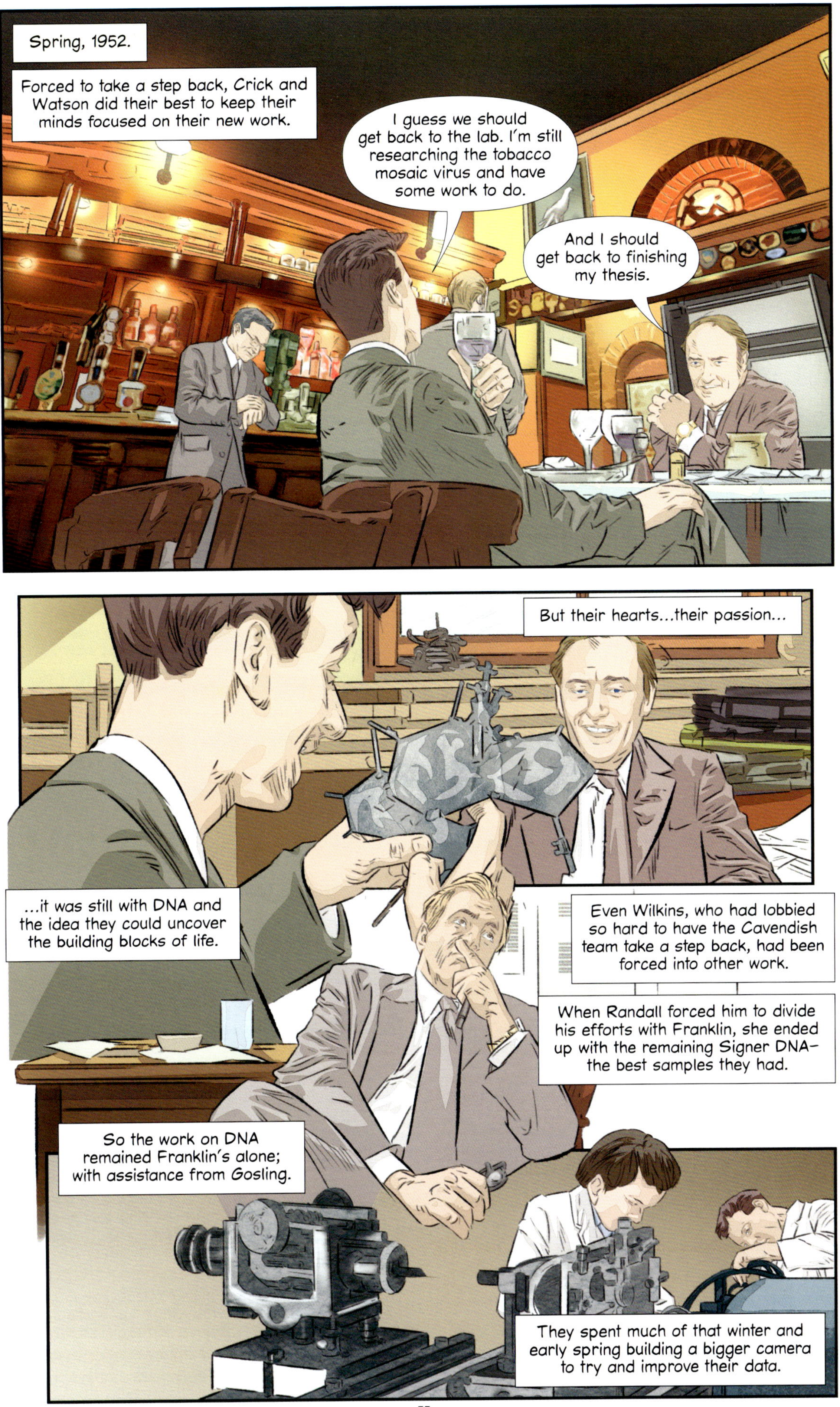
Spring, 1952.
Forced to take a step back, Crick and Watson did their best to keep their minds focused on their new work.
I guess we should get back to the lab. I'm still researching the tobacco mosaic virus and have some work to do.
And I should get back to finishing my thesis.
But their hearts...their passion...
...it was still with DNA and the idea they could uncover the building blocks of life.
Even Wilkins, who had lobbied so hard to have the Cavendish team take a step back, had been forced into other work.
When Randall forced him to divide his efforts with Franklin, she ended up with the remaining Signer DNA–the best samples they had.
So the work on DNA remained Franklin's alone; with assistance from Gosling.
They spent much of that winter and early spring building a bigger camera to try and improve their data.

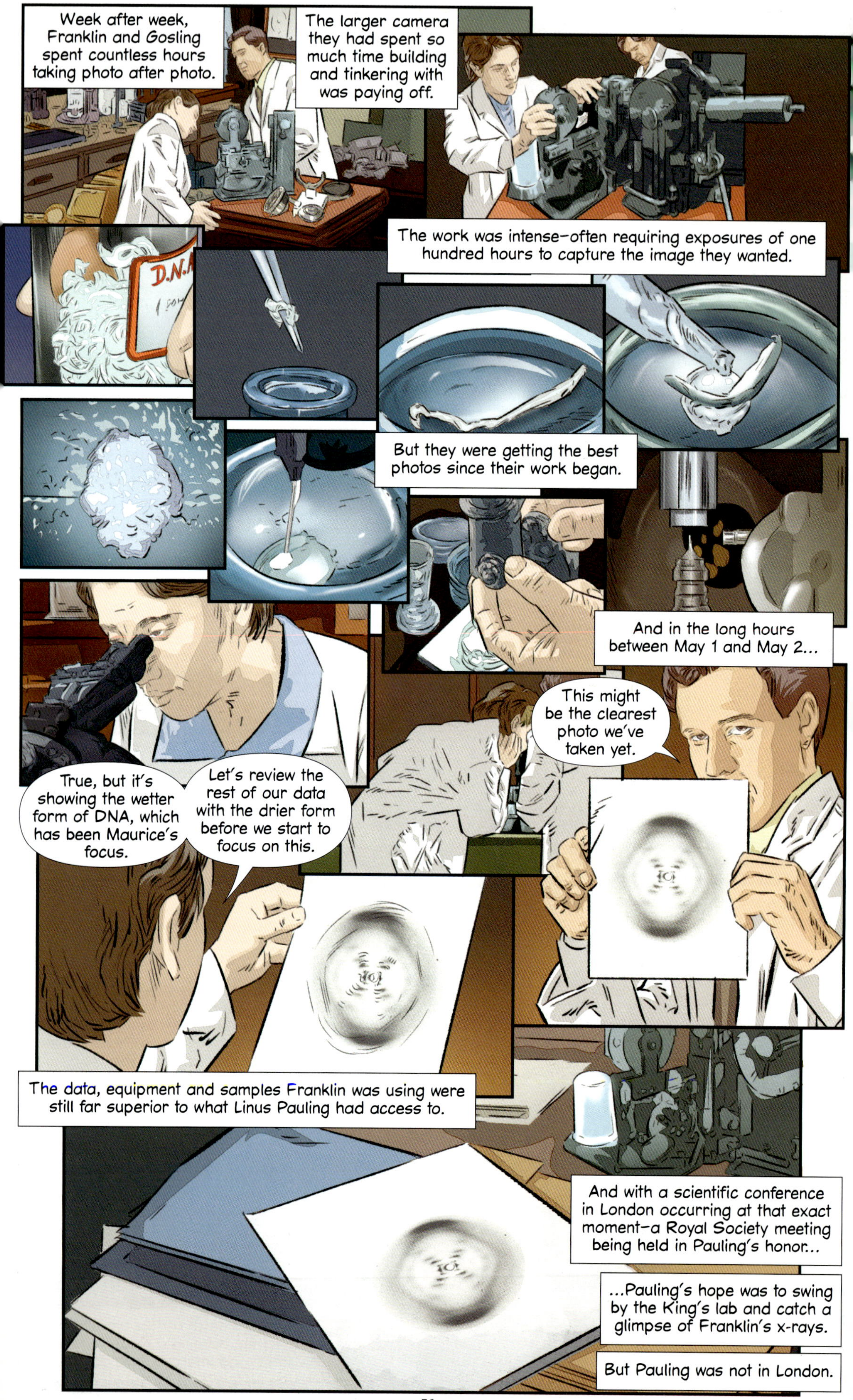

Week after week, Franklin and Gosling spent countless hours taking photo after photo.
The larger camera they had spent so much time building and tinkering with was paying off.
D.N.A
The work was intense–often requiring exposures of one hundred hours to capture the image they wanted.
But they were getting the best photos since their work began.
And in the long hours between May 1 and May 2...
This might be the clearest photo we've taken yet.
True, but it's showing the wetter form of DNA, which has been Maurice's focus.
Let's review the rest of our data with the drier form before we start to focus on this.
The data, equipment and samples Franklin was using were still far superior to what Linus Pauling had access to.
And with a scientific conference in London occurring at that exact moment–a Royal Society meeting being held in Pauling's honor...
...Pauling's hope was to swing by the King's lab and catch a glimpse of Franklin's x-rays.
But Pauling was not in London.

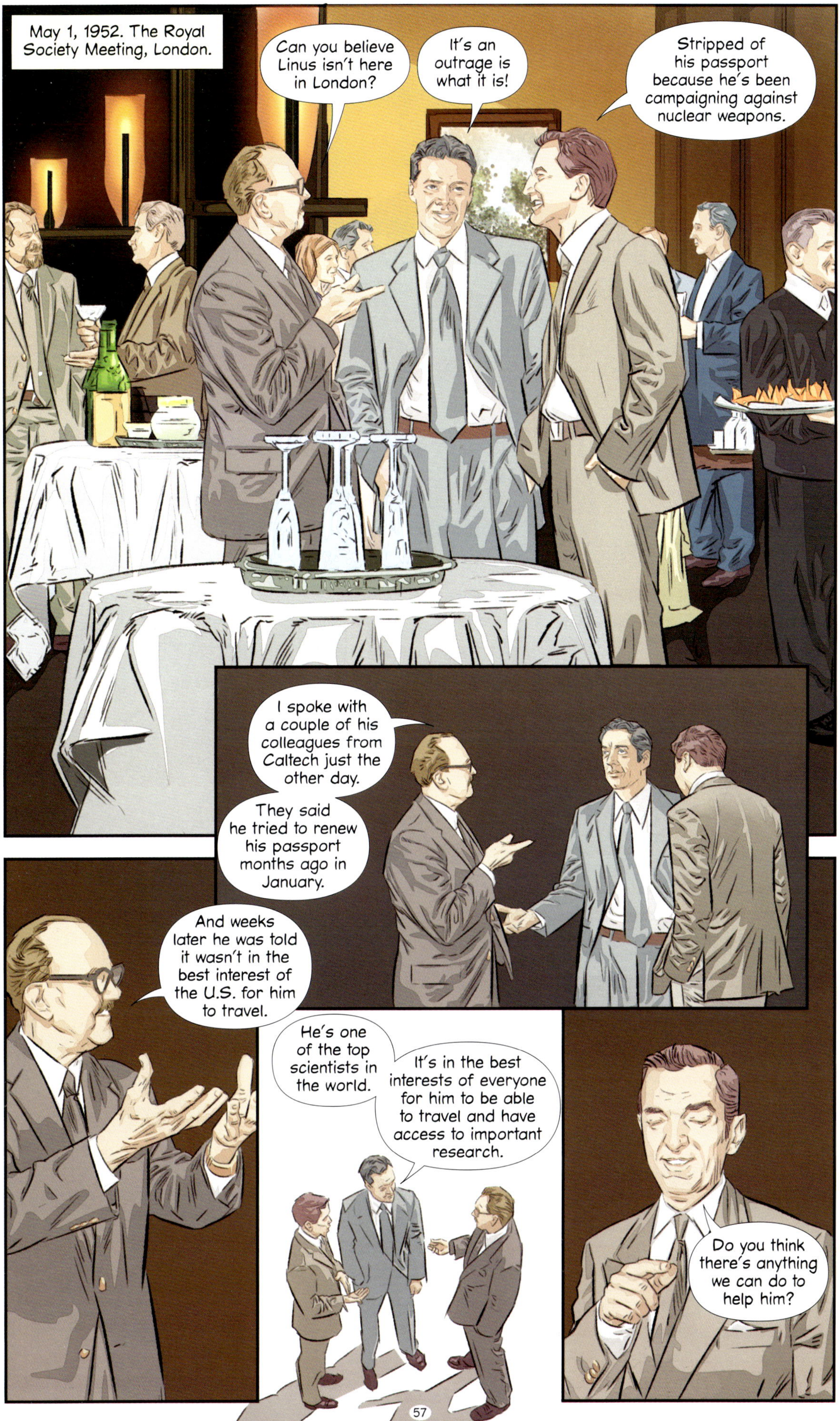
May 1, 1952. The Royal Society Meeting, London.
Can you believe Linus isn't here in London?
It's an outrage is what it is!
Stripped of his passport because he's been campaigning against nuclear weapons.
I spoke with a couple of his colleagues from Caltech just the other day.
They said he tried to renew his passport months ago in January.
And weeks later he was told it wasn't in the best interest of the U.S. for him to travel.
He's one of the top scientists in the world.
It's in the best interests of everyone for him to be able to travel and have access to important research.
Do you think there's anything we can do to help him?

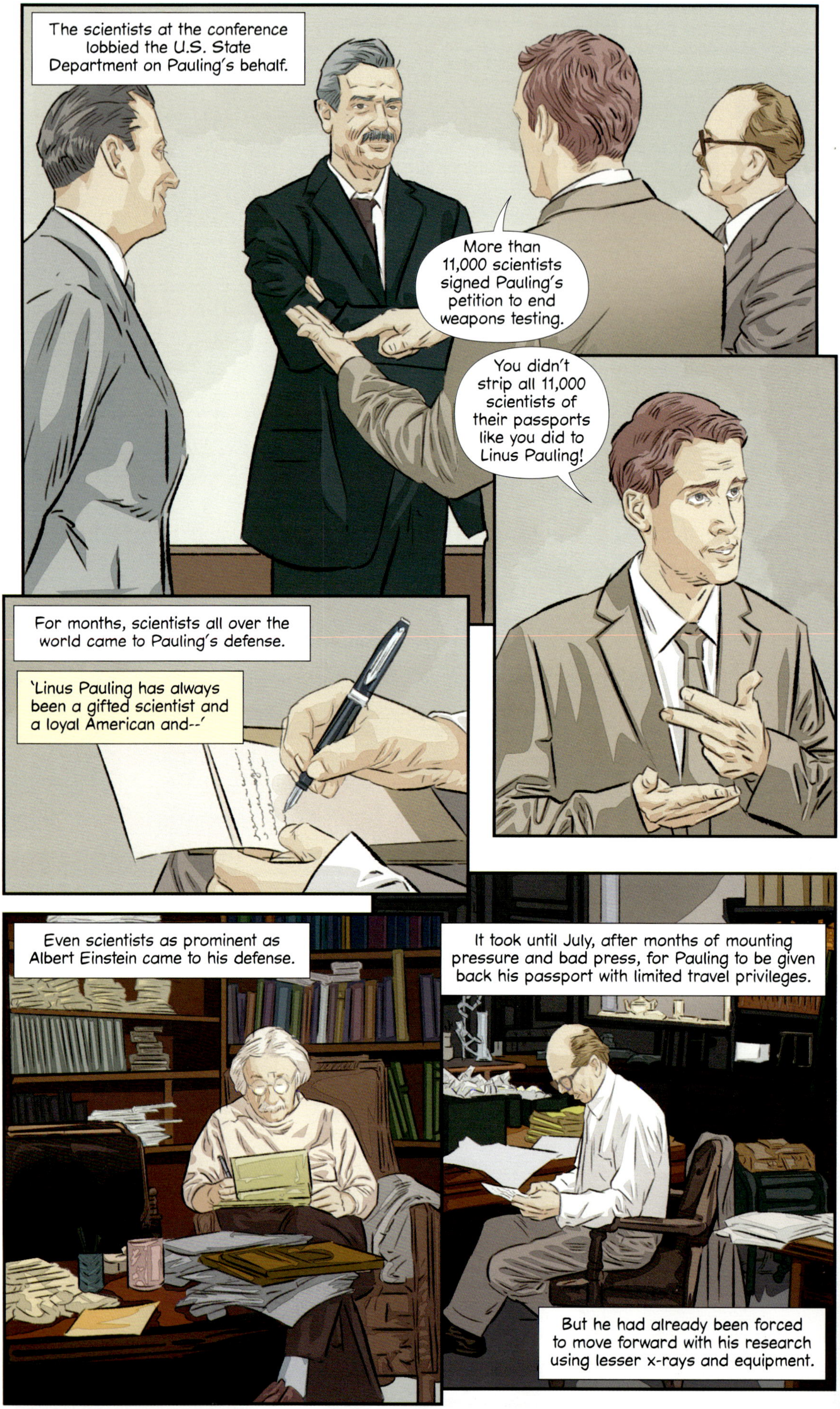

The scientists at the conference lobbied the U.S. State Department on Pauling's behalf.
More than 11,000 scientists signed Pauling's petition to end weapons testing.
You didn't strip all 11,000 scientists of their passports like you did to Linus Pauling!
For months, scientists all over the world came to Pauling's defense.
'Linus Pauling has always been a gifted scientist and a loyal American and--'
Even scientists as prominent as Albert Einstein came to his defense.
It took until July, after months of mounting pressure and bad press, for Pauling to be given back his passport with limited travel privileges.
But he had already been forced to move forward with his research using lesser x-rays and equipment.

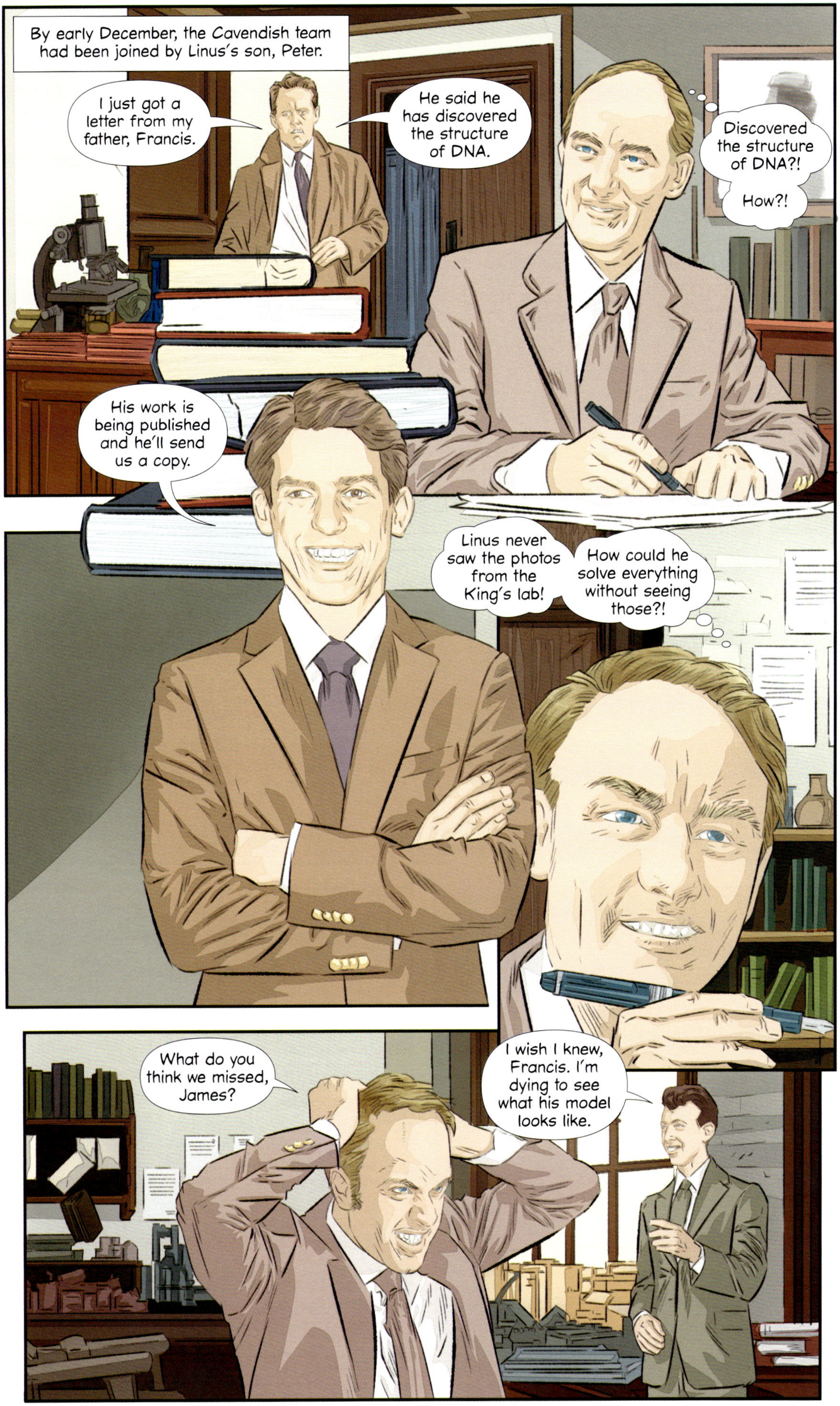
By early December, the Cavendish team had been joined by Linus's son, Peter.
I just got a letter from my father, Francis.
He said he has discovered the structure of DNA.
Discovered the structure of DNA?!
How?!
His work is being published and he'll send us a copy.
Linus never saw the photos from the King's lab!
How could he solve everything without seeing those?!
What do you think we missed, James?
I wish I knew, Francis. I'm dying to see what his model looks like.

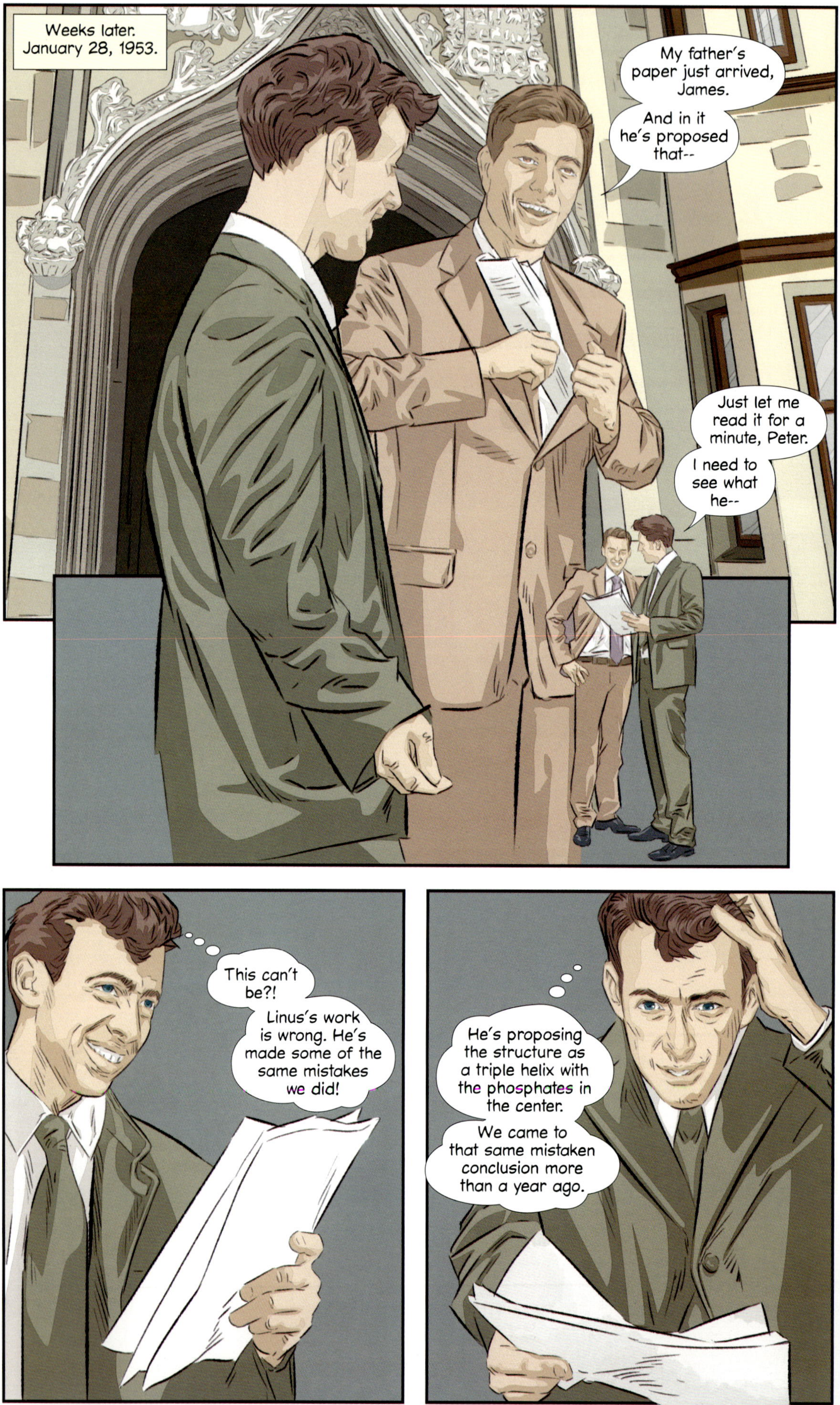
Weeks later. January 28, 1953.
My father's paper just arrived, James.
And in it he's proposed that--
Just let me read it for a minute, Peter.
I need to see what he--
This can't be?!
Linus's work is wrong. He's made some of the same mistakes we did!
He's proposing the structure as a triple helix with the phosphates in the center.
We came to that same mistaken conclusion more than a year ago.

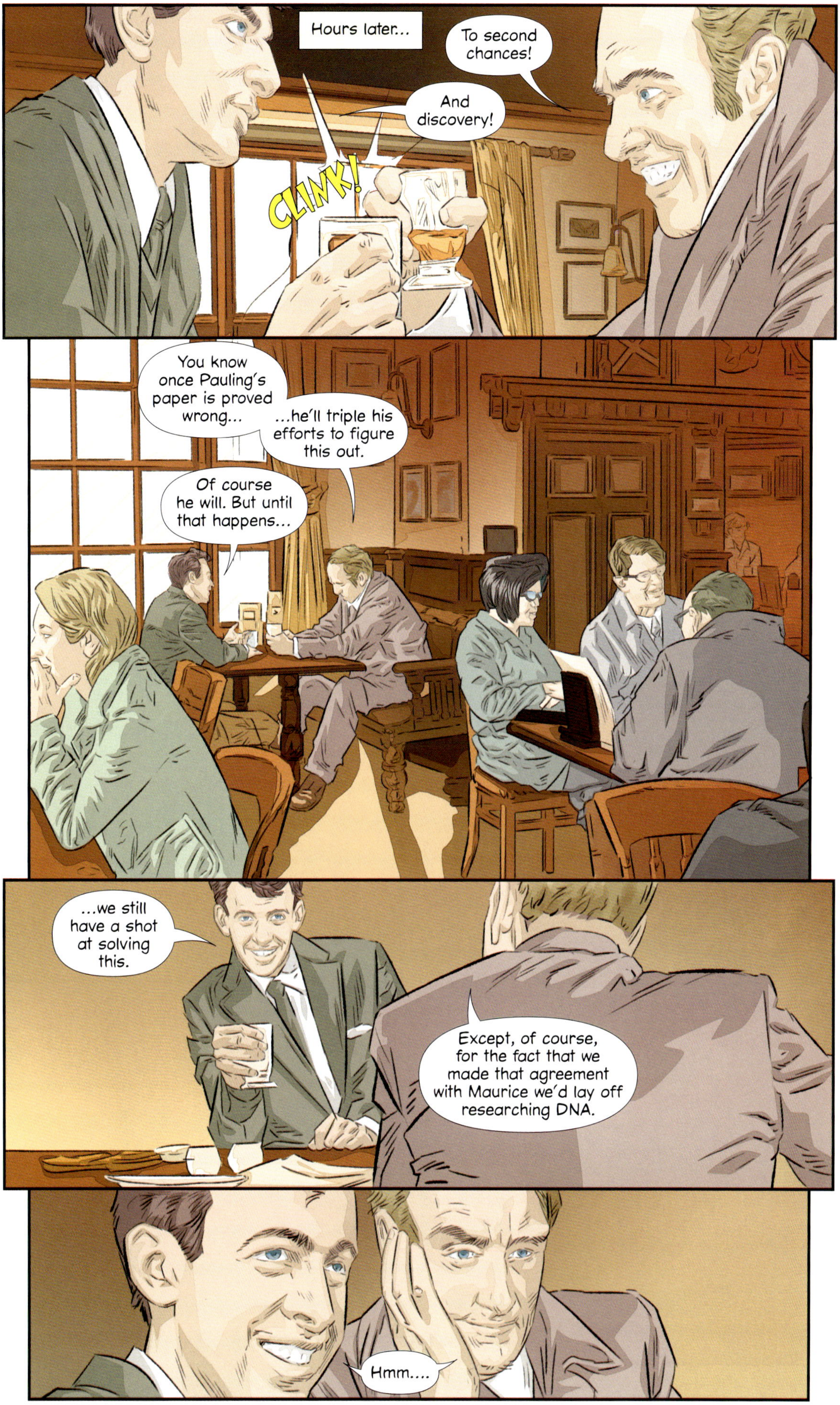

Hours later...
To second chances!
And discovery!
CLINK!
You know once Pauling's paper is proved wrong...
...he'll triple his efforts to figure this out.
Of course he will. But until that happens...
...we still have a shot at solving this.
Except, of course, for the fact that we made that agreement with Maurice we'd lay off researching DNA.
Hmm....

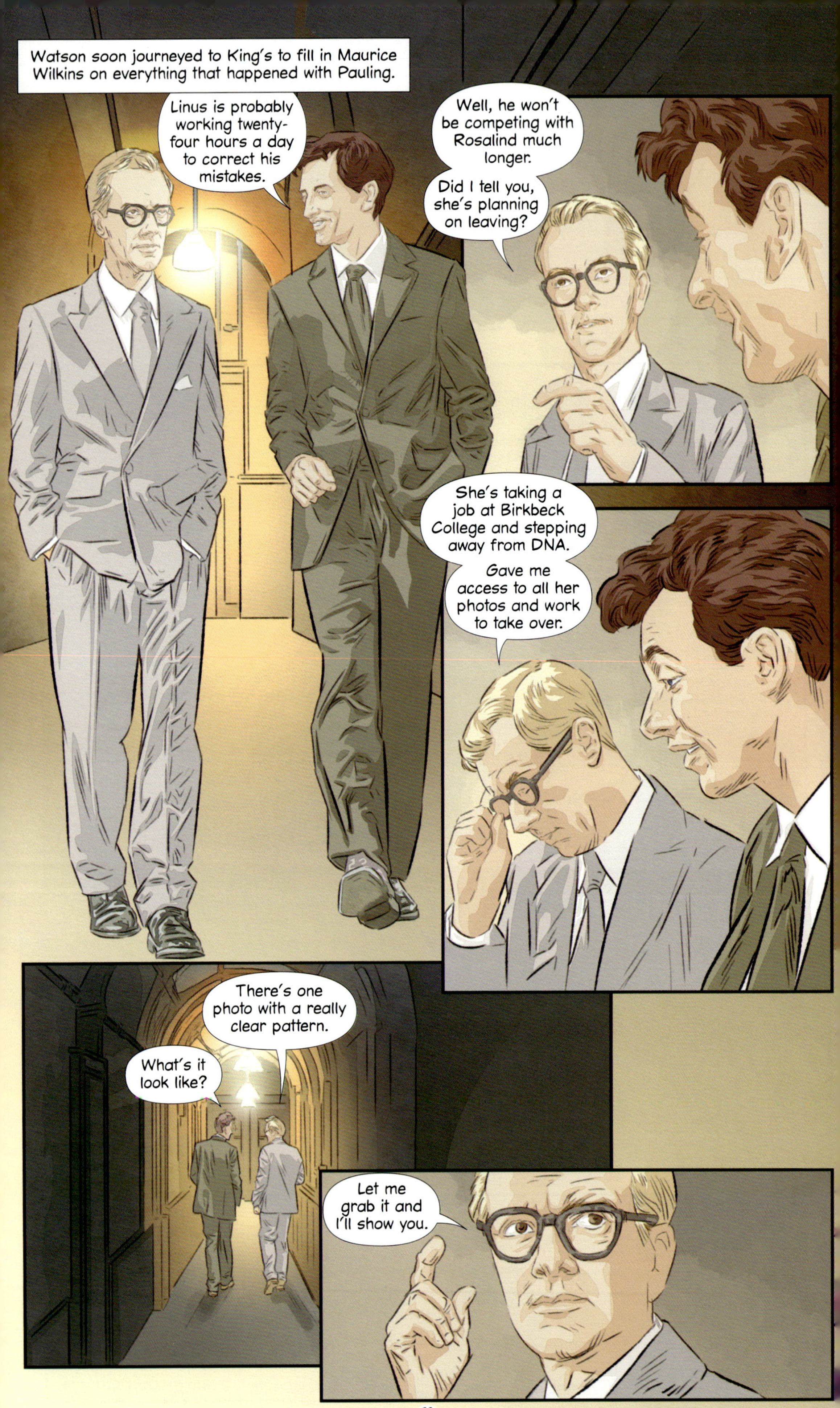

Watson soon journeyed to King's to fill in Maurice Wilkins on everything that happened with Pauling.
Linus is probably working twenty-four hours a day to correct his mistakes.
Well, he won't be competing with Rosalind much longer.
Did I tell you, she's planning on leaving?
She's taking a job at Birkbeck College and stepping away from DNA.
Gave me access to all her photos and work to take over.
There's one photo with a really clear pattern.
What's it look like?
Let me grab it and I'll show you.

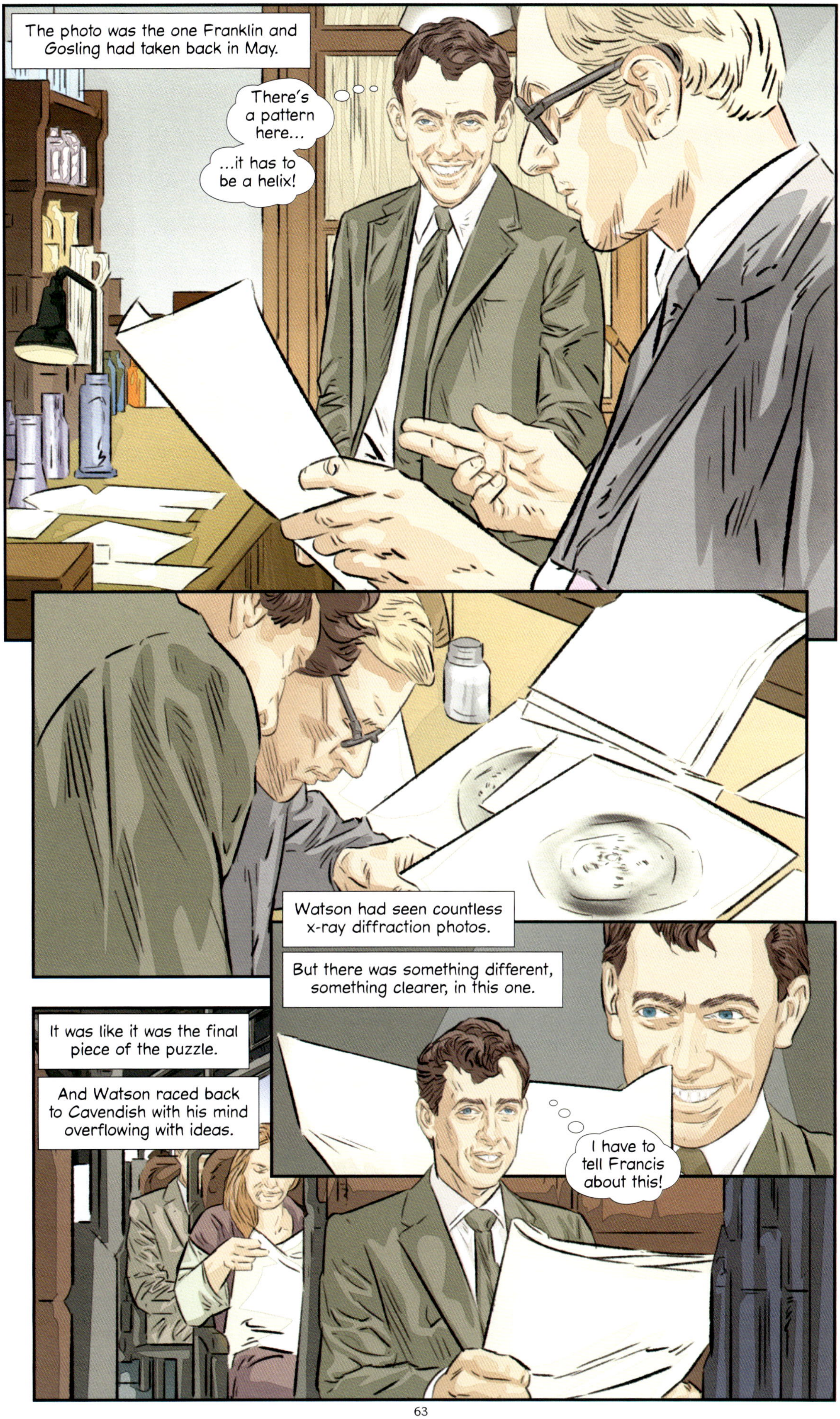

The photo was the one Franklin and Gosling had taken back in May.
There's a pattern here...
...it has to be a helix!
Watson had seen countless x-ray diffraction photos.
But there was something different, something clearer, in this one.
It was like it was the final piece of the puzzle.
And Watson raced back to Cavendish with his mind overflowing with ideas.
I have to tell Francis about this!

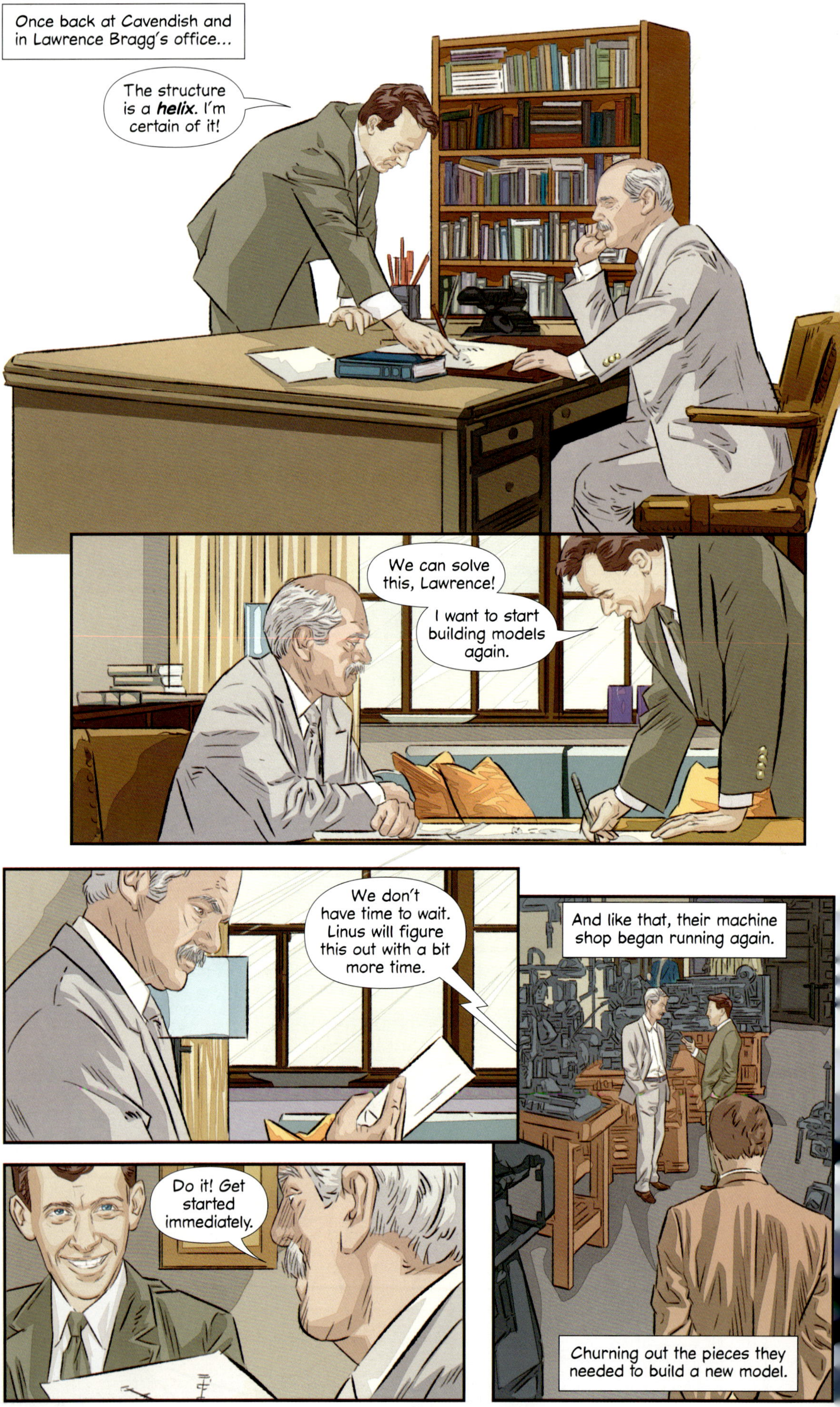
Once back at Cavendish and in Lawrence Bragg's office...
The structure is a **helix**. I'm certain of it!
We can solve this, Lawrence!
I want to start building models again.
We don't have time to wait. Linus will figure this out with a bit more time.
Do it! Get started immediately.
And like that, their machine shop began running again.
Churning out the pieces they needed to build a new model.

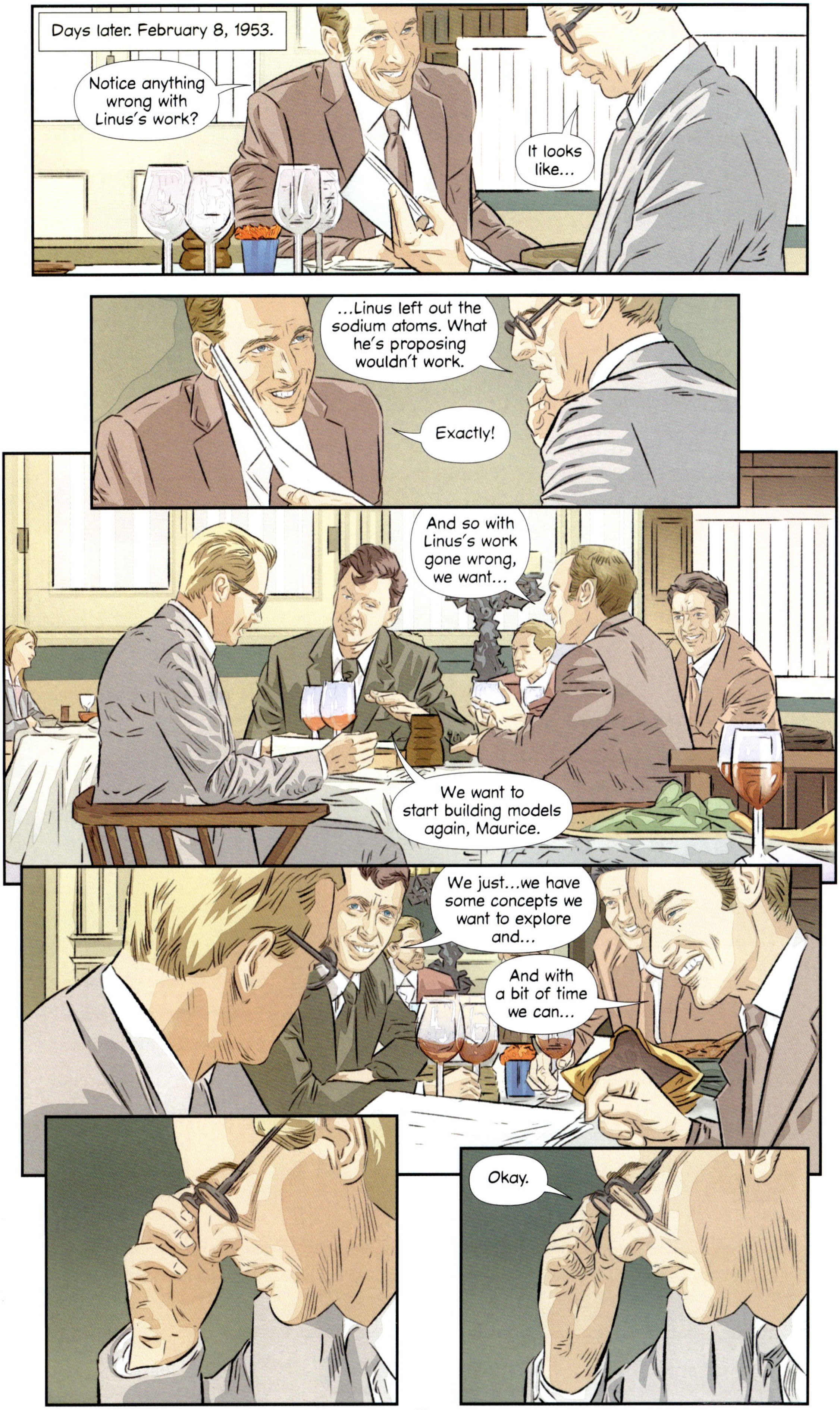
Days later. February 8, 1953.
Notice anything wrong with Linus's work?
It looks like...
...Linus left out the sodium atoms. What he's proposing wouldn't work.
Exactly!
And so with Linus's work gone wrong, we want...
We want to start building models again, Maurice.
We just...we have some concepts we want to explore and...
And with a bit of time we can...
Okay.

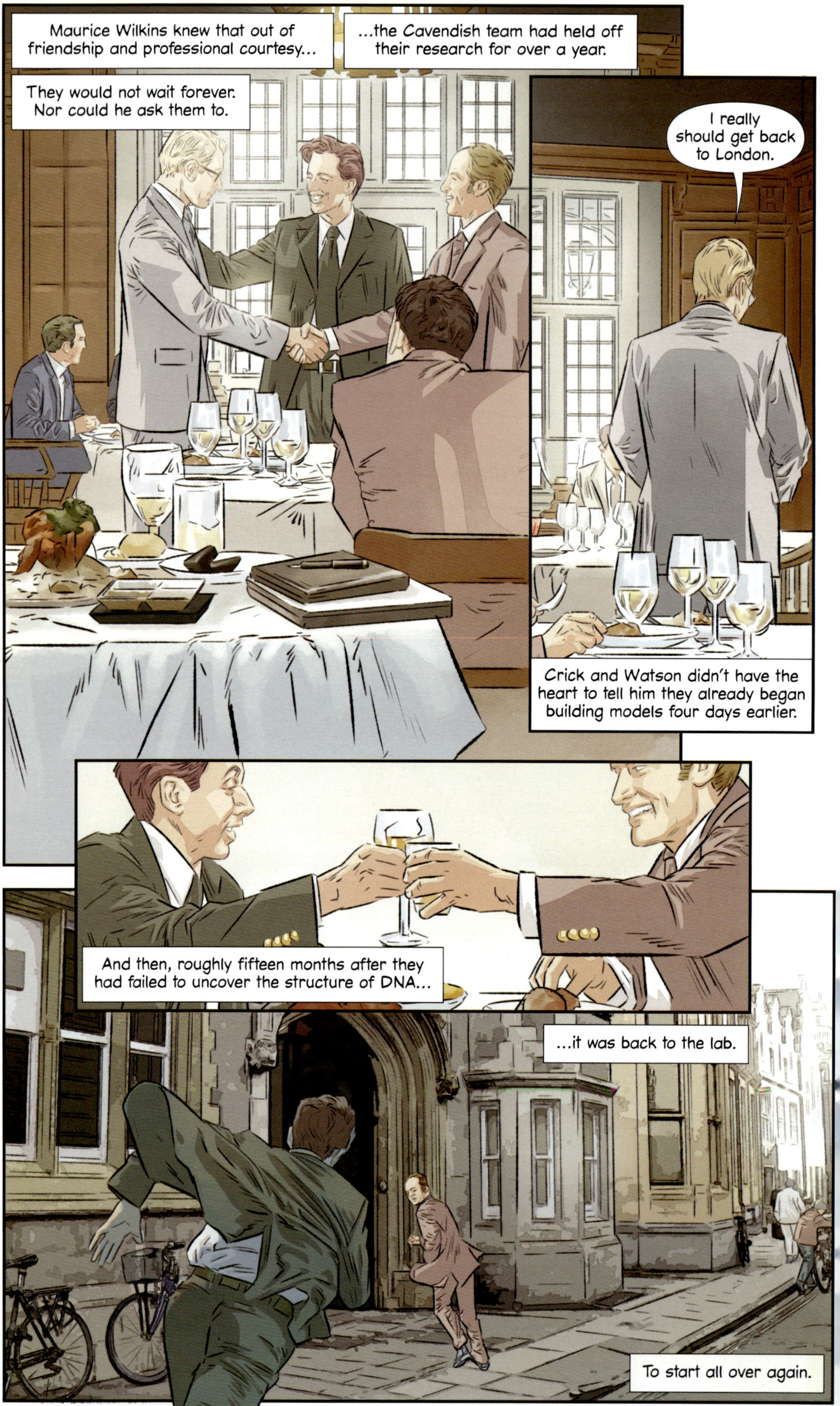
Maurice Wilkins knew that out of friendship and professional courtesy...
...the Cavendish team had held off their research for over a year.
They would not wait forever. Nor could he ask them to.
I really should get back to London.
Crick and Watson didn't have the heart to tell him they already began building models four days earlier.
And then, roughly fifteen months after they had failed to uncover the structure of DNA...
...it was back to the lab.
To start all over again.

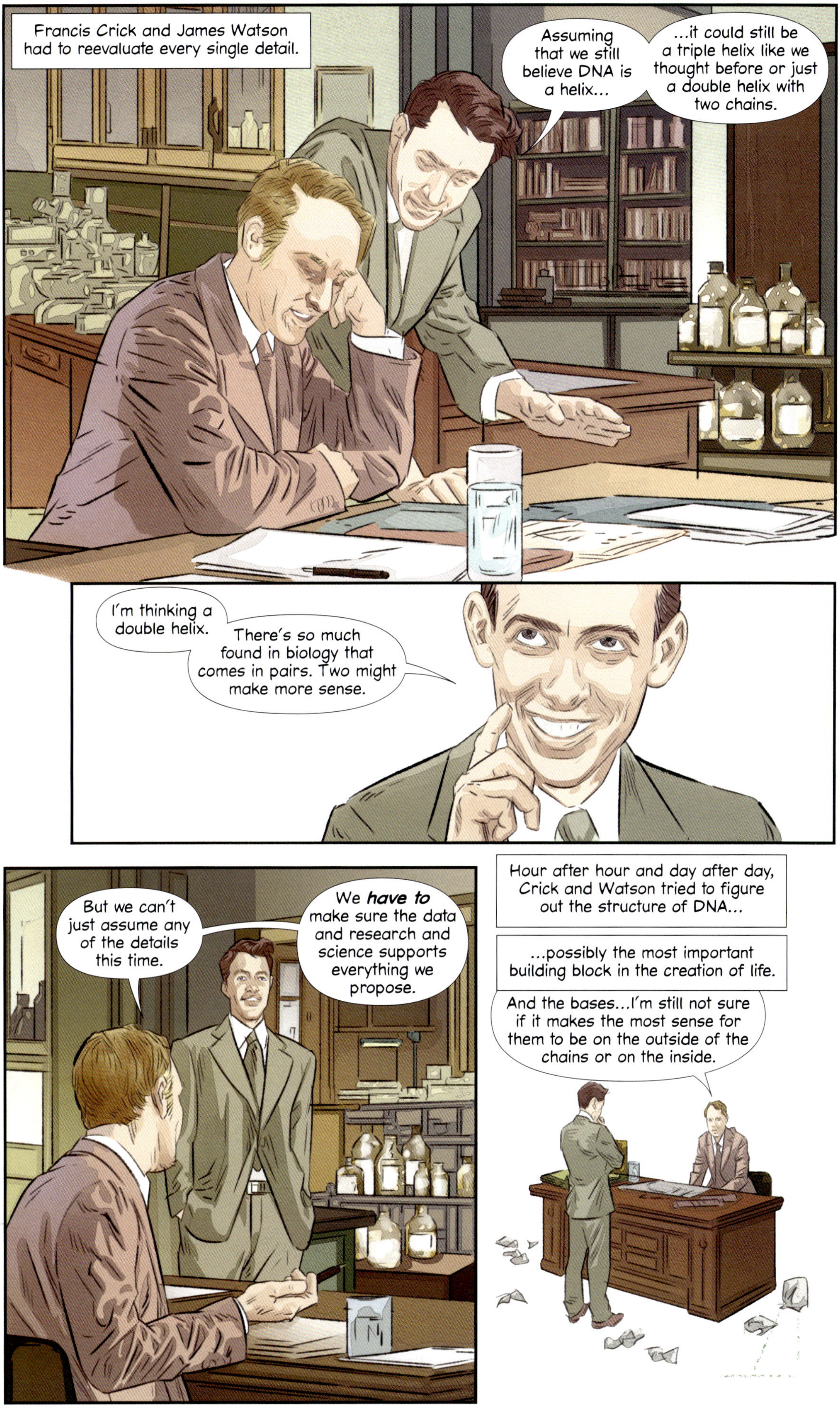
Francis Crick and James Watson had to reevaluate every single detail.
Assuming that we still believe DNA is a helix...
...it could still be a triple helix like we thought before or just a double helix with two chains.
I'm thinking a double helix.
There's so much found in biology that comes in pairs. Two might make more sense.
But we can't just assume any of the details this time.
We *have to* make sure the data and research and science supports everything we propose.
Hour after hour and day after day, Crick and Watson tried to figure out the structure of DNA...
...possibly the most important building block in the creation of life.
And the bases...I'm still not sure if it makes the most sense for them to be on the outside of the chains or on the inside.

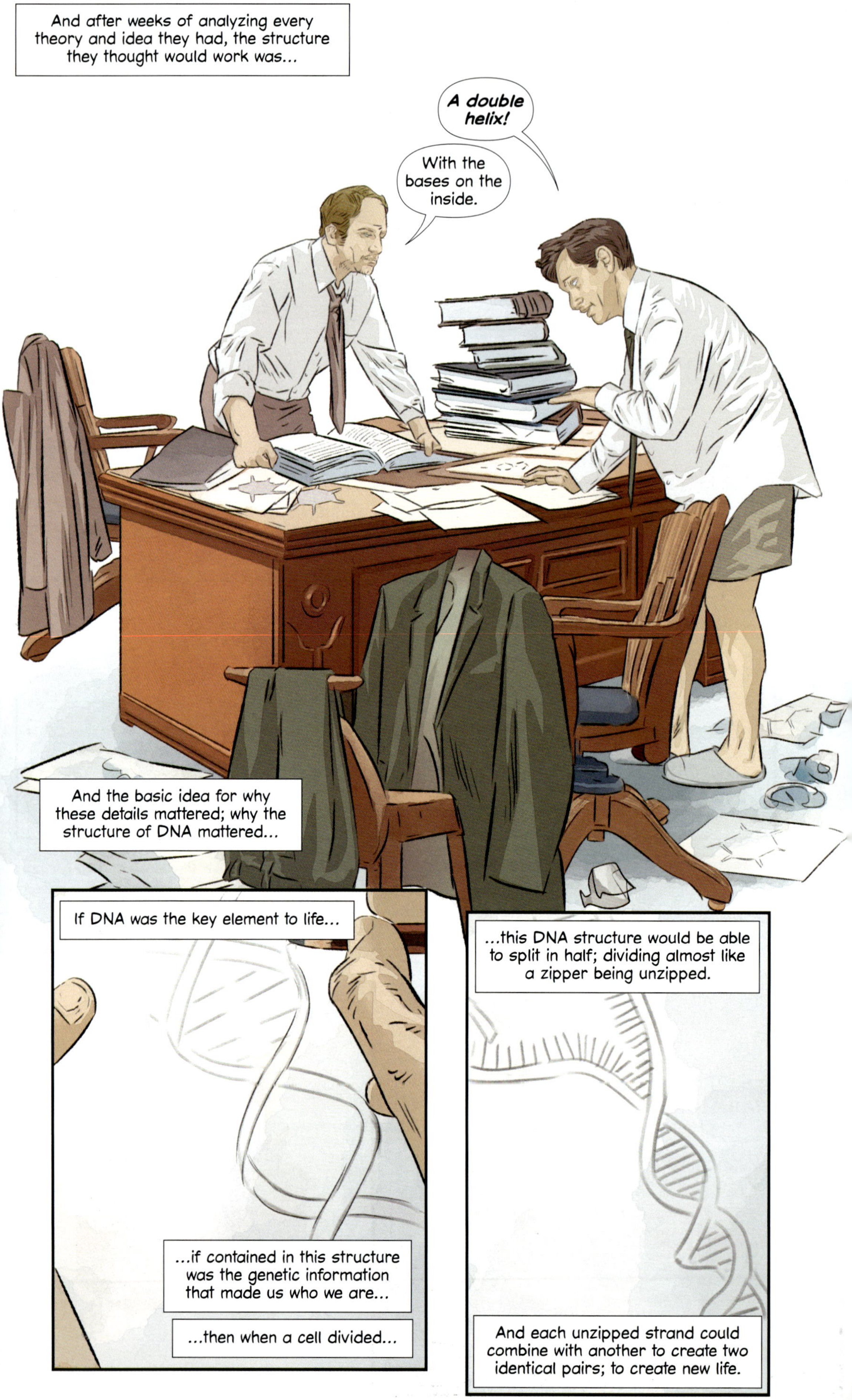
And after weeks of analyzing every theory and idea they had, the structure they thought would work was...
With the bases on the inside.
A double helix!
And the basic idea for why these details mattered; why the structure of DNA mattered...
If DNA was the key element to life...
...if contained in this structure was the genetic information that made us who we are...
...then when a cell divided...
...this DNA structure would be able to split in half; dividing almost like a zipper being unzipped.
And each unzipped strand could combine with another to create two identical pairs; to create new life.

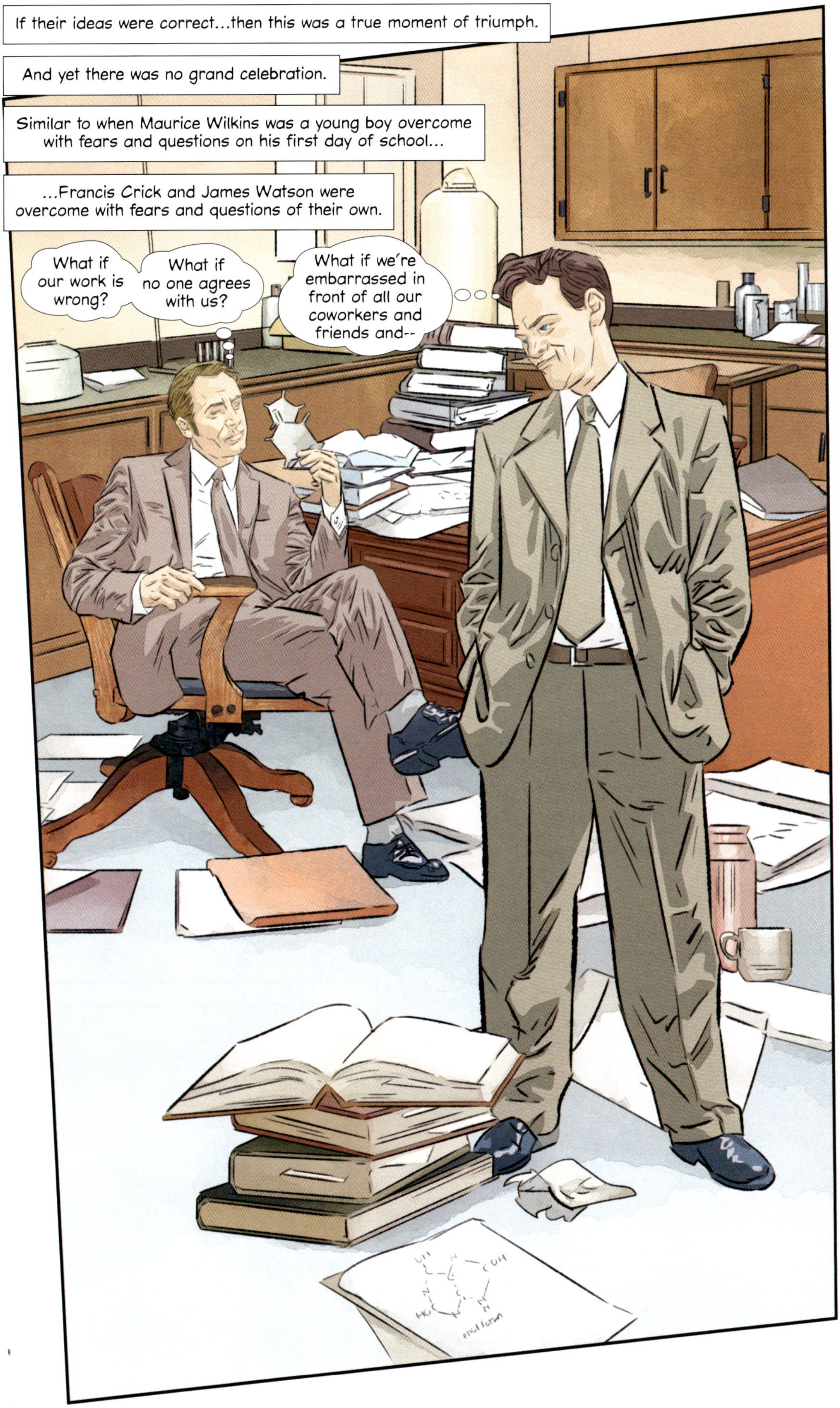
If their ideas were correct...then this was a true moment of triumph.
And yet there was no grand celebration.
Similar to when Maurice Wilkins was a young boy overcome with fears and questions on his first day of school...
...Francis Crick and James Watson were overcome with fears and questions of their own.
What if our work is wrong?
What if no one agrees with us?
What if we're embarrassed in front of all our coworkers and friends and--

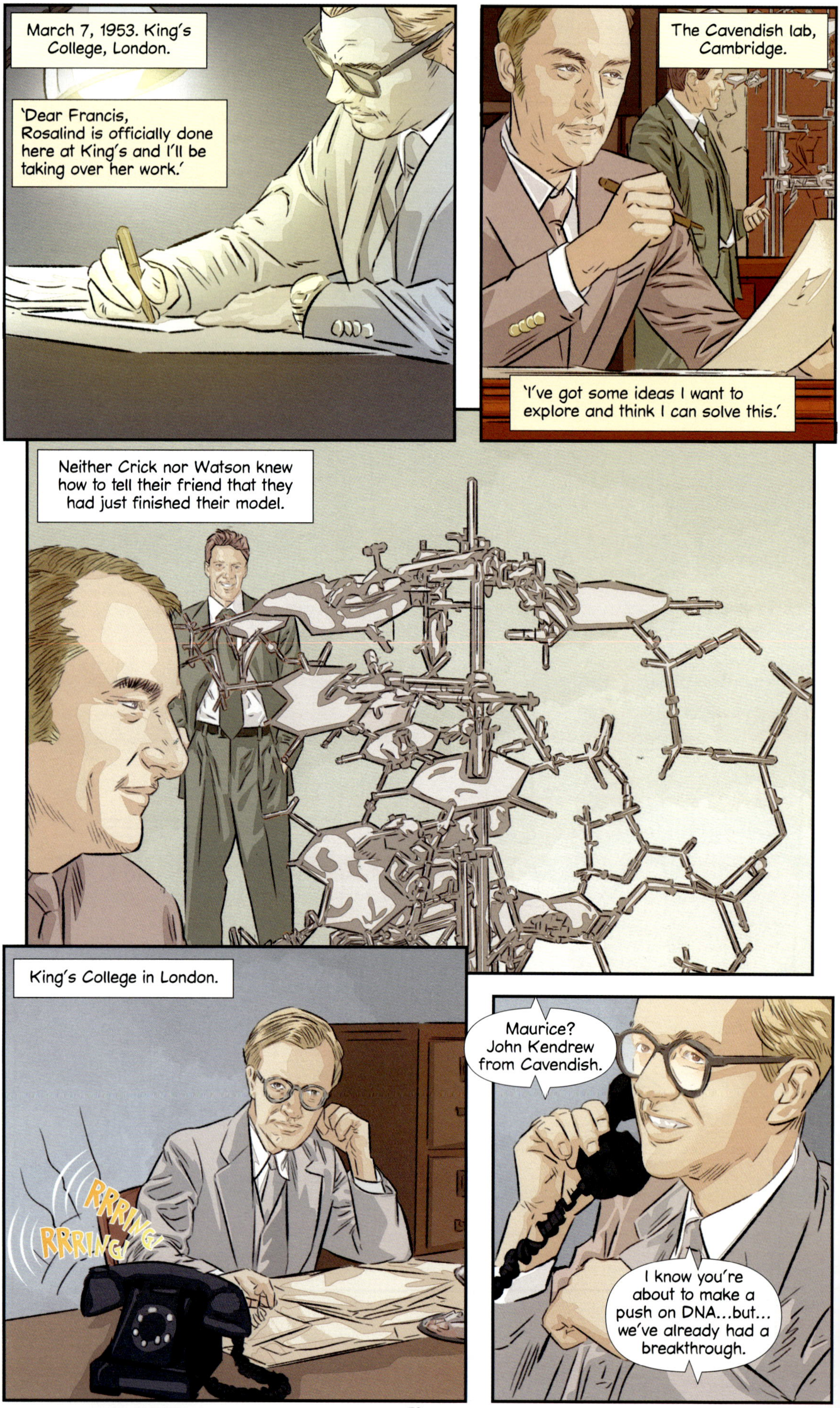
March 7, 1953. King's College, London.
'Dear Francis, Rosalind is officially done here at King's and I'll be taking over her work.'
The Cavendish lab, Cambridge.
'I've got some ideas I want to explore and think I can solve this.'
Neither Crick nor Watson knew how to tell their friend that they had just finished their model.
King's College in London.
RRRING! RRRING!
Maurice? John Kendrew from Cavendish.
I know you're about to make a push on DNA...but... we've already had a breakthrough.

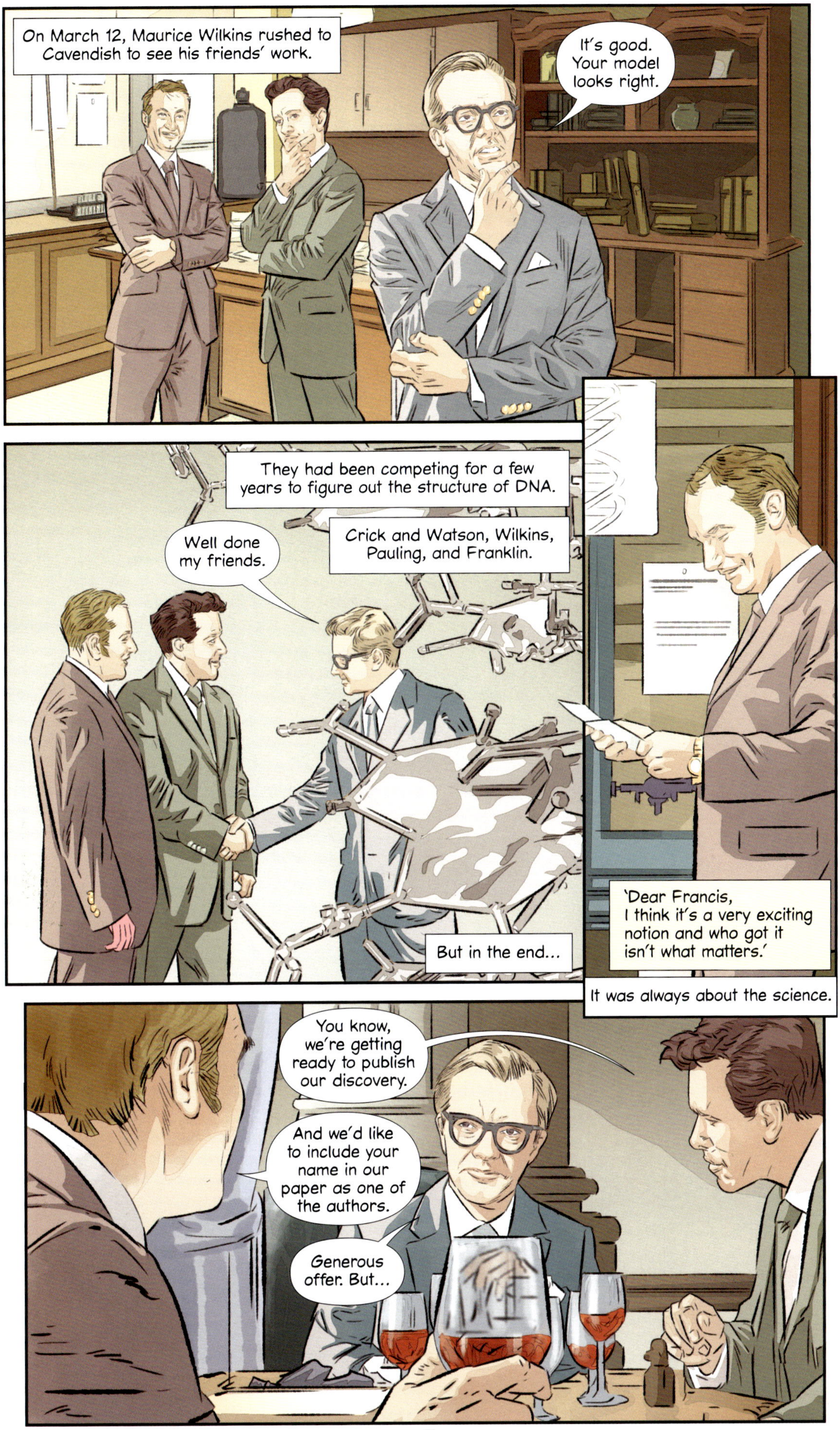
On March 12, Maurice Wilkins rushed to Cavendish to see his friends' work.
It's good. Your model looks right.
They had been competing for a few years to figure out the structure of DNA.
Crick and Watson, Wilkins, Pauling, and Franklin.
Well done my friends.
But in the end...
'Dear Francis, I think it's a very exciting notion and who got it isn't what matters.'
It was always about the science.
You know, we're getting ready to publish our discovery.
And we'd like to include your name in our paper as one of the authors.
Generous offer. But...

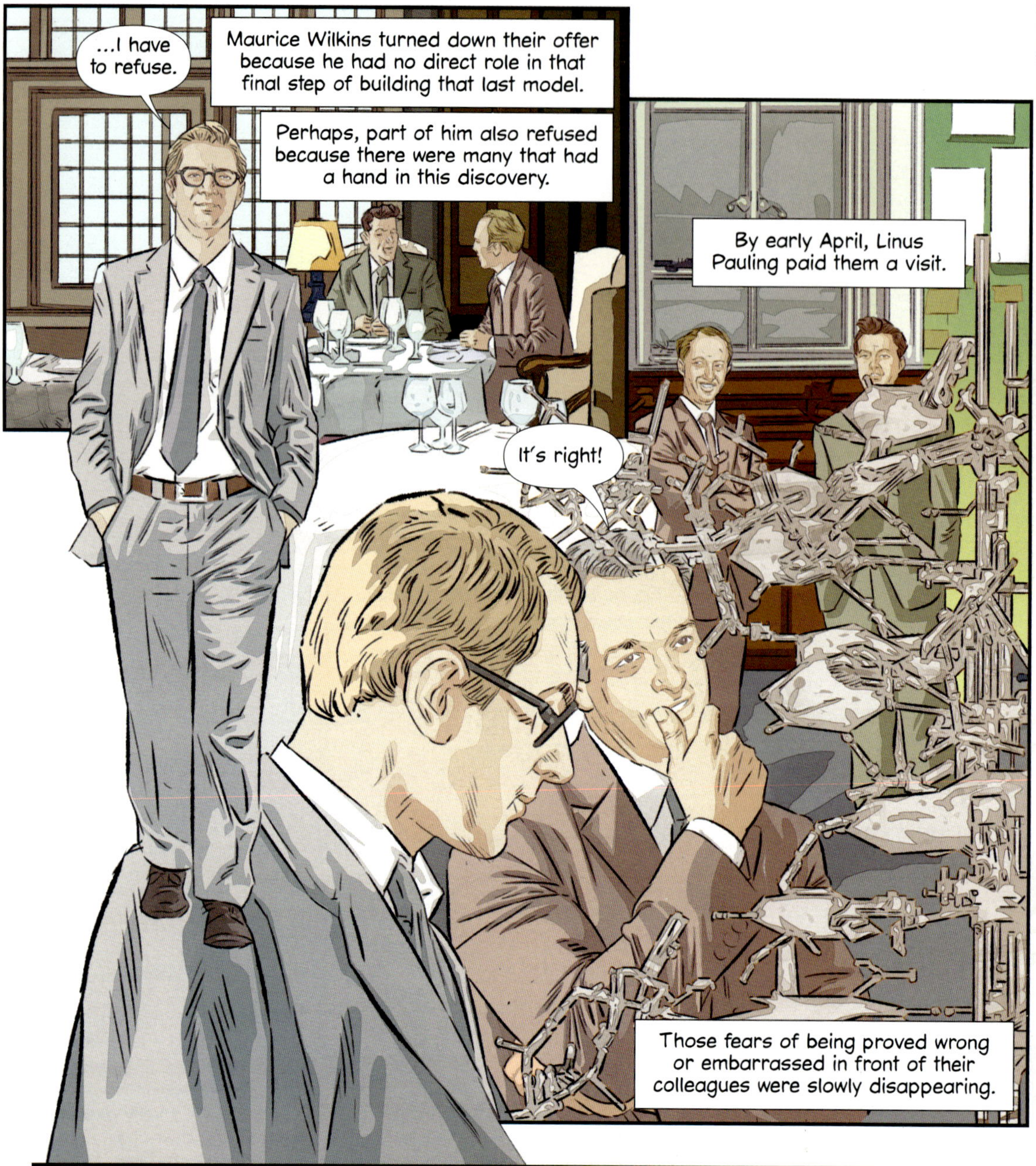
...I have to refuse.
Maurice Wilkins turned down their offer because he had no direct role in that final step of building that last model.
Perhaps, part of him also refused because there were many that had a hand in this discovery.
By early April, Linus Pauling paid them a visit.
It's right!
Those fears of being proved wrong or embarrassed in front of their colleagues were slowly disappearing.

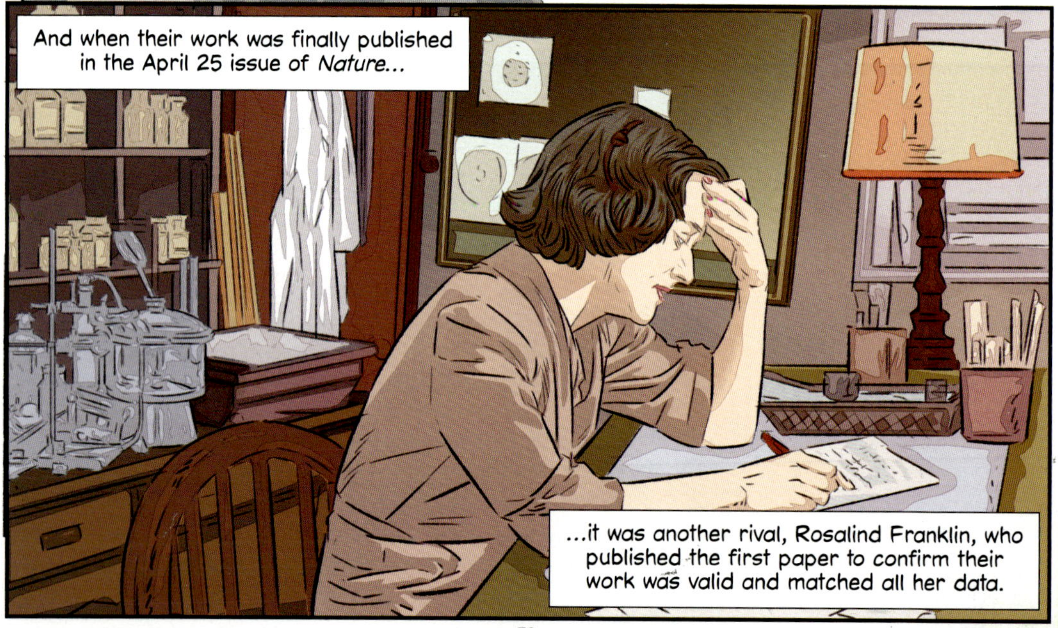
And when their work was finally published in the April 25 issue of *Nature*...
...it was another rival, Rosalind Franklin, who published the first paper to confirm their work was valid and matched all her data.

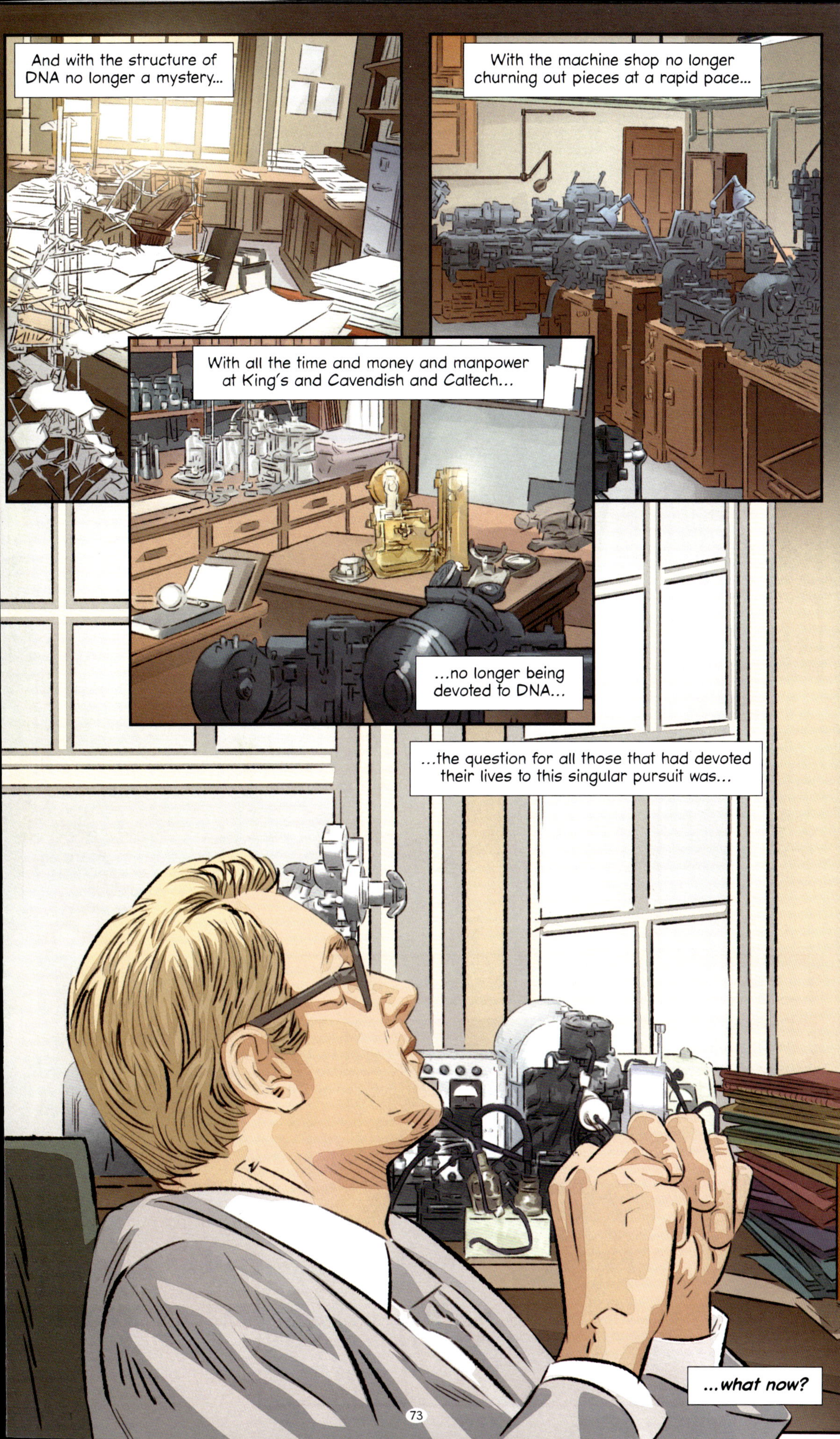
And with the structure of DNA no longer a mystery...
With the machine shop no longer churning out pieces at a rapid pace...
With all the time and money and manpower at King's and Cavendish and Caltech...
...no longer being devoted to DNA...
...the question for all those that had devoted their lives to this singular pursuit was...
...what now?

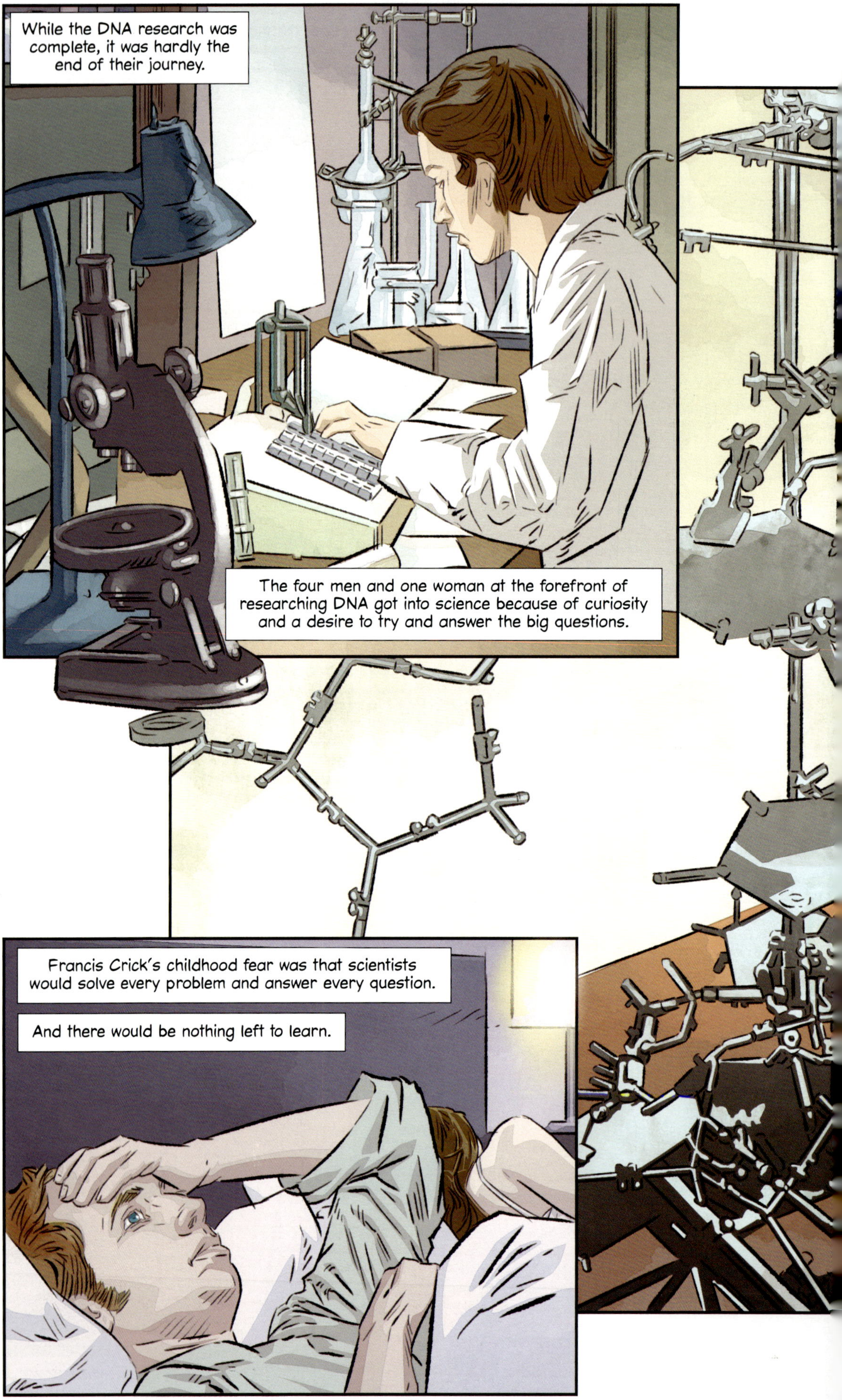
While the DNA research was complete, it was hardly the end of their journey.
The four men and one woman at the forefront of researching DNA got into science because of curiosity and a desire to try and answer the big questions.
Francis Crick's childhood fear was that scientists would solve every problem and answer every question.
And there would be nothing left to learn.

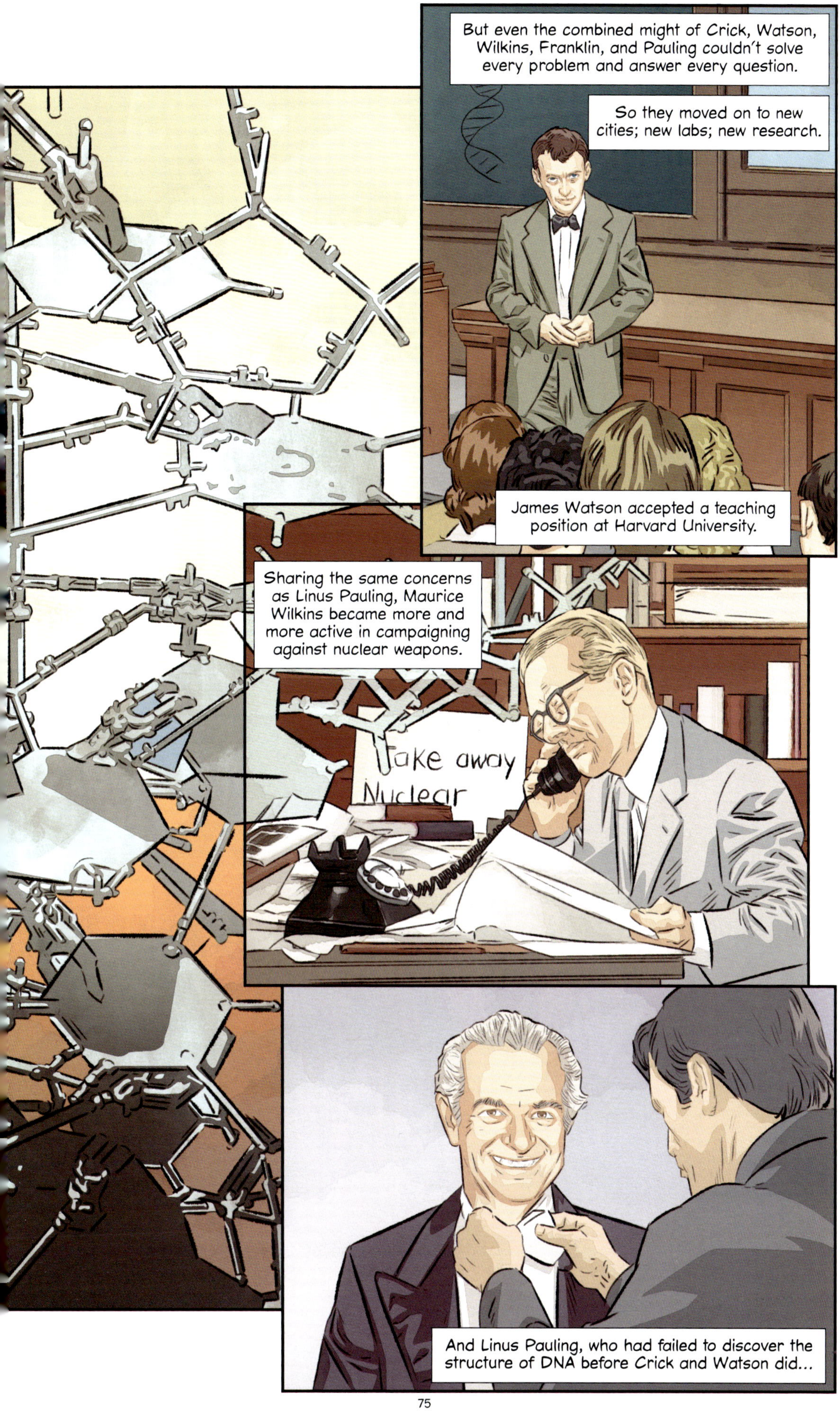
But even the combined might of Crick, Watson, Wilkins, Franklin, and Pauling couldn't solve every problem and answer every question.
So they moved on to new cities; new labs; new research.
James Watson accepted a teaching position at Harvard University.
Sharing the same concerns as Linus Pauling, Maurice Wilkins became more and more active in campaigning against nuclear weapons.
Take away
Nuclear
And Linus Pauling, who had failed to discover the structure of DNA before Crick and Watson did...

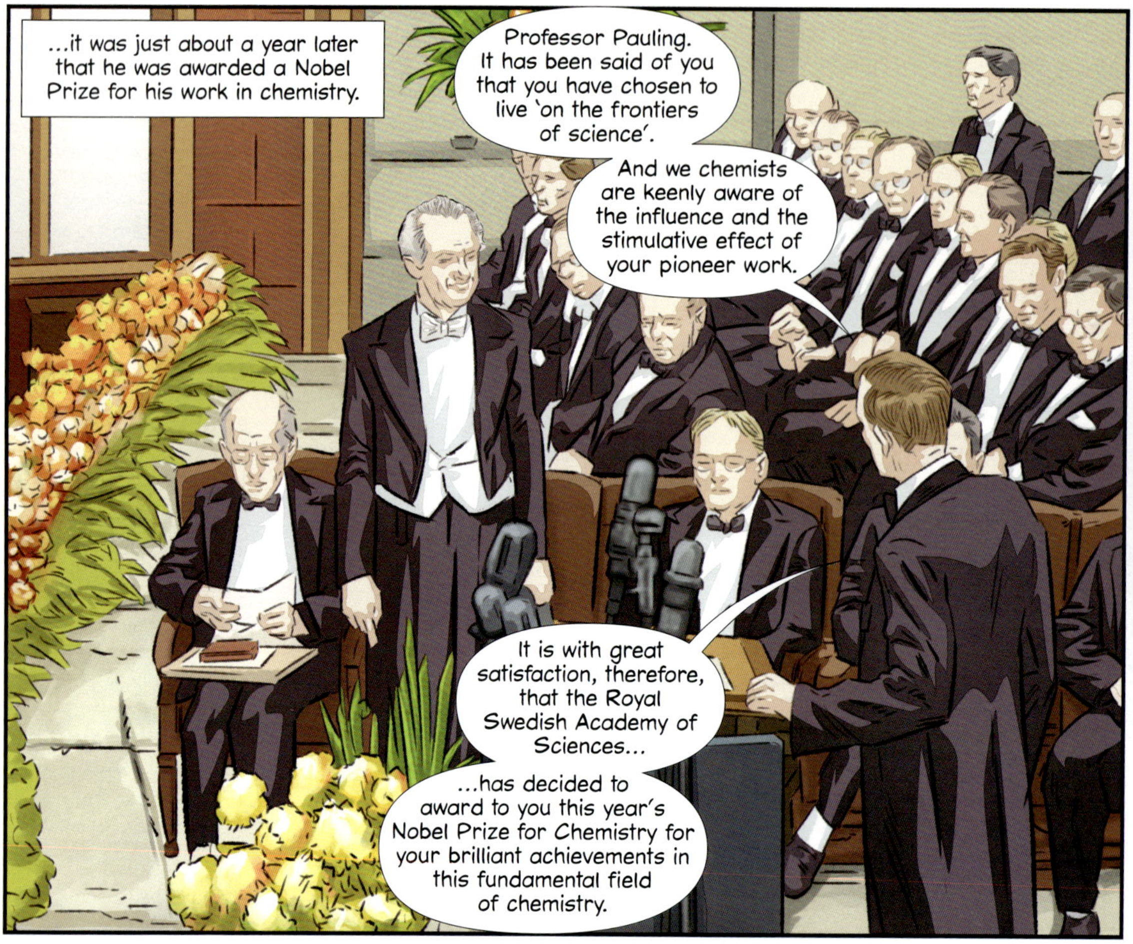
...it was just about a year later that he was awarded a Nobel Prize for his work in chemistry.
Professor Pauling. It has been said of you that you have chosen to live 'on the frontiers of science'.
And we chemists are keenly aware of the influence and the stimulative effect of your pioneer work.
It is with great satisfaction, therefore, that the Royal Swedish Academy of Sciences...
...has decided to award to you this year's Nobel Prize for Chemistry for your brilliant achievements in this fundamental field of chemistry.
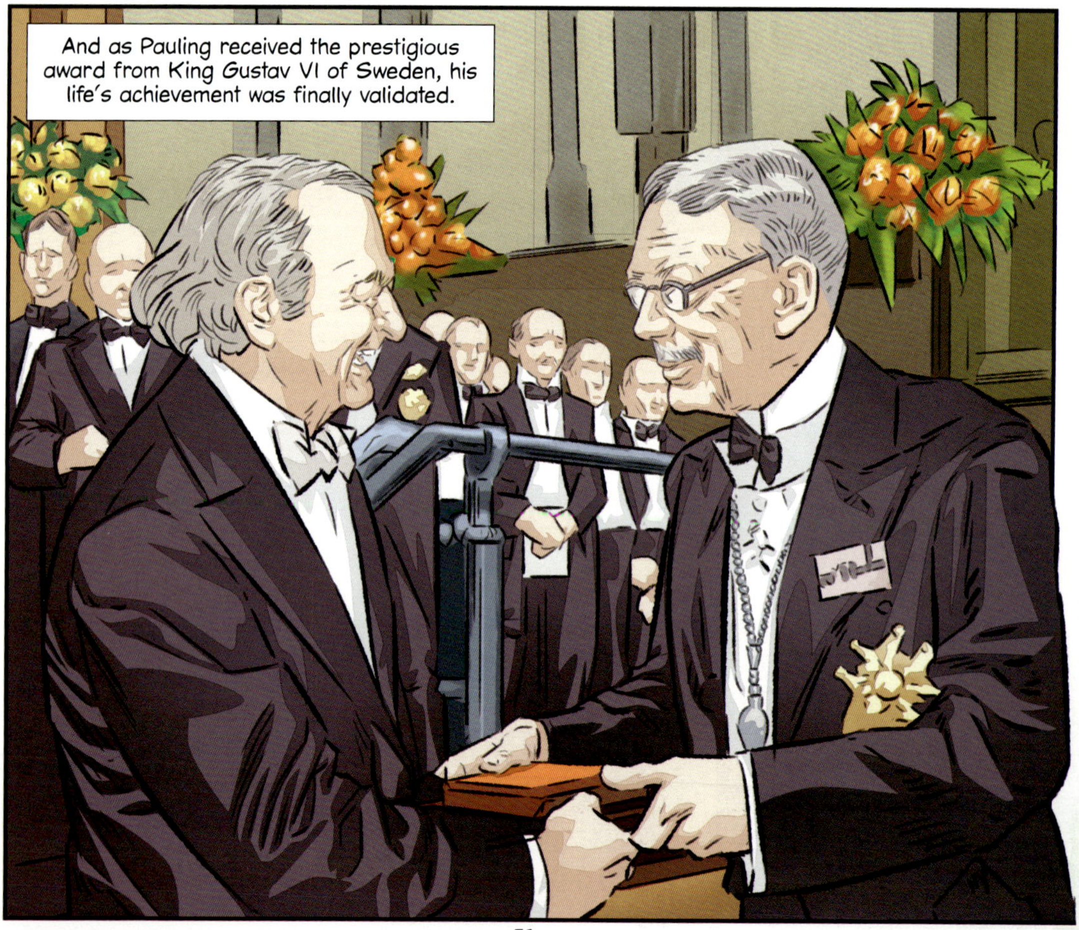
And as Pauling received the prestigious award from King Gustav VI of Sweden, his life's achievement was finally validated.

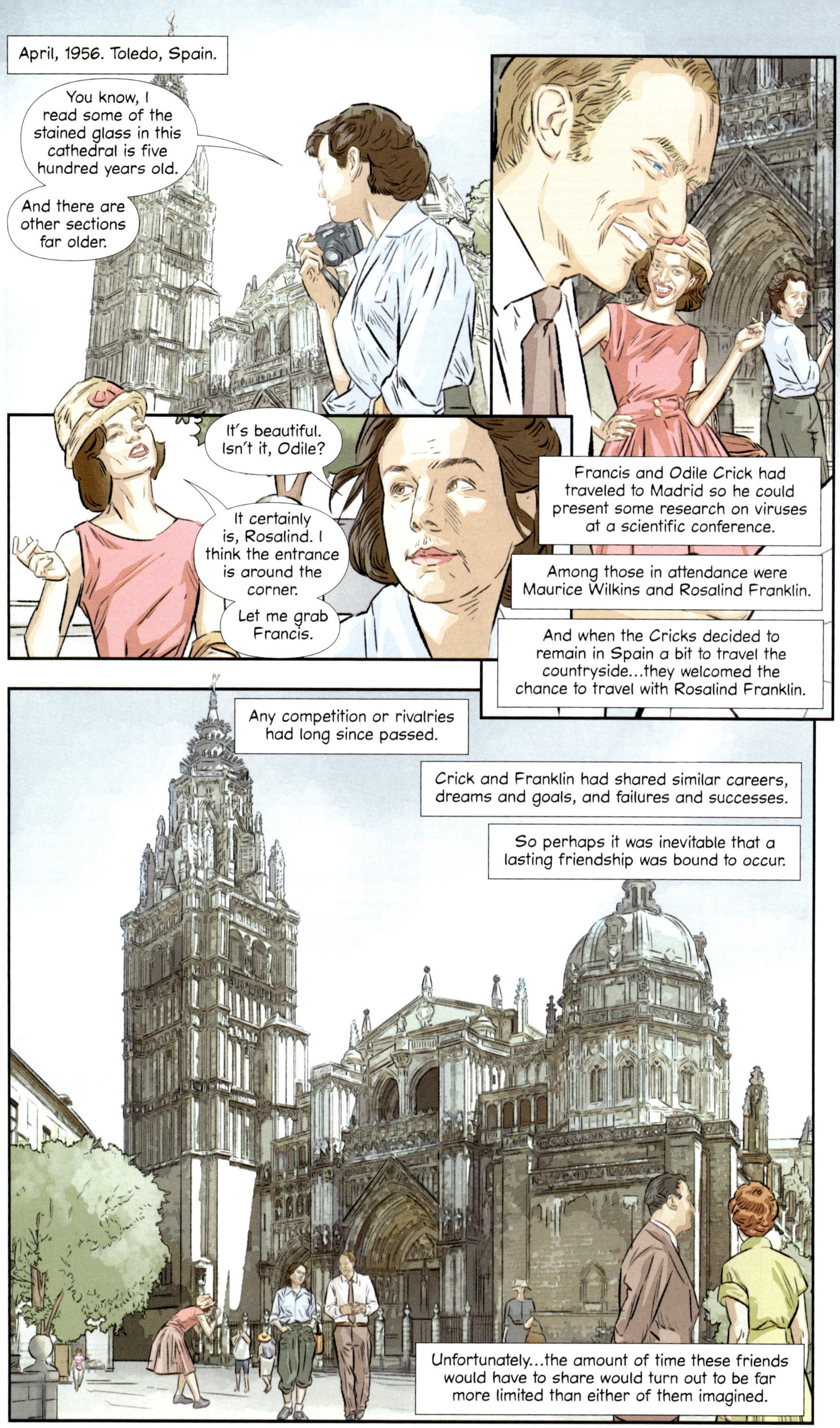
April, 1956. Toledo, Spain.
You know, I read some of the stained glass in this cathedral is five hundred years old.
And there are other sections far older.
Francis and Odile Crick had traveled to Madrid so he could present some research on viruses at a scientific conference.
Among those in attendance were Maurice Wilkins and Rosalind Franklin.
And when the Cricks decided to remain in Spain a bit to travel the countryside...they welcomed the chance to travel with Rosalind Franklin.
It's beautiful. Isn't it, Odile?
It certainly is, Rosalind. I think the entrance is around the corner.
Let me grab Francis.
Any competition or rivalries had long since passed.
Crick and Franklin had shared similar careers, dreams and goals, and failures and successes.
So perhaps it was inevitable that a lasting friendship was bound to occur.
Unfortunately...the amount of time these friends would have to share would turn out to be far more limited than either of them imagined.

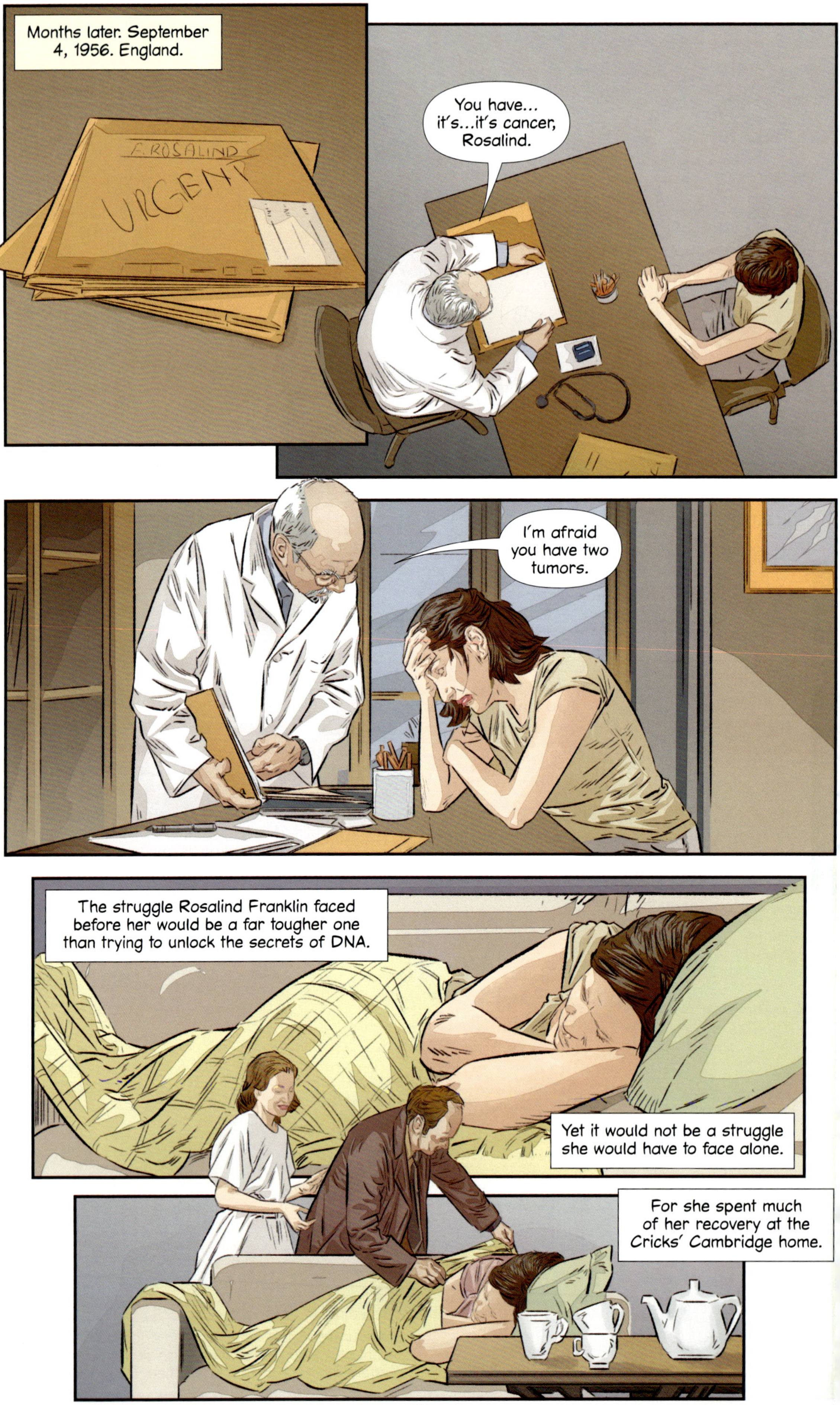
Months later. September 4, 1956. England.
ROSALIND
URGENT
You have... it's...it's cancer, Rosalind.
I'm afraid you have two tumors.
The struggle Rosalind Franklin faced before her would be a far tougher one than trying to unlock the secrets of DNA.
Yet it would not be a struggle she would have to face alone.
For she spent much of her recovery at the Cricks' Cambridge home.

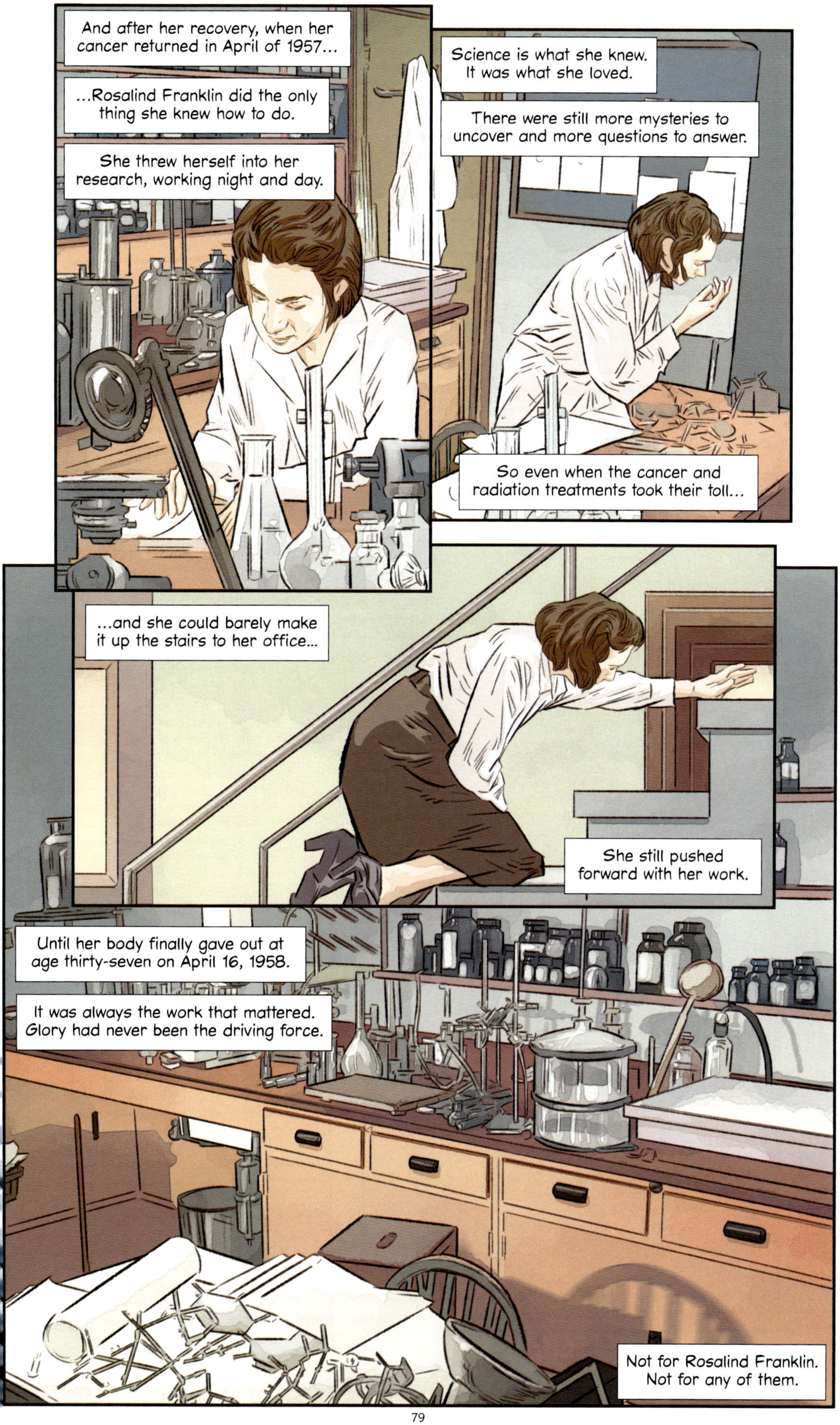
And after her recovery, when her cancer returned in April of 1957...
...Rosalind Franklin did the only thing she knew how to do.
She threw herself into her research, working night and day.
Science is what she knew. It was what she loved.
There were still more mysteries to uncover and more questions to answer.
So even when the cancer and radiation treatments took their toll...
...and she could barely make it up the stairs to her office...
She still pushed forward with her work.
Until her body finally gave out at age thirty-seven on April 16, 1958.
It was always the work that mattered. Glory had never been the driving force.
Not for Rosalind Franklin. Not for any of them.

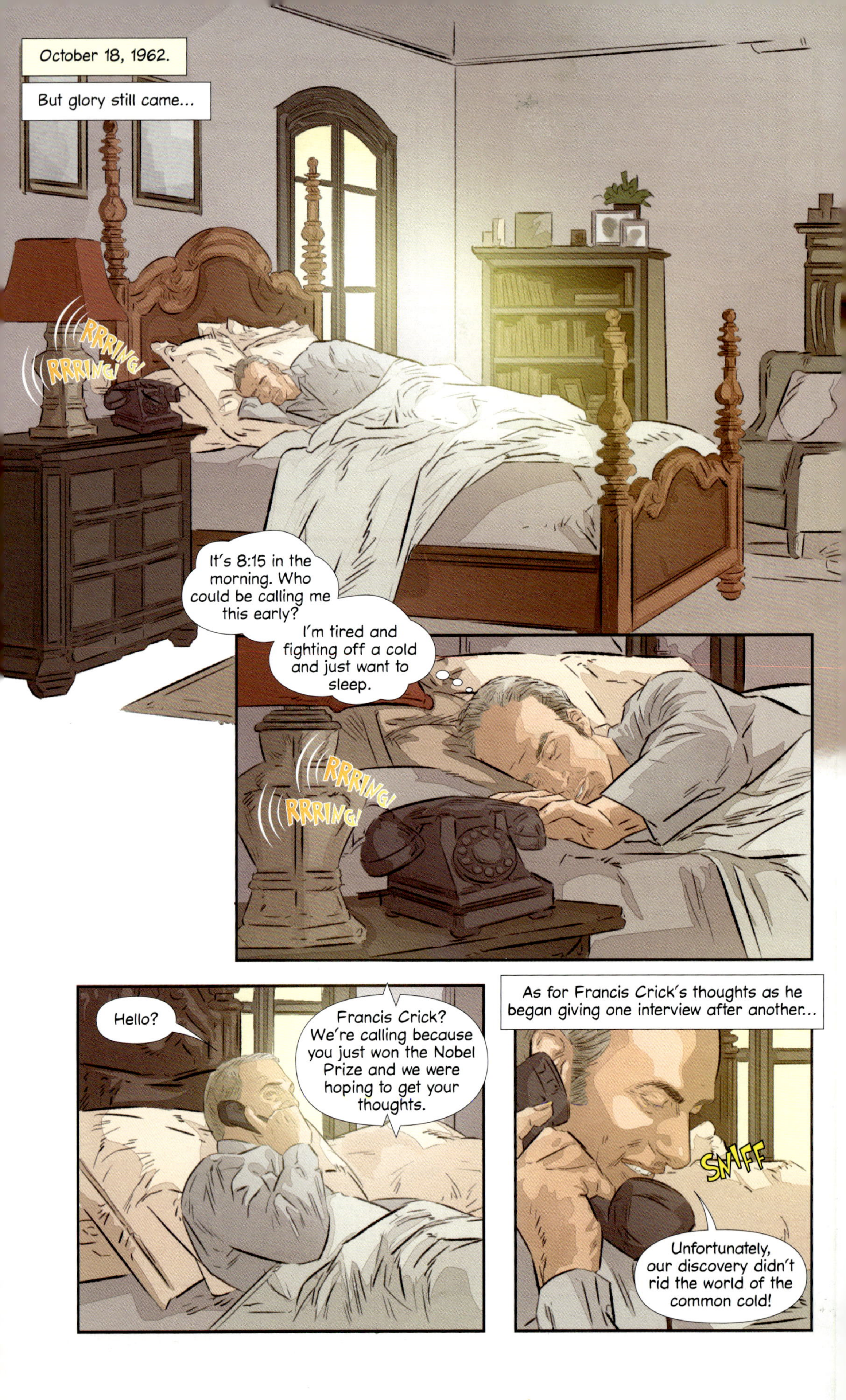
October 18, 1962.
But glory still came...
RRRING!
RRRING!
It's 8:15 in the morning. Who could be calling me this early?
I'm tired and fighting off a cold and just want to sleep.
RRRING!
RRRING!
Hello?
Francis Crick? We're calling because you just won the Nobel Prize and we were hoping to get your thoughts.
As for Francis Crick's thoughts as he began giving one interview after another...
SNIFF
Unfortunately, our discovery didn't rid the world of the common cold!

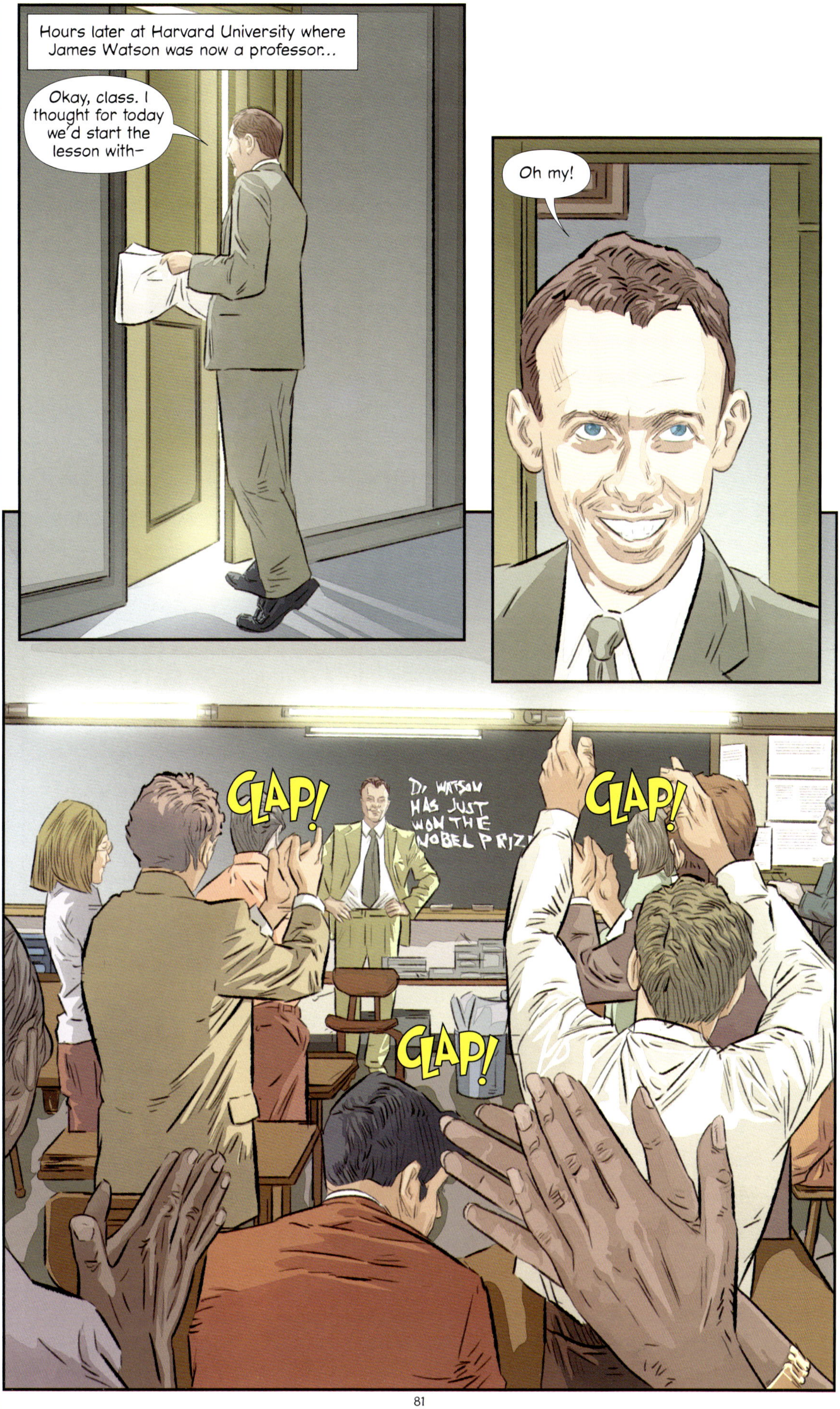

Hours later at Harvard University where James Watson was now a professor...
Okay, class. I thought for today we'd start the lesson with–
Oh my!
CLAP!
DR WATSON HAS JUST WON THE NOBEL PRIZ
CLAP!
CLAP!

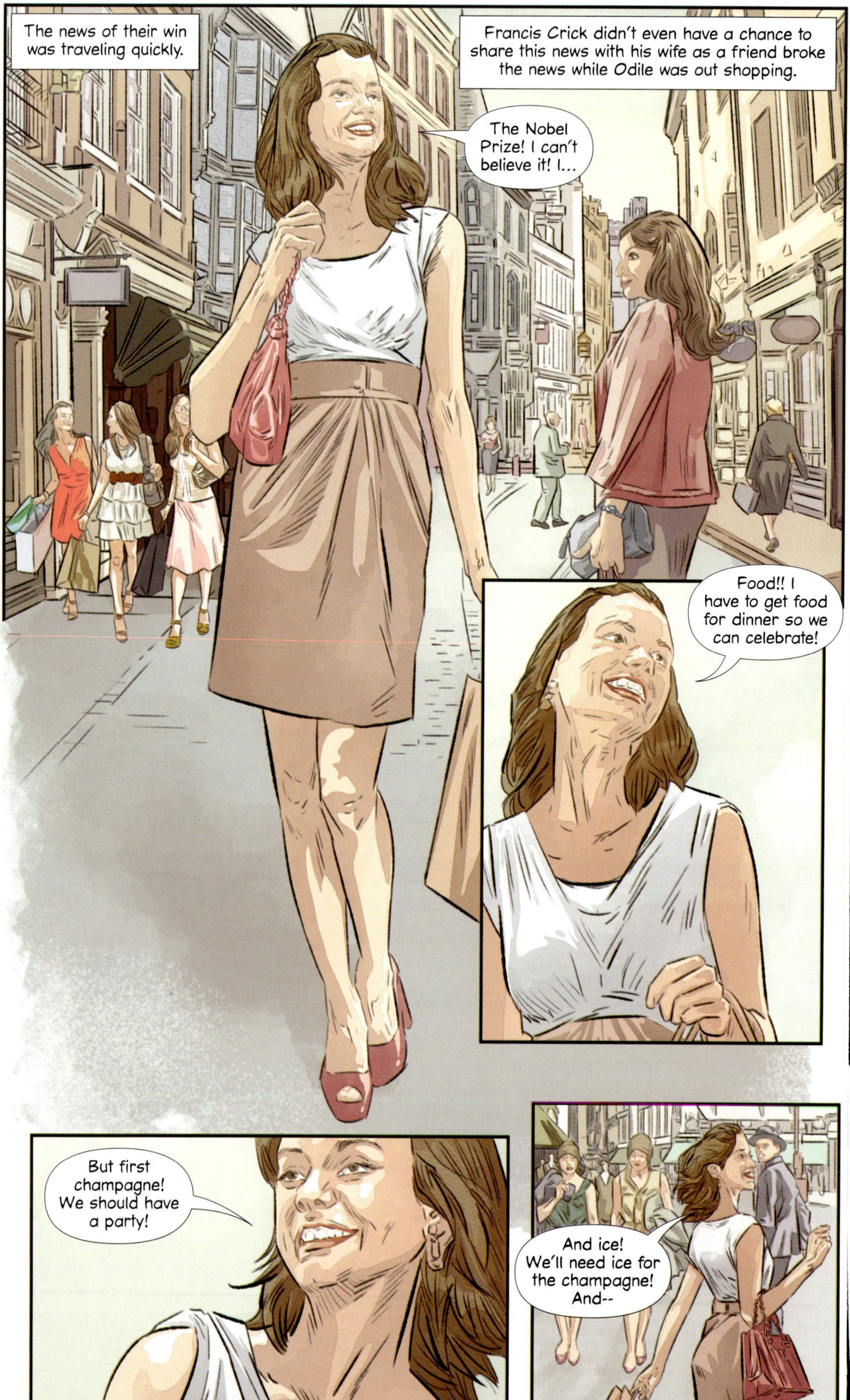
The news of their win was traveling quickly.
Francis Crick didn't even have a chance to share this news with his wife as a friend broke the news while Odile was out shopping.
The Nobel Prize! I can't believe it! I...
Food!! I have to get food for dinner so we can celebrate!
But first champagne! We should have a party!
And ice! We'll need ice for the champagne! And--

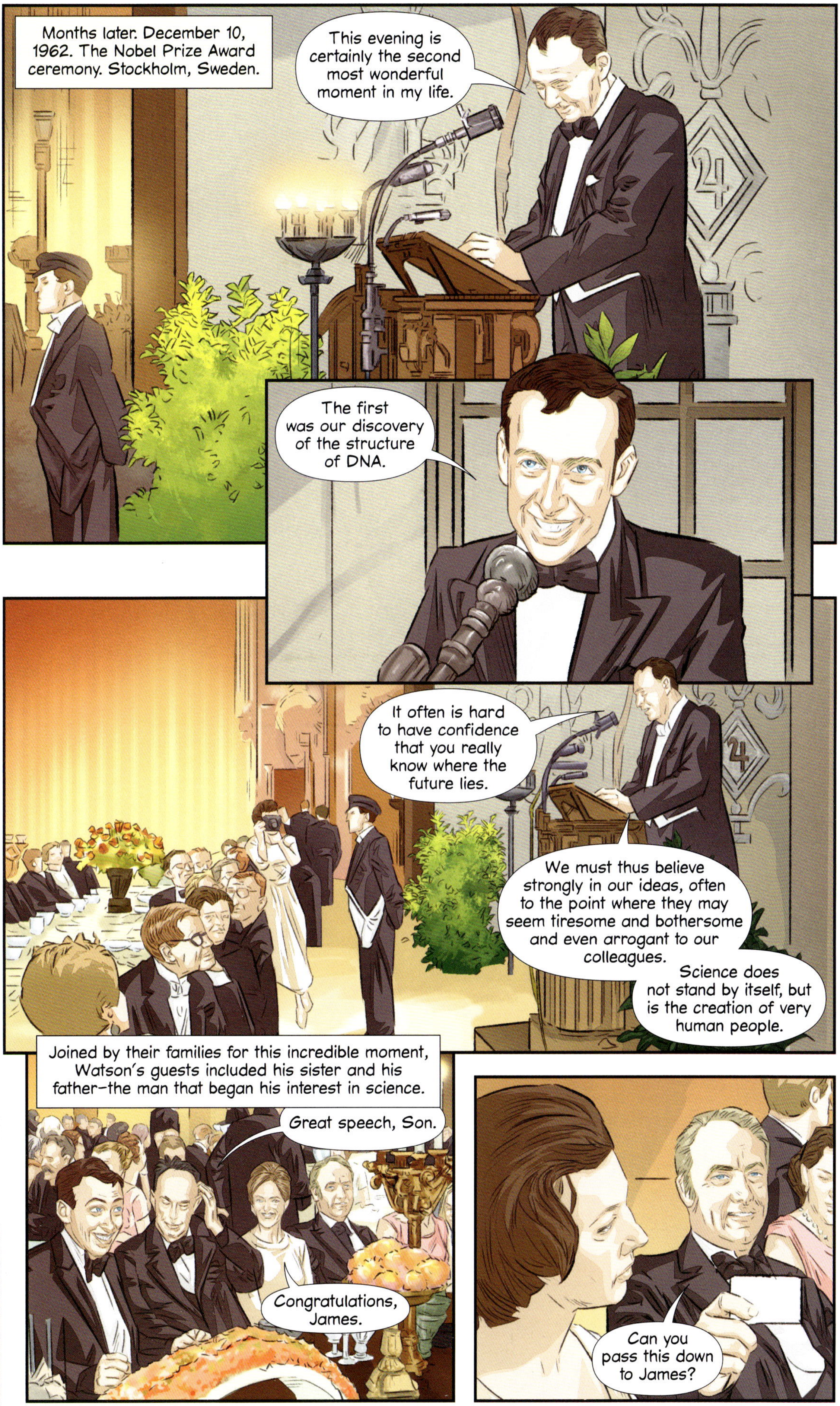
Months later. December 10, 1962. The Nobel Prize Award ceremony. Stockholm, Sweden.
This evening is certainly the second most wonderful moment in my life.
The first was our discovery of the structure of DNA.
It often is hard to have confidence that you really know where the future lies.
We must thus believe strongly in our ideas, often to the point where they may seem tiresome and bothersome and even arrogant to our colleagues.
Science does not stand by itself, but is the creation of very human people.
Joined by their families for this incredible moment, Watson's guests included his sister and his father–the man that began his interest in science.
Great speech, Son.
Congratulations, James.
Can you pass this down to James?

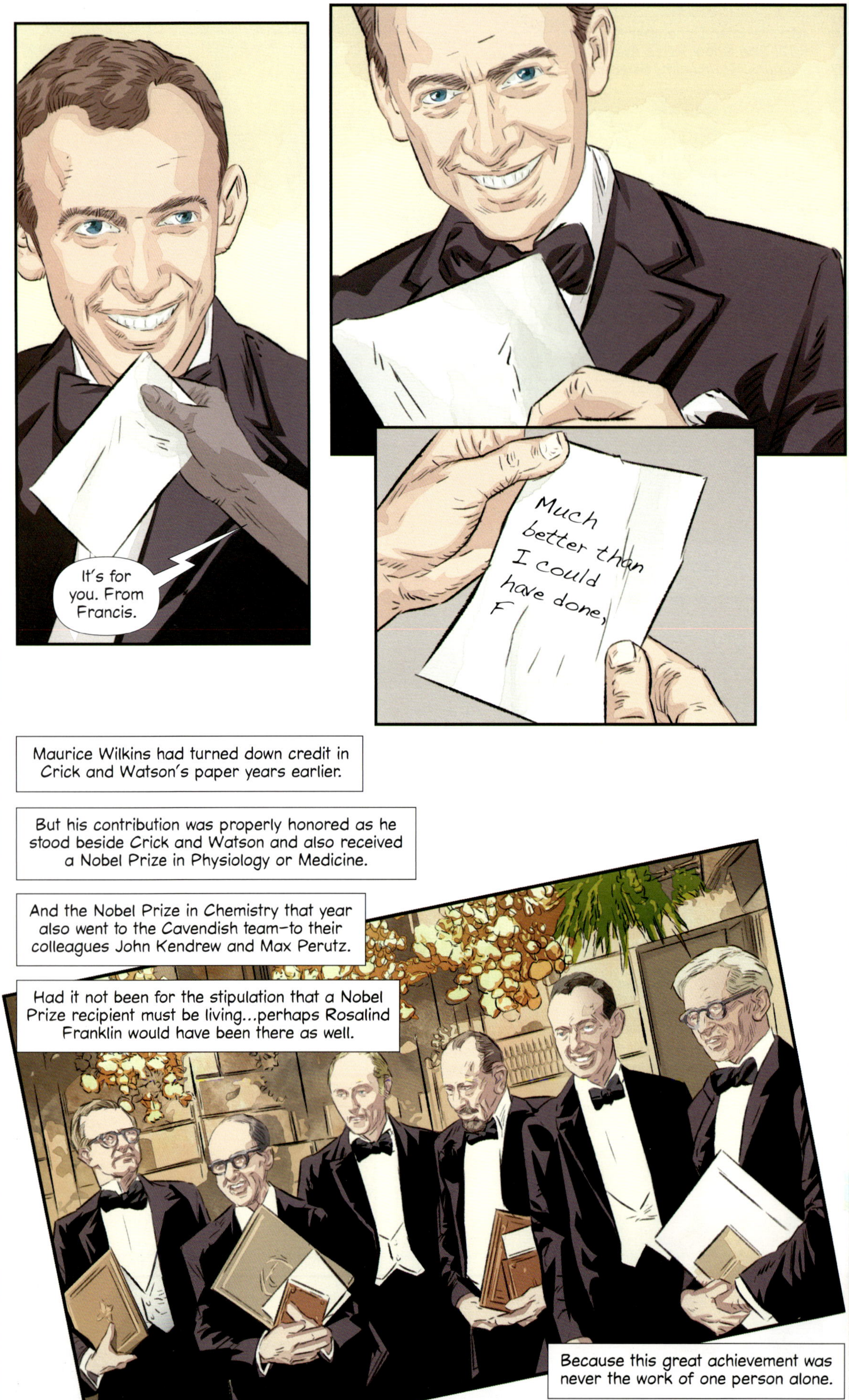
It's for you. From Francis.
Much better than I could have done, F
Maurice Wilkins had turned down credit in Crick and Watson's paper years earlier.
But his contribution was properly honored as he stood beside Crick and Watson and also received a Nobel Prize in Physiology or Medicine.
And the Nobel Prize in Chemistry that year also went to the Cavendish team—to their colleagues John Kendrew and Max Perutz.
Had it not been for the stipulation that a Nobel Prize recipient must be living...perhaps Rosalind Franklin would have been there as well.
Because this great achievement was never the work of one person alone.

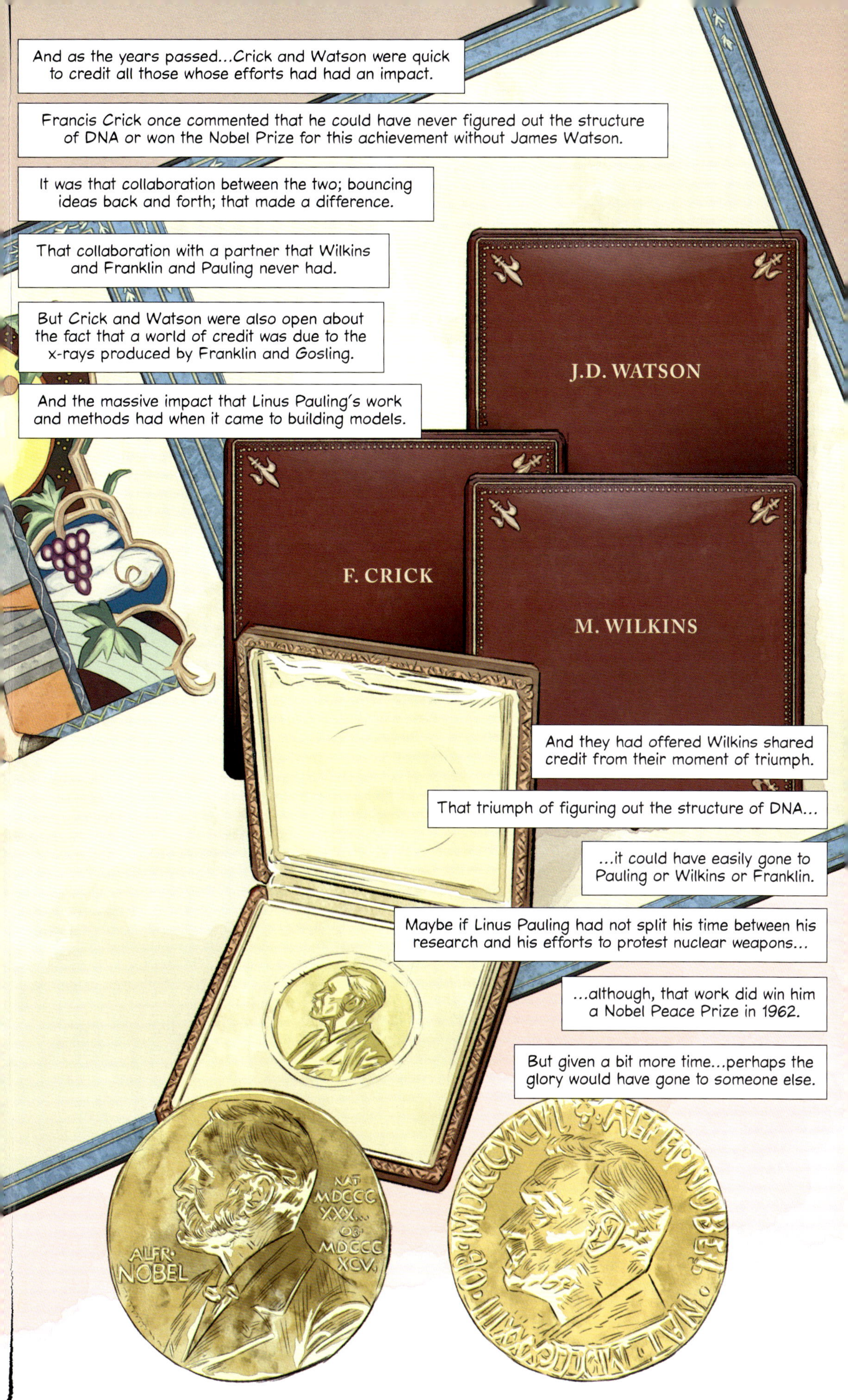
And as the years passed...Crick and Watson were quick to credit all those whose efforts had had an impact.
Francis Crick once commented that he could have never figured out the structure of DNA or won the Nobel Prize for this achievement without James Watson.
It was that collaboration between the two; bouncing ideas back and forth; that made a difference.
That collaboration with a partner that Wilkins and Franklin and Pauling never had.
But Crick and Watson were also open about the fact that a world of credit was due to the x-rays produced by Franklin and Gosling.
And the massive impact that Linus Pauling's work and methods had when it came to building models.
J.D. WATSON
F. CRICK
M. WILKINS
And they had offered Wilkins shared credit from their moment of triumph.
That triumph of figuring out the structure of DNA...
...it could have easily gone to Pauling or Wilkins or Franklin.
Maybe if Linus Pauling had not split his time between his research and his efforts to protest nuclear weapons...
...although, that work did win him a Nobel Peace Prize in 1962.
But given a bit more time...perhaps the glory would have gone to someone else.
ALFR. NOBEL

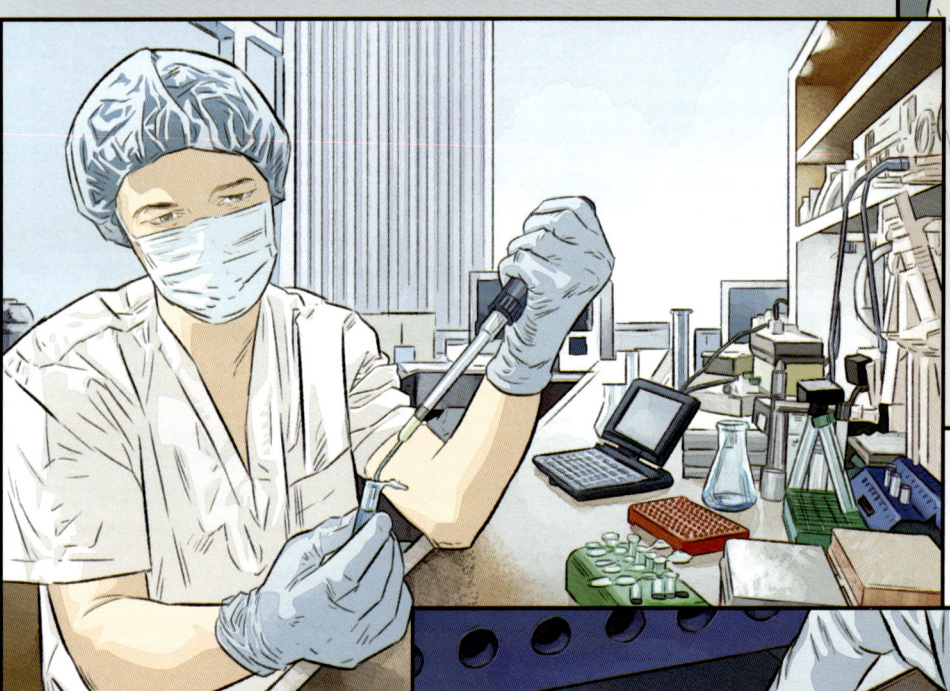

For all of the scientists that came before Crick and Watson...there was a belief that their work was a beginning; not an end.

The achievements of Mendel and Miescher and the Braggs and Avery... each breakthrough was a small step leading to something greater.

A small step in the journey to greatness.

And the truth is the same holds true for Crick and Watson's great achievement.

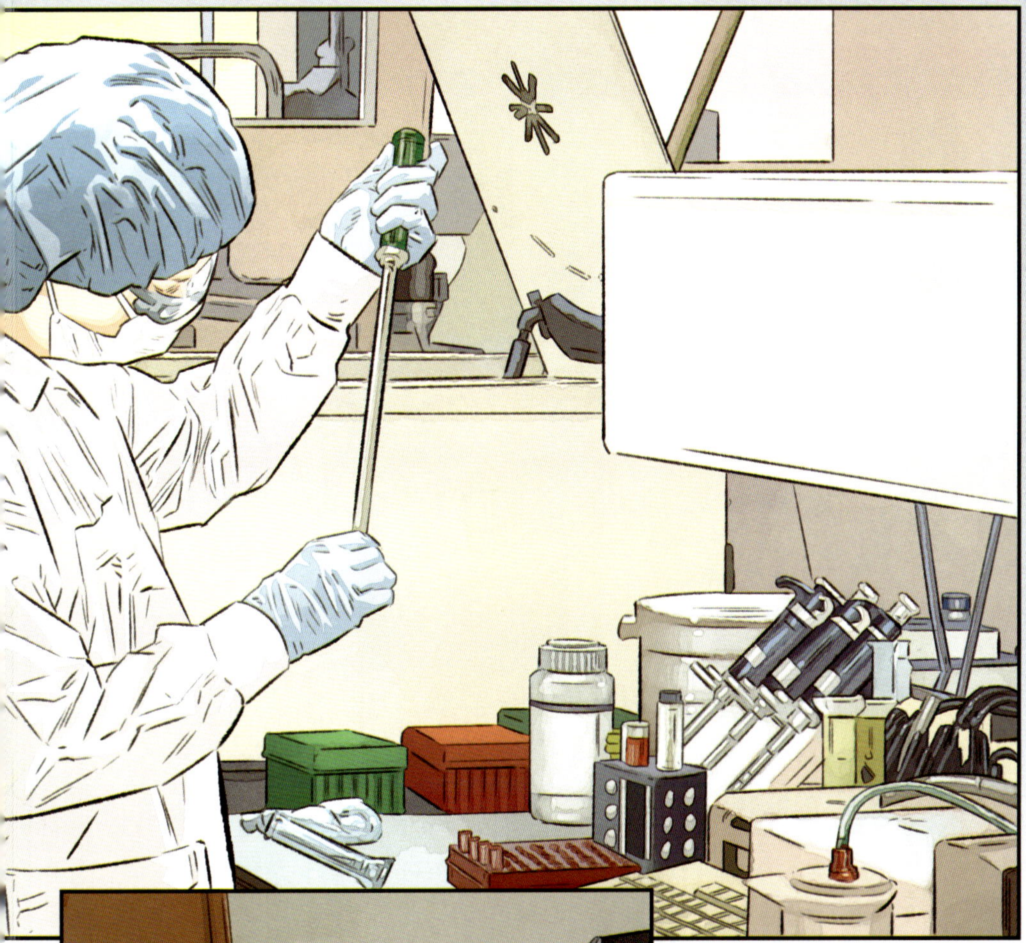

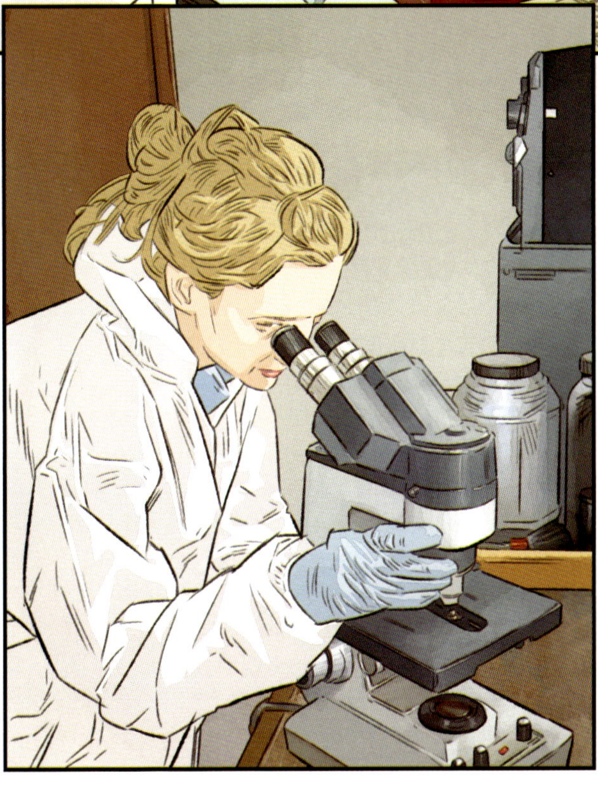

Uncovering the structure of DNA was not an end.

It was never about merely knowing the structure of DNA.

It was about the doors that were opened once that information was finally known.

From DNA fingerprinting and cloning to genetic screening and the ability to develop more powerful drugs to fight diseases...

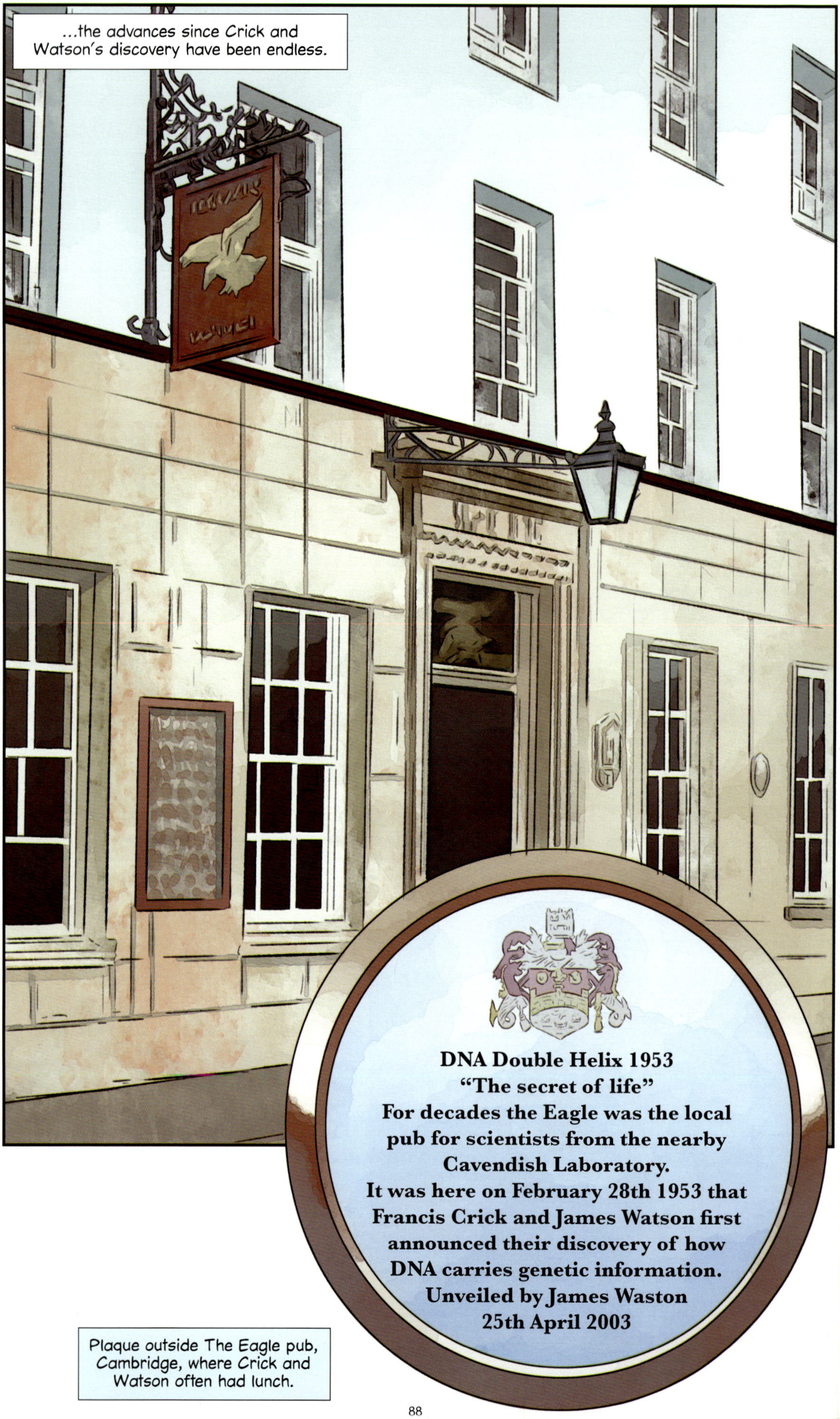
...the advances since Crick and Watson's discovery have been endless.
DNA Double Helix 1953
"The secret of life"
For decades the Eagle was the local pub for scientists from the nearby Cavendish Laboratory.
It was here on February 28th 1953 that Francis Crick and James Watson first announced their discovery of how DNA carries genetic information.
Unveiled by James Waston
25th April 2003
Plaque outside The Eagle pub, Cambridge, where Crick and Watson often had lunch.

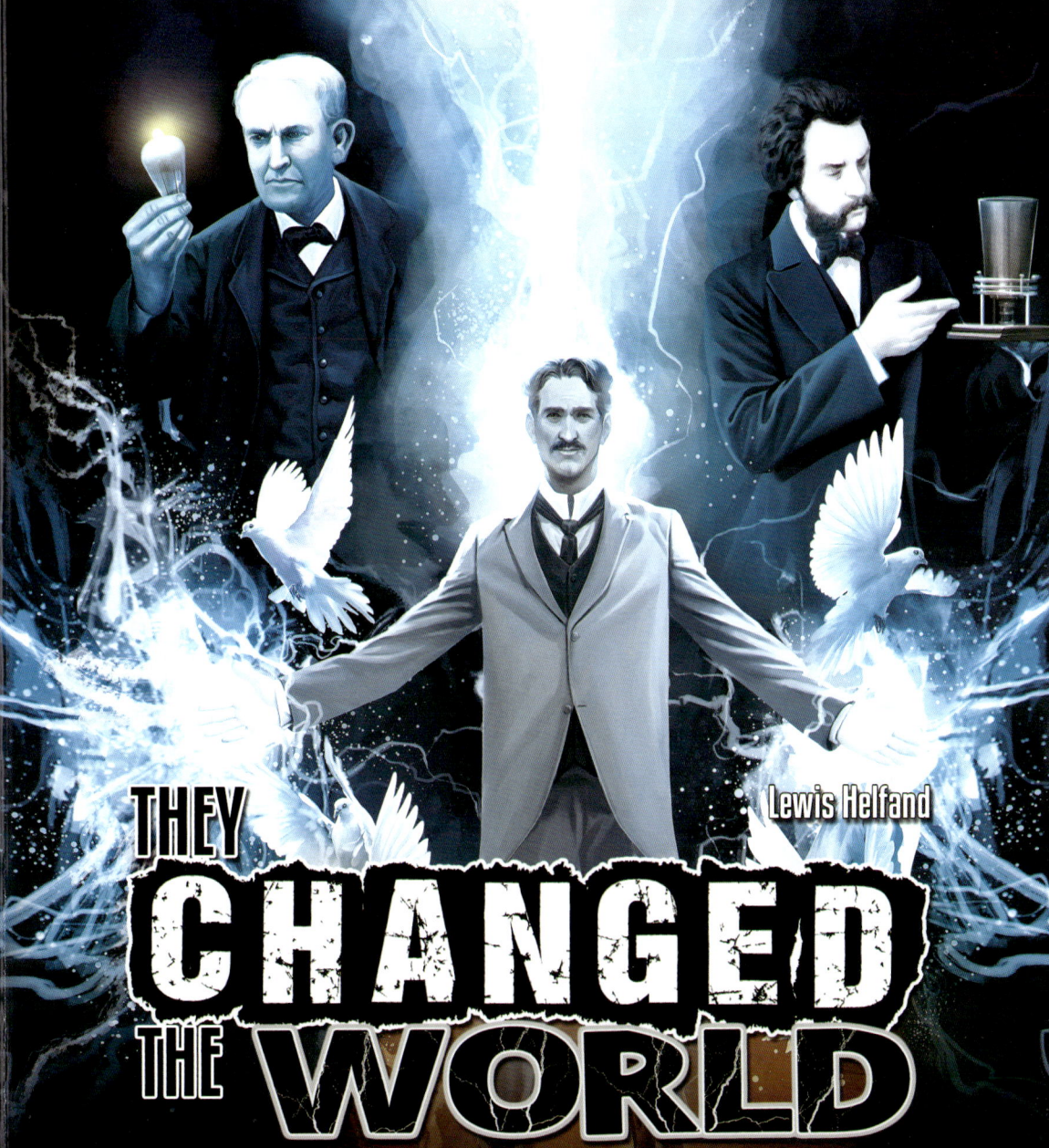

ALSO AVAILABLE

THEY CHANGED THE WORLD
EDISON - TESLA - BELL

Lewis Helfand

Three lives, one epic story. Find out how Alexander Graham Bell, Thomas Edison and Nikola Tesla changed the world we live in forever! Three men, three great minds with three completely different approaches to their work. As their paths cross, a rivalry grows and the men who revolutionized the fields of light, sound and vision compete with each other to become the leading genius of the age. Discover how these men tamed the forces of science in order to share its power with the world.

DNA-The Building Block of Life

1. What is the building block of life? At its most fundamental level, it is deoxyribonucleic acid, more commonly known as DNA. It is a hereditary material that is present in the cells of all living organisms. Most of the DNA of a person is located in the nucleus of a cell, but in some cases can also be found in the mitochondria (mitochondrial DNA or mtDNA). The DNA of a person is identical in all of his or her cells.

2. DNA stores information in the form of chemical bases known as adenine (A), guanine (G), cytosine (C), and thymine (T). A human DNA can comprise up to three billion bases, and more than 99 percent of those bases are identical in all people. It is the sequence in which they are arranged that determines the information available for creating and maintaining an organism.

3. DNA bases pair up with each other, A with T and C with G, to form units called base pairs. Each base is also attached to a sugar molecule and a phosphate molecule, together known as a nucleotide. Nucleotides are arranged in two long strands that form a spiral called a double helix, with the base pairs in the middle and the sugar and phosphate molecules on the sides.

4. DNA can replicate, or make copies of itself, with every strand in the double helix serving as a pattern for duplicating the sequence of bases. According to natural order, when cells divide, each new cell needs to have an exact copy of the DNA that was present in the old cell. This is how life forms replicate and reproduce.